Kenneth P. Norwick is a member of the New York law firm of Norwick & Schad and specializes in publishing and communications law. He is the author of *Lobbying for Freedom: A Citizen's Guide to Fighting Censorship at the State Level*, published in 1975, and he is the editor and principal author of a revised and expanded edition of that book, *Lobbying for Freedom in the 1980s: A Grass Roots Guide to Protecting Your Rights*, published in 1983. He is also the editor of *Your Legal Rights: Making the Law Work for You*, which was published in 1975. He has served as Legislative Director of the New York Civil Liberties Union and as Special Professor of Law at Hofstra Law School. He is a 1965 graduate of the University of Chicago Law School, where he was an editor of the *Law Review* and the founder and editor-in-chief of the law school's newspaper.

Jerry Simon Chasen is a New York attorney specializing in entertainment and publishing matters. He is an honors graduate of the New York University School of Law where he was an editor of the *Law Review*. Following graduation he clerked in the U.S. District Court in Manhattan. He was with the New York law firm of Greenbaum Wolff & Ernst until that firm's dissolution in 1982 and is now with the law firm of Linden & Deutsch. He is Counsel to the P.E.N. American Center and a member of the New York County Lawyers' Association

Law.

Henry .... orney
specializi .... munications la .... Libel
Defense .... Counsel to the firm of Karpatkin Pollet Perlmutter & Beil.

Other Bantam books in the series
Ask your bookseller for the titles you have missed

AN AMERICAN CIVIL LIBERTIES UNION HANDBOOK

THE RIGHTS
OF
AUTHORS AND ARTISTS

THE BASIC ACLU GUIDE TO THE
LEGAL RIGHTS OF AUTHORS AND ARTISTS

Kenneth P. Norwick
and
Jerry Simon Chasen
with
Henry R. Kaufman

General Editor of this series:
Norman Dorsen, President, ACLU

BANTAM BOOKS
TORONTO · NEW YORK · LONDON · SYDNEY

THE RIGHTS OF AUTHORS AND ARTISTS

*A Bantam Book / published by arrangement with
The American Civil Liberties Union*

Bantam edition / January 1984

Excerpt from *Synopsis of the Law of Libel and the Right of Privacy*
by Bruce W. Sanford (Rev. ed. 1981). Copyright © 1977, 1981 by
Baker and Hostetler, Washington, D.C. Courtesy of The World Almanac.

ISBN 0-553-23654-7

Published simultaneously in the United States and Canada

PRINTED IN THE UNITED STATES OF AMERICA

O   0 9 8 7 6 5 4 3 2 1

Acknowledgments

Several of our colleagues graciously agreed to review portions of this book and give us the benefit of their comments, and the book has been significantly enhanced by their contributions. We are especially grateful to Michael Bamberger, Harriette K. Dorsen, Joseph F. Gelband, Francis J. Harvey, Jr., Eugene V. Kokot, Tennyson Schad, Nancy F. Wechsler, and Roger L. Zissu. In addition, several people assisted in the research for the book, including Patrick Brown, Laura Dubetsky, Susan Lerner, and Edna Wells, and we are grateful for their contributions as well. As always, Rochelle Leib and Yung Jin Kim provided invaluable assistance throughout this project, and we are pleased to acknowledge that assistance here.

We also wish to acknowledge with gratitude and affection the guidance, support and friendship we have each received over the years from Harriet F. Pilpel.

KENNETH P. NORWICK
JERRY SIMON CHASEN

Contents

Preface

This guide sets forth your rights under the present law, and offers suggestions on how they can be protected. It is one of a continuing series of handbooks published in cooperation with the American Civil Liberties Union (ACLU).

Surrounding these publications is the hope that Americans, informed of their rights, will be encouraged to exercise them. Through their exercise, rights are given life. If they are rarely used, they may be forgotten and violations may become routine.

This guide offers no assurances that your rights will be respected. The laws may change and, in some of the subjects covered in these pages, they change quite rapidly. An effort has been made to note those parts of the law where movement is taking place, but it is not always possible to predict accurately when the law *will* change.

Even if the laws remain the same, their interpretations by courts and administrative officials often vary. In a federal system such as ours, there is a built-in problem of state and federal law, not to speak of the confusion between states. In addition, there are wide variations in the ways in which particular courts and administrative officials will interpret the same law at any given moment.

If you encounter what you consider to be a specific abuse of your rights, you should seek legal assistance. There are a number of agencies that may help you, among them, ACLU affiliate offices, but bear in mind that the ACLU is a limited-purpose organization. In many communities, there are federally funded legal service offices which provide assistance to persons who cannot afford the costs of legal representation. In general, the rights that the ACLU defends are freedom of inquiry and expression; due process of law; equal protection of the laws; and privacy. The authors in this series have discussed other rights (even though they sometimes fall outside ACLU's usual concern) in order to provide as much guidance as possible.

These books have been planned as guides for the people directly affected; therefore, the question and answer format. (In some areas there are more detailed works available for "experts.") These guides seek to raise the major issues and inform the nonspecialist of the basic law on the subject. The authors of these books are themselves specialists who understand the need for information at "street level."

If you encounter a specific legal problem in an area discussed in one of these handbooks, show the book to your attorney. Of course, he or she will not be able to rely exclusively on the handbook to provide you with adequate representation. But if your attorney hasn't had a great deal of experience in the specific area, the handbook can provide helpful suggestions on how to proceed.

NORMAN DORSEN, President
American Civil Liberties Union

Introduction

Because this book is entitled *The Rights of Authors and Artists,* a few disclaimers are necessary. First, although portions of the book should prove useful to all creative people, the book does not address the particular legal rights and problems of all authors and artists. Of necessity, lines had to be drawn and categories of creators excluded. Thus, the book does not deal separately with performing artists, those who create or arrange music, choreographers, directors, screenwriters, or photographers, among others. Instead, the book concentrates on those authors who write articles and books and those artists who create works of visual art. (For a comprehensive review of the law applicable to journalists, see *The Rights of Reporters,* by Joel M. Gora, which is a part of this series.)

Second, the book does not purport to provide the last word with respect to most of the issues it discusses. Especially where the applicable law can vary markedly from state to state, such an undertaking would have been impossible. Instead, the book attempts to provide an introduction to and overview of the basic legal rights of authors and artists. Readers who are confronted with specific legal problems may well find guidance in this book but should nevertheless obtain the assistance of a lawyer familiar with the applicable law in resolving those problems. In addition, the Authors Guild and PEN American Center, national organizations dedicated to protecting the interests of all authors, make available a wide variety of excellent materials, including extensive symposia, on issues of vital concern to authors. For further information contact the Guild at 234 West 44th Street, New York, New York 10036 and PEN at 47 Fifth Avenue, New York, New York 10003.

THE RIGHTS
OF
AUTHORS AND ARTISTS

I

The Constitutional Foundation

The Constitution of the United States is not only "the supreme law of the land," it is also the original source of all other law in this country. In Article I, for example, the Constitution spells out the "legislative powers" that are vested in the U.S. Congress. It is this article that grants to the Congress the principal power it has to enact the laws that ultimately affect the business and personal lives of all of us. And in the Bill of Rights, of course, the Constitution sets forth the fundamental rights and freedoms of all people in this country, rights and freedoms which cannot be denied or abridged by Congress in the laws it enacts or by any other branch or level of government.

Unlike most groups or categories of Americans, who do not find specific reference to their callings in the Constitution, authors and artists are doubly blessed: they can point to two separate, and most important, references to their activities in the Constitution. Indeed, these two constitutional provisions establish the foundation for the most important legal rights of all authors and artists.

The first reference, in clause 8 of section 8 of Article I, grants Congress the legislative power

> to promote the progress of science and useful arts,
> by securing for limited times to authors and inven-

1

tors the exclusive right to their respective writings and discoveries.[1]

This clause has empowered Congress to enact copyright laws, which have provided to authors and artists since the first Congress the essential protection they need to be able to continue to create. And although the clause refers only to "authors" and "writings," it is clear that, as the Supreme Court has put it, the copyright clause "may be interpreted to include any physical rendering of the fruits of creative, intellectual or aesthetic labor."[2] However, as will be discussed in Chapter II, it is clear that Congress has not, in the copyright laws it has passed, protected all the fruits of such labor that it might have.

The second reference to the activities of authors and artists is in the First Amendment, which provides that "Congress shall make no law . . . abridging the freedom of speech, or of the press." Especially since it is now clear that this provision applies as fully to state and local governments as it does to the federal government,[3] it is not difficult to agree with the Supreme Court when it described the First Amendment as "the matrix, the indispensable condition, of nearly every other form of freedom."[4]

The scope of the First Amendment is extensive. Most obviously, it applies to speech and writings on "political" matters; as late Supreme Court Justice Hugo L. Black put it:

In the First Amendment the Founding Fathers gave the free press the protection it must have to fulfill its essential role in our democracy. The press was to serve the governed, not the governors. The Government's power to censor the press was abolished so that the press would remain forever free to censure the Government.[5]

In addition, and perhaps of equal importance to most authors and artists, it is clear that the First Amendment is not limited to such "political speech." As the Supreme Court confirmed in a 1981 decision:

> Entertainment, as well as political and ideological speech, is protected; motion pictures, programs broadcast by radio and television and live entertainment, such as musical and dramatic works, fall within the First Amendment guarantee.[6]

Read literally, the First Amendment prohibits any law that would abridge the "freedom of speech, or of the press," which presumably includes all the creations of all authors and artists. But if anything is clear about the meaning of those words, it is that they do not mean what they seem to say and that the First Amendment has never been construed as "absolute" in its force and effect. Instead, as will be discussed more fully in Chapters IV and V, the First Amendment does not necessarily protect all speech and writings. Nevertheless, it and the copyright clause with the laws it has engendered are the sources and bulwarks of the most fundamental rights of authors and artists.

There is at least a potential conflict between the copyright clause and the First Amendment. Thus, the latter's prohibitions could be read to encompass the freedom to write or speak whatever one wishes, including the writings of others, while the copyright clause makes clear that Congress can prevent such borrowing. As Professor Melville Nimmer, a leading authority on copyright, has posed the dilemma:

> Does not the Copyright Act fly directly in the face of [the First Amendment's] command? Is it not precisely a "law" made by Congress which abridges the "freedom of speech" and "of the press" in that it punishes expressions by speech and press when such expressions consist of the unauthorized use of material protected by copyright?[7]

Somewhat surprisingly, the courts have not found it necessary to determine whether these two constitutional provisions do in fact conflict. However, it is generally assumed that if and when that effort becomes necessary, the courts will not find that the legal protections afforded authors and artists by copyright laws violate the First Amendment. Instead, the courts will reconcile whatever potential conflict exists. Indeed, many courts have at least implicitly done so through the "fair use" exception built into copyright law, by reference to the constitutional purpose of the copyright clause—i.e., to promote knowledge—and by adhering to the well established rule that copyright does not protect "ideas" but only "the particular selection and arrangement of ideas, as well as a given specificity in the form of their expression . . ."[8]

It seems clear that authors and artists will continue to be able to claim the protection of both the copyright law and the First Amendment. We shall now turn to the rights afforded under the copyright law.

NOTES

1. The derivation and history of the copyright clause has been summarized as follows: "When the framers of the United States Constitution met in Philadelphia to consider which powers might best be entrusted to the national government, there appears to have been virtual unanimity in determining that copyright should be included within the federal sphere. Although the committee proceedings which considered the copyright clause were conducted in secret, it is known that the final form of the clause was adopted without debate. Moreover, in Federalist Paper No. 43 James Madison found it necessary to devote but a single paragraph to the efficacy of both the copyright and patent powers. Stating that 'The utility of this power will scarcely be questioned,' he put the case for federal authority with respect to both copyrights and patents on the ground that 'The States cannot separately make effectual provision for either of the cases . . .' " *Nimmer on Copyright*, §1.01 at pp. 1–2–1–3 (1980) (hereinafter Nimmer).

2. *Goldstein v. California*, 412 U.S. 546, 561 (1973).

3. *See, e.g.*, *Gitlow v. New York*, 268 U.S. 652 (1925).

4. *Palko v. Connecticut*, 302 U.S. 319, 326 (1937) (opinion by Justice Cardozo). A recent history of the First Amendment written for the layperson is Hentoff, *The First Freedom: The Tumultuous History of Free*

Speech in America, Delacorte Press, 1980, which contains a useful bibliography.

5. *New York Times Co. v. United States,* 403 U.S. 713, 720 (1971) (the Pentagon Papers case) (concurring opinion).

6. *Schad v. Borough of Mount Ephraim,* 452 U.S. 61, 66 (1981).

7. Nimmer, §1.10[A] at p. 1–63.

8. Nimmer, §1.10[B] at pp. 1–73–74.

II

Copyright and Other Legal Rights

Pursuant to the power granted to it in Article I of the U.S. Constitution,[1] Congress enacted the first Copyright Act in 1790. Since then, there has always been such a law, with major revisions made when developments in communications rendered the existing law inapplicable or anachronistic. On January 1, 1978, the first major revision of our law in almost seventy years took general effect. The Copyright Act of 1976 was the result of more than twenty years of study, drafting, and compromise on the part of the various (and often conflicting) interests directly affected by any copyright law. The previous Copyright Act had been enacted in 1909—before sound motion pictures, radio, television, and, of course, computers; it was not relevant to modern-day communications and had not been for a long time.

This chapter will review the kinds of works that are eligible for copyright protection, the nature of the rights that copyright confers, the ''fair use'' doctrine, and the formalities that must be complied with to secure copyright protection. In addition, where necessary, the chapter will refer to the law as it existed prior to January 1, 1978, which in several respects was quite different from the present law. It will also discuss the kinds of legal protection available to authors and artists outside the Copyright Act.

What do we mean by copyright?

Copyright is a form of legal protection afforded in this and other countries to a wide variety of creative works. It is a property right that one "owns," much as one owns a car, a horse, or shares of stock; it is a kind of monopoly that the law gives to creative people with respect to their creations.

Under current law, only one kind of copyright is available to creative people for virtually all creative works—the protection afforded by the federal Copyright Act of 1976. Such works either enjoy the protection of the Act or they have no copyright protection. Before 1978 there were two systems of copyright available to authors and artists: the first, known as common law copyright, was available through state decisional law and applied to works that had never been published or otherwise publicly disseminated; the second, the federal Copyright Act of 1909, applied mainly to published works.[2] With the enactment of the 1976 act, virtually all prior systems of common law copyright were abolished.[3] In legal parlance, the new act substantially "pre-empted" state common law copyright protection.

The protection the Copyright Act gives a copyright owner is extensive.[4] Anyone who uses a copyrighted work without the authority of its owner in a way that constitutes an infringement may be subject to civil remedies including an injunction,[5] forfeiture of the infringing items,[6] and the obligation to pay to the copyright owner all profits from the infringement,[7] money damages,[8] and the owner's attorneys' fees.[9] In appropriate cases the infringer can also be subject to criminal penalties.[10] Further questions in this chapter deal with infringement.

What kinds of works can be protected by copyright under the Act?

Section 102 of the Act states:

Copyright protection subsists . . . in original works of authorship fixed in any tangible medium of expression, now known or later developed, from which they can be perceived, reproduced, or otherwise communicated, either directly or with the aid of a machine or device.[11]

There are two fundamental requirements for copyright protection: the work must be "original" and it must be "fixed" in a "tangible medium of expression."

What does the requirement of "originality" entail?

It may seem foreboding, but this requirement is relatively undemanding. To be original enough a work does not have to be novel, unique, or ingenious, as a patentable invention must be.[12] Instead, it need only have been created or originated by an "author" rather than found or identically copied from another work, and it must present more than a trivial variation on prior works from which it is derived.[13] Perhaps the best summation of originality was provided by Judge Learned Hand, who wrote that "if by some magic a man who had never known it were to compose anew Keats's Ode on a Grecian Urn, he would be an 'author,' and, if he copyrighted it, others might not copy that poem, though they might of course copy Keats's."[14]

To illustrate how limited the requirement of originality is, the Copyright Act states that compilations or anthologies of previously copyrighted (or public domain) works are eligible for copyright, the requisite originality being in the selection and ordering of the works. Similarly, a collage composed of found objects is the original work of an artist who has created the work through a process of selection and arrangement, and is copyrightable.

Every work must be evaluated to determine if it is sufficiently original. There is no one formulation or standard that articulates the requirement. The courts have found that mezzotint reproductions of 18th- and 19th-century paintings,[15] a scale model reproduction of Rodin's "Hands of God" sculpture,[16] and computer answer sheets for standardized tests [17] needed some degree of judgment, skill, and expertise for their creation and so were "original" enough to be eligible for copyright.

What is required for a work to be "fixed in a tangible medium of expression"?

According to the Copyright Act:[18]

A work is "fixed" in a tangible medium of expression when its *embodiment in a copy* . . . by or under the authority of the author, is *sufficiently permanent or stable to permit it to be perceived, reproduced, or otherwise communicated for a period of more than transitory duration.* [Italics added.]

9

The statutory definition is intentionally broad so that it will be applicable to modes of expression, developed in the future, that are unknown today. Preparatory works such as sketches, drafts, models, and notes, as well as finished works such as manuscripts, paintings, sculptures, motion pictures, and audio- and video-tapes, satisfy the fixation requirement. But, for example, oral recitations or performances, however original and otherwise eligible for federal copyright, do not satisfy the fixation test. An unauthorized taping of an oral recitation would not be eligible for copyright, since the statutory definition requires the "embodiment" to be "by or under the authority of the author." (Even though such an unfixed rendition will not qualify for federal copyright protection, it may—as is discussed on pages 37-40—qualify for other forms of legal protection.)

What kinds of works are protected?

Section 102 of the Act provides a partial answer: "Works of authorship include the following categories: (1) literary works; (2) musical works, including any accompanying words; (3) dramatic works, including any accompanying music; (4) pantomimes and choreographic works; (5) pictorial, graphic, and sculptural works; (6) motion pictures and other audiovisual works; and (7) sound recordings."[19] Most of those terms—e.g., "literary works" and "pictorial, graphic, and sculptural works"—are given more specific definitions in the Act. "Literary works," for example, are defined as "works, other than audiovisual works, expressed in words, numbers, or other verbal or numerical symbols or indicia, regardless of the nature of the material objects, such as books, periodicals, manuscripts, phonorecords, film, tape, disks, or cards, in which they are embodied."[20]

Significantly, the seven categories listed in section 102 do not exhaust the kinds of works that may qualify for copyright protection. The introduction to the listing contains the word "include," which the Act defines as being "illustrative and not limitative." Still, not every creative work necessarily qualifies for copyright protection.

What isn't protected by copyright?

Unfortunately, there is no clear and concise answer. The

1976 Copyright Act provides several categories or descriptions of works that are not subject to copyright protection. But as with so many areas of the law, the precise meaning of the statutory language is frequently difficult to discern and is open to interpretation and debate.

Section 102(b) provides:

> In no case does copyright protection . . . extend to any idea, procedure, process, system, method of operation, concept, principle, or discovery, regardless of the form in which it is described, explained, illustrated, or embodied in such work.[21]

This is a very important limitation of the availability of copyright protection. The traditional statement of this rule is that copyright protects only the "expression" of an idea and not the idea itself.[22] It is often far from clear just when the noncopyrightable "idea" becomes the copyrightable "expression" of that idea. For example, in one famous case the author of the play *Abie's Irish Rose* sued the producer of a motion picture entitled *The Cohens and the Kellys* for copyright infringement. Both works involve the marriage of a Jewish man to an Irish woman; their fathers oppose the marriage but ultimately come to bless it. The court rejected the copyright claim, declaring:

> Upon any work, and especially upon a play, a great number of patterns of increasing generality will fit equally well, as more and more of the incident is left out. The last may perhaps be no more than the most general statement of what the play is about, and at times might consist only of its title; but there is a point in this series of abstractions where they are no longer protected, since otherwise the playwright could prevent the use of his ideas, to which, apart from their expression, his property is never extended.[23]

Hypothetically, a novel dealing with the life and times of a Mafia "godfather" would not necessarily infringe the copyright of Mario Puzo's *The Godfather*, and a comic strip or motion picture about a man of extraordinary strength who can fly would not necessarily infringe the copyrights protecting *Superman*.[24]

On a more prosaic level, the U.S. Copyright Office, the federal agency responsible for administering the Copyright Act, has articulated the idea/expression distinction as follows:

> Copyright protection extends to a description, explanation, or illustration of an idea or system assuming that the requirements of the copyright law are met. Copyright in such a case protects the particular literary or pictorial form in which an author chooses to express himself. However, it gives the copyright owner no exclusive rights in the idea, plan, method, or system involved.
>
> Suppose, for example, that an author copyrights a book explaining a new system for food processing. The copyright in the book . . . will prevent others from publishing the author's text and illustrations describing the author's ideas for machinery, processes, and merchandising methods. However, it will not give him any rights against others who adopt the ideas for commercial purposes, or who develop or use the machinery, processes, or methods described in the book.[25]

At some point in the continuum a subsequent author's use of another author's "ideas" may well violate the copyright in that author's work, since at some point the first author's combination of "ideas" becomes protectable expression for copyright purposes. Just when that point will be reached is impossible to say in general. Each case depends on its own circumstances.

What about an author's research, and the discovery of facts?

Facts, as such, are not protectable by copyright, even if they are newly discovered by an author. Copyright only protects the original, creative work of an author; discovered facts do not meet that requirement. As a recent case put it:

> Obviously, a fact does not originate with the author of a book describing the fact. Neither does it originate

with one who "discovers" the fact. "The discoverer merely finds and records. He may not claim that the facts are 'original' with him although there may be originality and hence authorship in the manner of reporting, i.e., the 'expression' of the facts.". . .Thus, since facts do not owe their origin to any individual, they may not be copyrighted and are part of the public domain available to every person.[26]

Similarly, an author's research—no matter how diligent or important—cannot be copyrighted. As that same case explained:

> The valuable distinction in copyright law between facts and the expression of facts cannot be maintained if research is held to be copyrightable. There is no rational basis for distinguishing between facts and the research involved in obtaining facts. To hold that research is copyrightable is no more or no less than to hold that the facts discovered as a result of research are entitled to copyright protection.[27]

Hoehling v. Universal City Studios, Inc., involved a nonfiction book entitled *Who Destroyed the Hindenberg?*, in which the author presented at length the results of his exhaustive research and his theory of what happened to the German dirigible. When a movie was produced on the same subject, propounding the same theory, the author sued for copyright infringement. Even though it was admitted that the book was used in the making of the movie, the federal court of appeals in New York rejected the suit, holding that both the author's research and his theory were not protected by copyright. As the court put it:

> In works devoted to historical subjects, it is our view that a second author may make significant use of prior work, so long as he does not bodily appropriate the expression of another. . . . This principle is justified by the fundamental policy undergirding the copyright laws—the encouragement of contributions to recorded knowledge. The "financial reward guaranteed to the copy-

right holder is but an incident of this general objective, rather than an end in itself.'' . . . Knowledge is expanded as well, by granting new authors of historical works a relatively free hand to build upon the work of their predecessors.[28]

Legal protection for ideas, apart from copyright, is discussed later in this chapter.

What about names, titles, and short phrases?

According to the Copyright Office, ''To be protected by copyright, a work must contain at least a certain minimum amount of authorship in the form of original literary, musical, or graphic expression. Names, titles, and other short phrases do not meet these requirements.''[29]

The Office has provided a listing of kinds of phrases that do not qualify for copyright. It includes ''names or pseudonyms of individuals (including a pen name or stage name),'' ''titles of works,'' and ''catchwords, catch phrases, mottoes, slogans, or short advertising expressions.'' To emphasize the point, the Office states that this ineligibility ''is true even if the name, title, or short phrase is novel, distinctive, or lends itself to a play on words.''

But here too, at some point a short phrase, perhaps even a title, will be ''long'' enough to qualify for copyright. Just how ''long'' is ''long enough'' is impossible to state in a single formulation. Instead, determination of claims to copyright will again require case-by-case evaluation.

What about works of the United States government?

The Copyright Act expressly provides that ''Copyright protection . . . is not available for any work of the United States Government,'' which the Act defines as ''a work prepared by an officer or employee of the United States Government as a part of that person's official duties.''[30]

It should be fairly easy, most of the time, to determine whether a particular work merits this exclusion. Statements and reports issued by congressional committees or federal agencies, and opinions of the federal courts, clearly are not eligible for copyright and may be used freely by anyone who so desires. Sometimes the determination may not be so easy. One leading case involved the copyrightability of speeches of an admiral of the U.S. Navy that were written and delivered on his own time but typed by his navy assistant on navy equipment and stationery on navy time. The court ruled that the speeches did not qualify as "works of the United States Government," and thus could be copyrighted by the admiral, because they were not given as a part of his official duties but as an individual.[31] Presumably, then, a congressman's speech on the floor of the House would not be eligible for copyright, but his speech to a college audience might be. However, the mere fact that material is included in the Congressional Record does not mean anyone can use it, since it may have been quoted there and created by someone other than an officer or employee of the U.S. Government.

A more difficult issue is whether copyright can be secured in works prepared under a government contract or grant. The Act is deliberately silent on this point, it being Congress's intent to allow each government agency to make its own determination on copyrightability for each situation. Congress anticipated that if the agency hired an outside person or firm to do the work "merely as an alternative to having one of its own employees prepare the work," the right to copyright would not be granted.[32] It is foreseeable, however, that many contracted works will be eligible for copyright. Plainly, the matter is open to negotiation, and authors who are considering doing work under the auspices of the federal government should ensure that their work will be copyrightable.

What about works in the public domain?

This answer is somewhat circular: Works that are in the public domain are not eligible for copyright protection. A work is in the public domain when it is not protected by copyright, either because its copyright term has expired or because it failed to obtain or was otherwise ineligible for copyright protection. Generally, works in the public domain can be freely copied by anyone. All of Shakespeare's works, for instance, are in the public domain. Once a work falls into the public domain, there is no way to return it to copyright protection.

Can characters be protected by copyright?

Definitely, if they are in pictorial form. Pictorial renditions of Mickey Mouse, Dick Tracy, Wonder Woman, and other created characters are eligible.[33]

It is more difficult for literary characters—i.e., those depicted in words but not pictorially—to meet the level of expression required for copyright protection. For example, some courts have held that such characters are protectable if they "constitute the story being told" rather than only being the "vehicle" for telling the story.[34]

Applying this reasoning, one court held that Dashiell Hammett's conveyance of the copyright in the first Sam Spade story, *The Maltese Falcon,* to Warner Brothers did not transfer a copyright in the Spade character, so that Hammett was free to continue to use Spade in his work.[35] One of the most famous judicial statements on the issue came from Judge Learned Hand in the *Abie's Irish Rose* case:

> If Twelfth Night were copyrighted, it is quite possible that a second comer might so closely imitate Sir Toby Belch or Malvolio as to infringe, but it would not be enough that for one of his characters he cast a riotous knight who kept wassail to the discomfort of the household, or a vain and foppish steward who became amorous of his mistress. There would be no more than Shakespeare's "ideas" in the play, as little capable of monopoly as Einstein's Doctrine of Relativity, or Darwin's theory of the Origin of Species. It follows that the less developed the characters, the less they can be copyrighted; that is the penalty an author must bear for marking them too indistinctly.[36]

Thus, a well delineated literary character will be protectable by copyright.

What is a derivative work?

One of the five "exclusive rights" (discussed more fully below) that copyright confers on a copyright owner is the right "to prepare derivative works based upon the copyrighted work."[37]

The Act defines a "derivative work" as "a work based upon one or more preexisting works, such as a translation, musical arrangement, dramatization, fictionalization, motion picture version, sound recording, art reproduction, abridgment, condensation, or any other form in which a work may be recast, transformed, or adapted." It adds that "a work consisting of editorial revisions, annotations, elaborations, or other modifications which, as a whole, represent an original work of authorship, is a 'derivative work.' "[38]

Thus, whenever a book is translated into another language or abridged, or a movie is based on a book or a play, or a television series is based on a movie, or a book is based on a short story or magazine article, the resulting works are derivative works which the original copyright owner can control. Conversely, derivative works created without the consent of the copyright owner infringe the copyright of the original work.

The derivative work is entitled to a separate copyright. However, the Act states that the copyright in the derivative work "extends only to the material contributed by the author of such work, as distinguished from the preexisting material employed in the work, and does not imply any exclusive right in the preexisting material," and that it "is independent of, and does not affect or enlarge the scope, duration, ownership, or subsistence of, any copyright protection in the preexisting material."[39] In other words, it is only the new matter in the derivative work that is protected by its copyright.

As a result of these provisions, it is possible that a derivative work (such as a movie version or translation of a book) can be protected by its own copyright even if the underlying book is no longer copyrighted. This protection is limited: others are free to create their own movie versions or translations of the same underlying book—as long as they do not copy from a previous copyrighted movie version or translation.

What about collections of separate works, such as an almanac, an anthology, or an issue of a magazine?

The Copyright Act has provisions for "compilations" and "collective works." A compilation is "a work formed by the collection and assembling of preexisting materials or of data that

17

are selected, coordinated, or arranged in such a way that the resulting work as a whole constitutes an original work of authorship." Furthermore, "The term 'compilation' includes collective works."[40]

A collective work is "a work, such as a periodical issue, anthology, or encyclopedia, in which a number of contributions, constituting separate and independent works in themselves, are assembled into a collective whole."[41]

Thus—unlike derivative works, which by definition require adaptation and change of the underlying copyrighted work—in a compilation or collective work the presumption is that no changes have been made to the underlying material. As with derivative works, the Act makes clear that compilations (including collective works) can have their own copyrights, but the copyrights are independent from and do not affect the existence, duration, or effectiveness of the copyright in the underlying material.[42]

What specific rights does a copyright confer?

As indicated at the beginning of this chapter, copyright grants to its owner a form of legal monopoly over his or her work. It is not an absolute monopoly, however: it consists of specific "exclusive rights."

The Copyright Act lists five exclusive rights that belong to a copyright owner. They are:

(1) to reproduce the copyrighted work in copies;

(2) to prepare derivative works based upon the copyrighted work;

(3) to distribute copies . . . of the copyrighted work to the public by sale or other transfer of ownership, or by rental, lease, or lending;

(4) in the case of literary, musical, dramatic, and choreographic works, pantomimes, and motion pictures and other audiovisual works, to perform the copyrighted work publicly; and

(5) in the case of literary, musical, dramatic, and choreographic works, pantomimes, and pictorial, graphic, or sculptural works . . . to display the copyrighted work publicly.[43]

Thus the copyright grants to its owner, in large measure, the right to control the destiny of the copyrighted work. The owner can determine whether to expose it to the public, and if it is exposed, the owner can control—at least initially—the persons and means through which the exposure will take place. Any right the copyright owner possesses can be transferred to others.

These exclusive rights do not give the copyright owner complete control. The Act provides specified limitations, e.g., that libraries and archives have certain rights to reproduce copyrighted works without the copyright owner's consent.[44] In addition, the owner of an authorized copy of a copyrighted work—e.g., a book purchased in a bookstore—can do whatever he or she wishes with the copy, including reselling it, without the copyright owner's consent.[45] Probably the most significant limitation of the exclusive rights of the copyright owner is in the "fair use" doctrine.

What is "fair use"?

Although the concept of "fair use" was not expressly recognized in the copyright acts before the present one, it has long been an integral part of the law, as interpreted by the courts.[46] Faced with claims of infringement that seemed unfair or unrealistic, or inconsistent with the Constitutional purpose of copyright to promote knowledge and perhaps with the spirit if not the letter of the First Amendment, the courts had little difficulty creating a "fair use" limitation on the rights of copyright owners to prevent unauthorized use. A judicially created doctrine of "fair use" was well established in the law of copyright before the 1976 Copyright Act.

The Act expressly recognized a "fair use" limitation, providing that "notwithstanding" the grant of exclusive rights enumerated in the law, "the fair use of a copyrighted work . . . for purposes such as criticism, comment, news reporting, teaching (including multiple copies for classroom use), scholarship, or research, is not an infringement of copyright."[47] In the congressional reports accompanying the 1976 act, the drafters of the law provided other, more explicit examples of fair use:

quotation of excerpts in a review or criticism for purposes of illustration or comment; quotation of short passages in a scholarly or technical work, for illustration or clarification of the author's observations; use in a parody of some of the content of the work parodied; summary of an address or article, with brief quotations, in a news report; reproduction by a library of a portion of a work to replace part of a damaged copy; reproduction by a teacher or student of a small part of a work to illustrate a lesson; reproduction of a work in legislative or judicial proceedings or reports; incidental and fortuitous reproduction, in a news reel or broadcast, of a work located in the scene of an event being reported.[48]

As with many other concepts at the heart of copyright law, it is much easier to describe "fair use" in general than to give it a specific, concise, usable definition. "Indeed," it has been stated, "since the doctrine is an equitable rule of reason, no generally applicable definition is possible, and each case raising the question must be decided on its own facts."[49]

To assist in this effort, Congress has provided in the 1976 act four factors which "are to be considered" in "determining whether the use made of a work in any particular case is a fair use":

(1) the purpose and character of the use, including whether such use is of a commercial nature or is for nonprofit educational purposes;

(2) the nature of the copyrighted work;

(3) the amount and substantiality of the portion used in relation to to the copyrighted work as a whole ; and

(4) the effect of the use upon the potential market for or value of the copyrighted work.[50]

The first factor is self-explanatory. Plainly, even an extensive use for the purpose of criticism or scholarship will be viewed far differently in terms of fair use than the same—or even a lesser—use for the purpose of competing with the original copyrighted work or saving the second user the bother of having to create his or her original work.

The second factor—the nature of the copyrighted work being used—also requires little comment. In the vast gamut of works eligible for copyright, some, obviously, lend themselves far more readily than others to unauthorized use. A newspaper article or photograph reporting a political debate or a police raid—although entitled to copyright protection—seems far more susceptible to fair use by others than a poem, painting, or letter to one's spouse. If a copyrighted work is out of print or otherwise not readily accessible, unauthorized use of the work is more likely to be fair use. Perhaps conversely, whether a work is not yet—but is about to be—published may also be quite pertinent. Indeed, an important recent case dealt with the fairness of unauthorized use by a magazine of excerpts from an about-to-be published book in a situation where similar use after publication might well be deemed fair.[51]

The third factor—the amount and substantiality of the portion used in relation to the copyrighted work as a whole—usually generates the most questions by potential users, e.g., writers and publishers who want to include portions of the copyrighted work of others in their work. Invariably, they ask: How many words, how many pages, how many illustrations, can we use without having to get permission from the copyright owner? There is no one answer to this question. Fair use determination can only be made after evaluating all the factors set forth in the Act, as well as the surrounding circumstances. Nevertheless, it is obvious that the more one takes—especially as that taking represents an increasingly significant fraction of the entire copyrighted work— the less likely it is that the use will be found fair. The quality or significance of what is taken is also relevant.

The final factor—and the one that the courts often consider the most important—is "the effect of the use upon the potential market for or value of the copyrighted work." As one court put it, the central question in the determination of fair use is "whether the infringing work *tends* to diminish or prejudice the potential sale of plaintiff's work."[52]

In a recent case the sex-oriented weekly magazine *Screw* had published a full-page version of an advertisement that might have been sponsored by the Pillsbury Company. Almost exact copies of Pillsbury's copyrighted "Doughboy" and "Doughgirl" characters were portrayed—in the words of the federal judge who decided the case—"engaged in sexual intercourse and fellatio" beneath a headline containing an excerpt from Pillsbury's copyrighted jingle, "Nothing says lovin' like something from the oven and Pillsbury says it best." In a case that sought more than a million dollars in damages, the court ruled that *Screw*'s use of Pillsbury's copyrighted material was protected by the doctrine of fair use.

After applying the four statutory factors discussed above—indeed, after finding that under the third factor *Screw* had used "more of the copyrighted works than was necessary for its purposes"—the Court concluded that because Pillsbury had "failed to introduce more than a sliver of evidence supporting its claim of economic harm" caused by the alleged infringement, and because "the court is not inclined to fill this void by presuming economic injury from the acknowledged commercial value of these works," *Screw*'s use was not copyright infringement. The Court stated its conclusion as follows:

> In the court's judgment . . . the fact that the defendants used more than was necessary to accomplish the desired effect does not foreclose a finding of fair use. . . . [A]ll four factors must be considered together . . . Special emphasis, however, is placed on the fourth factor. [Pillsbury's] failure to show any appreciable harm to the potential market for or the value of its copyrighted works bears significantly upon the relative fairness of [*Screw*'s] unauthorized use of these copyrighted works. There is no showing that [*Screw*] intended to fill the demand for the original or that its presentation had this effect. One of the principal purposes of the Copyright Act is to preserve the profit motive for creating original works. Under this Act, the author's or creator's investment in a work and the ability to capitalize on this investment are entitled to protection. The same Act, however, creates a safe harbor for infringing uses which in Congress' collective judgment serve too important a

purpose to permit suppression. The court does not condone the manner in which [*Screw*] chose to assault the corporate citadel, but value judgments have no place in this analysis. The court concludes that [*Screw*'s] use of [Pillsbury's] copyrighted works was protected under the fair use doctrine.[53]

What about satire and parody?

One price an author or artist must pay for creating a successful work is that somebody, somewhere, may want to satirize it. Anyone familiar with television programs like the *Tonight Show* and *Saturday Night Live,* or magazines like *Mad,* is well aware that satire and parody of popular (and copyrighted) works is an important aspect of contemporary entertainment and communication. Whether such satires and parodies violate copyright is a serious and not necessarily easy question.

As might be expected, the courts have been confronted with many cases in which a copyright owner has claimed that a satire or parody of his work infringed his copyright, including a Jack Benny spoof of the Charles Boyer-Ingrid Bergman movie *Gaslight;*[54] pornographic versions of such characters as Mickey and Minnie Mouse;[55] *Mad* magazine's versions of the lyrics to such classic songs as "A Pretty Girl Is Like a Melody" (Louella Schwartz Describes Her Malady);[56] a musical play entitled *Scarlett Fever* which offended the owners of *Gone with the Wind;*[57] and *Screw* magazine's use of the Pillsbury jingle and doughdolls (just described). As might not be expected, the results in these cases have been anything but consistent, with some courts finding infringement and others finding fair use. In some cases the courts have ruled that the satirist may only use so much of the original work as is necessary to "evoke" it to his or her audience, while in other cases the courts have permitted much greater use so long as the satire does not injure the market for the original.[58] Again, each case depends upon its own facts and the court's evaluation of the four fair use factors discussed above.

Who owns the copyright in a work?

With two exceptions, which will be discussed in the next answer, the Act provides that "copyright in a work . . . vests

23

initially in the author or authors of the work."[59] Although the Act does not separately define the term "author," it does refer to "works of authorship," which were discussed above. Thus the person who originally creates a work of authorship—the writer of an article or book, the painter of a painting, the sculptor of a work of sculpture—owns the copyright.

The current Copyright Act has changed the law so that copyright protection attaches to a work automatically upon its creation. (Before, an unpublished work was protected, if at all, under the common law copyright principles of the states, with federal copyright protection, in the main, available only after the work was published.)[60]

What are the two exceptions to the author's ownership in the copyright to his or her work?

The first exception, works of the United States government, has already been discussed. Under the Act, such works are not entitled to copyright protection.[61] The second, and very important, exception is "works made for hire."

What is a "work made for hire," and who owns the copyright in it?

The Copyright Act describes two kinds of work made for hire. The first is "a work prepared by an employee within the scope of his or her employment."[62] The works of authors and artists who are employed by newspaper, magazine or book publishers, advertising agencies, TV or motion picture producers, or any other employer for that matter, are works made for hire if they are created in the course of employment (which essentially means as a part of the job). It is usually but not always easy to determine whether an author or artist is such an employee. In doubtful cases, factors that will be considered include the existence of a relationship going beyond the creation of the particular work; the payment of wages or other remuneration; the right of the employer to decide and supervise how the work is performed; the existence of an express employment contract; regular work hours and a regular workplace; and the employer's right to suspend or dismiss the employee.[63]

The second kind of work for hire is defined as "work

specially ordered or commissioned for use as a contribution to a collective work, as part of a motion picture or other audiovisual work, as a translation, as a supplementary work, as a compilation, as an instructional text, as a test, as answer material for a test, or as an atlas, if the parties expressly agree in a written instrument signed by them that the work shall be considered a work made for hire.''[64] Supplementary work is defined as ''a work prepared for publication as a secondary adjunct to a work by another author for the purpose of introducing, concluding, illustrating, explaining, revising, commenting upon, or assisting in the use of the other work, such as forewords, afterwords, pictorial illustrations, maps, charts, tables, editorial notes, musical arrangements, answer material for tests, bibliographies, appendices, and indexes.''[65] An ''instructional text'' is a ''literary, pictorial, or graphic work prepared for publication with the purpose of use in systematic instructional activities.''[66]

This second kind of ''work for hire'' has three significant aspects. First, works for hire are limited to the kinds set forth in the definition. Full-length books (other than instructional texts), plays, motion pictures, musical compositions, and almost all kinds of works of visual art (except illustrations for another work) can never be works for hire, which most often are articles or chapters for inclusion in magazines or books, illustrations for magazines or books, translations, or secondary contributions to a longer work, as described in the definition.

Second, the work has to be ''specially ordered or commissioned.'' It will usually be clear that this requirement has been satisfied, but sometimes this may be open to question, in which event an evaluation of the surrounding circumstances will be necessary. As Nimmer has put it, ''The key factor would appear to be whether the 'motivating factor in producing the work was the [person requesting preparation of the work] who induced [its] creation. . . .' ''[67]

Third, the ''for hire'' status must be confirmed in writing by the creator and employer. It is not clear whether the writing must be signed before the work is created; at least some publishers believe it is enough if the writing is signed much later, perhaps as an endorsement to the check used to pay for the work. But if the intention of the parties is to create a work-for-hire relationship, prudence suggests that the writing be executed at the time the work is first commissioned, at least pending court decisions on the matter. It is also best for the parties to state expressly that the work is "considered a work for hire."

The owner of the copyright in a work made for hire is the employer, not the creator. The creator has only the rights that may be contained in the contract between the parties for the work.

What happens when a work has two or more authors?

Under the Act, "the authors of a joint work are co-owners of copyright in the work"; a joint work is defined as "a work prepared by two or more authors with the intention that their contributions be merged into inseparable or interdependent parts of a unitary whole."[68] Co-owners are equal owners unless a contract between them says otherwise.[69]

Joint ownership of a work is discussed further in Chapter III, section B.

What can a copyright owner do with his or her copyright?

Pretty much anything the owner wants to. As indicated above, copyright is a form of property. Like other property, it may be sold, mortgaged, leased, licensed, bequeathed by will, or even given away, and of course it can simply be held on to by its owner.[70]

The present copyright law, unlike the 1909 law, allows the exclusive rights that comprise the copyright to be sold separately.[71] (Under the 1909 law, separate rights emanating from the copyright could be "licensed" but the copyright itself was deemed "indivisible" and could only be owned by *one* party at a time.) For example, the owner of the copyright in a novel can sell (or otherwise transfer) the exclusive right to publish it in book form to one or more publishers, sell (or otherwise transfer) the right to base a movie on it to somebody else, and retain all other rights. When one exclusive right is transferred by the copyright owner, the recipient owns the right for all purposes, including the right to bring suit for infringement.

When a copyright owner wishes to sell (or otherwise transfer) one or more of the exclusive rights in the copyright, the Act provides that there must be "an instrument of conveyance, or a note or memorandum of the transfer . . . in writing and signed by the owner of the rights conveyed or such owner's duly authorized agent."[72] The transfer of a non-exclusive right, however, does not have to be in writing to be valid.[73]

Does ownership of the physical work carry with it ownership of its copyright?

No. It used to be presumed that the ownership of a work of art included the right to reproduce it and own all other rights in the work.[74] But that presumption was changed by statute in some states[75] and was eliminated in the 1976 Copyright Act, which provides that "[t]ransfer of ownership of any material object," including the original of a work of art, "does not of itself convey any rights in the copyrighted work embodied in the object," and, conversely, that "transfer of ownership of a copyright or of any exclusive rights under a copyright" does not "convey property rights in any material object."[76]

A significant exception involves the exclusive right "to display the copyrighted work [of visual art] publicly." The sale of the physical work does not automatically carry with it the copyright in the work, which the artist retains, but it does transfer the "display" part of the copyright.[77]

How long does copyright protection last?

The answer to this simple question is not so simple. It depends on whether the work was protected by federal statutory copyright before January 1, 1978, on whether it is a work for hire, and on whether it is an "anonymous" or "pseudonymous" work.

Except for works for hire and anonymous or pseudonymous works, copyright in works that were not published by January 1, 1978, or were created after that date, lasts the life of the author plus 50 years.[78] In the case of joint authors, this means 50 years after the death of the last surviving author.[79] (Copyright for works that were unpublished on January 1, 1978, does not expire until December 31, 2002, even if the author has been dead for 50 years before then; if such works are published on or before December 31, 2002, the copyright will last until December 31, 2027.[80]) Anonymous or pseudonymous works and works made for hire keep their copyright· for 75 years from the year of first publication or 100 years from the year of creation, whichever expires first.[81]

For works that were protected by federal statutory copyright before January 1, 1978, which includes all works published with copyright before then, the term is different. The old copyright law provided two 28-year terms of protection generally beginning on the date of publication. Failure to renew for the second (renewal) term would cause the work to fall into the public domain.[82] The 1976 act made two changes. First, the second term was extended to 47 years, making the total duration of copyright protection 75 years.[83] Second, the old law required renewal within the exact last year, i.e., between the 27th and 28th anniversaries of the publication date.[84] The 1976 act extended the first term to the end of the calendar year during which it would otherwise have expired. The outside renewal date is thus the December 31 after the old date.[85]

Who is the beneficiary of the renewal term?

The answer requires an appreciation of the purpose of the renewal term. Because it is difficult, if not impossible, to estimate accurately the commercial value of a work before its initial publication, Congress in the 1909 Copyright Act sought to protect the creator by providing two periods of copyright protection, with the creator being able to reclaim the rights to the work at the end of the first term. Further, Congress sought to protect the creator's family by providing a succession of beneficiaries who would own the renewal term of copyright if the author died during the first term: "the author of such work, if still living, or the widow, widower, or children of the author, if the author be not living, or if such author, widow, widower, or children be not living, then the author's executors, or in the absence of a will, his or her next of kin."[86]

This system did not work well, for several reasons. First, failure properly to renew often resulted in unwitting forfeiture of copyright protection and dedication of the work to the public. Second, the courts held that authors' grants of rights in the expected renewal term made during the first term, even in the very first grant of rights, were effective and enforceable if the grantor was alive when the renewal term began.[87] It then became common practice for the recipient of rights during the first term to obtain a grant of renewal rights at the same time.

The 1976 act retained the renewal term system for works already in their first term on January 1, 1978, but Congress was determined to revise the system for works that first acquired copyright under the new act's provisions. The new act therefore contains a single term of copyright but the copyright owner has specific rights to terminate transfers of rights during that term.

How can a copyright owner terminate an earlier grant of rights?

The 1976 Act grants the copyright owner (or a specified list of beneficiaries) the right to terminate prior transfers at certain times and under certain circumstances. Its provisions are too complicated to be fully described here; instead, we shall summarize some of the most important elements.

There are different termination provisions for transfers executed before and after January 1, 1978, the day the 1976 act took effect.[88]

With respect to transfers—which term includes sales of the entire copyright as well as exclusive and non-exclusive licenses of selected rights executed by an individual author/copyright owner—that were made before January 1, 1978, when the two-term system was in effect, the new act, in the words of Barbara Ringer, the Register of Copyrights when the 1976 act took effect,

> permits an author (or certain heirs of a dead author) to reclaim rights under a copyright after the copyright has run 56 years. Since the new law extends the length of subsisting copyrights from the 56-year maximum provided in the 1909 Act to a new maximum of 75 years, the potential period covered by these terminations will usually be 19 years. However, for those copyrights that have already been given interim extensions beyond the 56-year maximum (under nine Acts of Congress between 1962 and 1974), the years

remaining to be covered by a possible termination will be less than 19, and in some cases as few as five.[89]

With respect to transfers made after January 1, 1978, the 1976 Act

establishes a system under which the author (or certain members of a dead author's family) can terminate the grant of rights and reclaim the copyright after a specified period. Generally the minimum period will be 35 years from the date the grant was executed, but it can be longer (up to 40 years) in certain cases involving publishing rights. Exercise of this right is optional and is subject to a number of conditions and qualifications. However . . . the right cannot be assigned away or waived in advance; the statute says: "Termination of the grant may be effected notwithstanding any agreement to the contrary, including an agreement to make a will or to make any future grant."

Furthermore:

The earliest date anyone might be able to file an advance notice of termination will be January 1, 2013. The day may seem a long way off, but this should not deter anyone from keeping accurate records or establishing appropriate tickler files now.[90]

Finally, Ms. Ringer observed that terminations of transfers made before and after 1978 "are subject to a complex assortment of conditions, time limits, and procedural requirements but, assuming these are met, the right to terminate will exist regardless of any contrary agreements."[91]

Are there any legal formalities that must be complied with to obtain and maintain copyright protection?

No, and yes. On creation of a work, nothing need be done to secure copyright protection, which is automatic. However, the Act contains requirements that must be complied with if and when a work is published and if and when an owner wants to be able to sue for infringement. The formalities are notice, registration and deposit, and recordation.

What are the notice requirements of the Copyright Act?

The Act provides that "[w]henever a work . . . is published in the United States or elsewhere by authority of the copyright owner, a notice of copyright . . . shall be placed on all publicly distributed copies from which the work can be visually perceived, either directly or with the aid of a machine or device."[92] Publication, for these purposes, means "the distribution of copies . . . of a work to the public by sale or other transfer of ownership, or by rental, lease, or lending."[93] The Act states that notice of copyright must consist of:

(1) the symbol © (the letter C in a circle), or the word "Copyright", or the abbreviation "Copr."; and

(2) the year of first publication of the work; in the case of compilations or derivative works incorporating previously published material, the year date of first publication of the compilation or derivative work is sufficient. The year date may be omitted where a pictorial, graphic, or sculptural work, with the accompanying text matter, if any, is reproduced in or on greeting cards, postcards, stationery, jewelry, dolls, toys, or any useful articles; and

(3) the name of the owner of copyright in the work, or an abbreviation by which the name can be recognized, or a generally known alternative designation of the owner.[94]

The Act provides that the notice "shall be affixed to the copies in such manner and location as to give reasonable notice of the claim of copyright."[95] (The old Copyright Act required that the notice appear at specified places on a work.) The Copyright Office has promulgated regulations that set forth permissible kinds of notice, but the Act makes clear that other means of notice may also be sufficient. The Office has also declared that the notice should be permanently legible to an ordinary user of the work and not concealed from view upon reasonable examination.

What happens if notice is omitted or in error?

Fortunately, the consequences under the 1976 act are not as severe as under the 1909 act, where omission of notice caused the work to go into the public domain.[96] The new act provides that if the notice has been omitted from "no more than a relatively small number of copies" distributed to the public, or if it contains certain errors, the copyright owner can preserve the copyright in the work by taking certain steps that are spelled out in the Act, including (1) registering the work with the Copyright Office within five years of the publication without notice and (2) attempting to correct the missing or erroneous notice.[97]

What are the notice requirements for a contribution to a magazine?

Under the Act, a contribution to a magazine—a "collective work"—may, but is not required to, bear its own notice of copyright. If the contribution does not contain its own notice, the Act provides that an overall notice for the entire work "is sufficient to satisfy the [notice] requirements . . . with respect to the separate contributions it contains . . . regardless of the ownership of copyright in the contributions and whether or not they have been previously published."[98] The only exception to this rule is for advertisements placed by anyone other than the publisher, which must contain their own notice.[99] Moreover, the single notice does not affect the copyright in that contribution, which —unless the contribution is a work made for hire or unless an agreement has been reached that provides otherwise—will be owned by the creator and not the publisher whose name almost always appears in the single notice. The Act also makes clear that "[i]n the absence of an express transfer of the copyright or of any rights under it, the owner of copyright in the collective work is presumed to have acquired only the privilege of reproducing and distributing the contribution as part of that particular collective work, any revision of that collective work, and any later collective work in the same series."[100]

What does registration involve?

Registration means the filing of a prescribed form with the Copyright Office, together with, in most cases, one or two copies of the work, and the payment of the prescribed fee.[101] (Generally, unpublished works require one copy, while published works require two.) If the Copyright Office determines that the work is eligible for copyright, it issues a certificate of copyright to the copyright owner. Published and unpublished works may be registered. The Copyright Office will upon request furnish anyone with copies of its numerous circulars on the new law and its procedures as well as copyright application forms. The Office will also answer telephone inquiries. The address is Information and Publications Section, Copyright Office, Library of Congress, Washington, D.C. 20559, and its telephone number is (202) 287–8700.

Registration is not required for a work to be protected by copyright, but is required before a copyright owner may sue for infringement.[102] There are, however, specific inducements to early registration. For example, registration may take place after the infringement, but then the copyright owner may not be entitled to an award of statutory damages or attorneys' fees in the infringement suit,[103] remedies which are discussed below. If a copyright owner contemplates the possibility of an infringement action, it is important that the work be registered as early as possible.

How does one know what form to use?

Somewhat surprisingly, the forms promulgated by the Copyright Office do not correspond to the enumeration of "works of authorship" set forth in the Copyright Act, but relate generally to the nature of the work. Form TX is used for all kinds of printed textual material; form VA, for works of visual art; form PA, for works of the performing arts; and form SR, for sound recordings. Renewals use form RE, and supplementary and correcting information is registered with form CA. Obviously, some works fit into more than one category; then the owner should choose the one which best applies (there are no penalties for using the wrong form). When the form is completed it is sent, along with the necessary deposit and payment, to the Copyright Office.

Must a copy of a work of visual art be deposited?

No. The Act authorizes the Copyright Office to promulgate regulations pursuant to which "identifying material" may be deposited in lieu of a copy of the actual work.[104] The Office's regulations state that it will accept "photographic prints, transparencies, photostats, drawings or similar two dimensional reproductions or renderings of the work, in a form visually perceivable without the aid of a machine or device."[105] With respect to pictorial or graphic works, "[s]uch material shall reproduce the actual colors employed in the work," but for all other works the material may be in black and white.[106]

Except for holograms, only one set of complete identifying material is required. A set of complete identifying material is defined as consisting of "as many pieces of identifying material as are necessary to show clearly the copyrightable content of the work for which deposit is made or for which registration is sought." All the pieces of identifying material in a set must be of uniform size. Transparencies must be at least 35mm, and if they are less than $3'' \times 3''$ they must be fixed on cardboard, plastic, or similar mounts to facilitate identification and storage. Identifying material other than transparencies should be not less than $3'' \times 3''$ and not more than $9'' \times 12''$. The Copyright Office expresses a preference for $8'' \times 10''$. At least one piece of the set must, on the frame, back, mount, or elsewhere, indicate the title and dimensions of the work. If the work has been published with a notice of copyright, the notice and its position on the work must be clearly shown on at least one piece of identifying material. If the size or position of the notice makes it necessary, a separate drawing or similar reproduction may be submitted.

What is "recordation"?

Recordation is the filing—recording—of certain documents with the Copyright Office. It is not a condition of copyright protection, but it is a prerequisite to bringing a suit for infringement.

As the Act puts it, "[a]ny transfer of copyright ownership or other document pertaining to a copyright may be recorded in the Copyright Office if the document . . . bears the actual signature of the person who executed it, or if it is accompanied by a sworn or official certification that it is a true copy of the original, signed document."[107] Recordation provides "constructive notice" of the facts stated in the document, and will establish priority between conflicting transfers.[108]

The only document that the law requires be recorded is a notice of termination of a previous transfer, which must "be recorded in the Copyright Office before the effective date of termination, as a condition to its taking effect."[109]

What constitutes infringement?

As defined by the Act, "[a]nyone who violates any of the exclusive rights of the copyright owner," subject to the doctrine of fair use and the other express limitations on those rights contained in the Act, "is an infringer of the copyright."[110] The Act does not further define what constitutes such a violation. Plainly, a copyrighted work would be infringed by reproducing it in whole or in any substantial part, and by duplicating it exactly or by simulation. Moreover, it is also clear that adapting a copyrighted work into a different medium—e.g., basing a movie on a novel—will also constitute infringement.

However, as indicated above in the discussion of the "originality" needed for copyright protection, similarity is not enough to establish infringement. As Nimmer has put it, "[T]he rights of a copyright owner are not infringed if a subsequent work, although substantially similar, has been independently created without reference to the prior work. Thus absent copying there can be no infringement of copyright regardless of the extent of similarity."[111]

It is not always easy to prove such copying, but it can be established by circumstantial evidence. Thus, if the plaintiff can show that the defendant had access to the copyrighted work, and that there are substantial similarities between the two works, a finding of infringement could well follow. But if the defendant can prove that he or she actually copied from a different work, or that the parts copied from the plaintiff are not copyrightable, then there can be no infringement. The copying need not be verbatim.

As long as the defendant's work is substantially similar to that of the plaintiff's, and is the product of copying rather than independent effort, it will constitute an infringement of the plaintiff's "expression." Similarity which is not "substantial," even if due to copying, is a noninfringing use of the plaintiff's "ideas."[112]

What should a copyright owner do upon discovering an infringement?

First, try to stop it. Sometimes the infringement is innocent—for one reason or another, the infringer is not aware that his or her use constitutes an infringement; in most of these cases the infringer will readily agree to stop, and perhaps to make amends. Innocence is no defense to an infringement action, but it will probably affect the nature and extent of the recovery obtained by the copyright owner in an infringement action.

However, the copyright owner will often conclude that a lawsuit must be brought. Indeed, it is the availability of such a suit that gives copyright protection its "teeth" and makes copyright a respected and valuable right.

What are the remedies available to a copyright owner in an infringement action?

Under the Act, a copyright owner can secure an injunction against continuation of the infringement, including, in appropriate cases, a "preliminary injunction" before the case goes to trial;[113] the impoundment and destruction of the infringing items;[114] an award of the owner's damages and the infringer's profits,[115] or in the alternative an award of "statutory damages";[116] and in the discretion of the court an award of the owner's attorney's fees.[117]

With respect to the award of actual damages and the infringer's profits, the Act provides:

The copyright owner is entitled to recover the actual damages suffered by him or her as a result of the infringement, and any profits of the infringer that are attributable to the infringement and are not taken into account in computing the actual damages. In establishing the infringer's profits, the copyright owner is required to present proof only of the infringer's gross revenue, and the infringer is required to prove his or her deductible expenses and the elements of profit attributable to factors other than the copyrighted work.[118]

It is often difficult for a copyright owner to prove actual damages and/or profits realized from the infringement. Recognizing this, Congress—in both the 1909 Copyright Act and the current one—allowed the owner to elect instead an award of "statutory damages." As the Act puts it,

> the copyright owner may elect, at any time before final judgment is rendered, to recover, instead of actual damages and profits, an award of statutory damages for all infringements involved in the action, with respect to any one work, for which any one infringer is liable individually, or for which any two or more infringers are liable jointly and severally, in a sum of not less than $250 or more than $10,000 as the court considers just.[119]

The Act also provides that if the infringement "was committed willfully," the maximum award of statutory damages can be $50,000, and if the infringement was innocent—i.e., "the infringer was not aware and had no reason to believe that his or her acts constituted an infringement of copyright," the minimum award of statutory damages can be $100.[120]

The Act also provides that the court, in its discretion, may grant to the copyright owner an award of his or her costs of litigation, including attorneys' fees. Statutory damages and attorneys' fees, it is important to remember, will not be available unless the copyright owner complies with the registration provisions discussed earlier in this chapter.

Finally, under certain circumstances, including willful infringement "for purposes of commercial advantage or private financial gain," the infringer can be subject to criminal penalties as well.[121]

Are there rights protecting the work of authors and artists other than those stemming from the Copyright Act?

Yes. As stated above, the Copyright Act of 1976 pre-empts all other copyright protection for works that meet its requirements. Thus an original work of authorship that is fixed in a tangible medium of expression will either have copyright protection under the federal Copyright Act or none at all.

But what about original works of authorship that are not so fixed, such as a recited poem or story, an improvised performance of a skit or play or dance, or an oral description of a visual design or work of art? Since these works are not eligible for protection under the Copyright Act, it seems likely that they are still protected from infringement under state common law copyright provisions.

Short phrases and titles, which are not eligible for federal copyright protection, may be protected by the federal trademark law and the trademark and unfair competition laws of the states. A phrase like "Where there's life, there's Bud," or a title like *E.T.*, will almost certainly be entitled to protection by non-copyright laws, which have as their purpose preventing customer confusion or the erosion of the value of a trade name or identity.[122] The principal requirement here is that the phrase or title be distinctive and that it be associated in the public's mind with a particular source or a particular work. This means that the title of a literary work is probably not entitled to protection unless and until it has achieved such a direct association, which the law somewhat confusingly calls "secondary meaning."

Every state has laws against "unfair competition," and to some extent such laws may still operate against the "misappropriation" of another's work, notwithstanding the Copyright Act's "pre-emption" of "all legal or equitable rights that are equivalent to any of the exclusive rights within the general scope of copyright."[123] The extent of this protection will have to await adjudication by the courts.

There are at least some indications from the courts that protection will be afforded apart from copyright when an author's work is misused or abused. In one important case,[124] the group Monty Python sought an injunction against a television network that intended to broadcast severely edited versions of three of its programs, even though the network had obtained permission to air the programs. The group contended that the network's editing "impaired the integrity" of its work and that this violated the permission the network had obtained and the legal rights of the group.

The federal Court of Appeals in New York ruled that "the unauthorized editing of the underlying work, if proven, would constitute an infringement of the copyright in that work similar to any other use of a work that exceeded the license granted by the proprietor of the copyright."[125] Also, and even more significantly, the court declared that it seemed likely that the group would establish that "the cuts made constituted an actionable mutilation of Monty Python's work." This legal claim, the court said, "finds its roots in the continental concept of *droit moral*, or moral right, which may generally be summarized as including the right of the artist to have his work attributed to him in the form in which he created it."[126] The court continued:

> American copyright law, as presently written, does not recognize moral rights or provide a cause of action for their violation, since the law seeks to vindicate the economic, rather than the personal, rights of authors. Nevertheless, the economic incentive for artistic and intellectual creation that serves as the foundation for American copyright law . . . cannot be reconciled with the inability of artists to obtain relief for mutilation or misrepresentation of their work to the public on which the artists are financially dependent. Thus courts have long granted relief for misrepresentation of an artist's work by relying on theories outside the statutory law of copyright, such as contract law . . . or the tort of unfair competition. . . . Although such decisions are clothed in terms of proprietary right in one's creation, they also properly vindicate the author's personal right to prevent the presentation of his work to the public in a distorted form.[127]

The court indicated that the "garbled" editing of the group's work violated its rights under the federal Lanham Act, which the court said protects against "misrepresentations that may injure [a person's] business or personal reputation, even where no registered trademark is concerned."[128] As the court concluded, "[I]t is sufficient to violate the [Lanham] Act that a representation of a

39

product, although technically true, creates a false impression of the product's origin."[129]

Although the language the court used strongly suggests that authors and artists have significant legal protection for the integrity of their work apart from copyright, and although such protection is much to be desired, it is not clear that such protection is generally available today. The broad declarations of the Monty Python case have not as yet been applied to enough situations where creators have suffered similar injury so as to lead to useful legal precedents. (The concept of *droit moral* is discussed further in Chapter III, section D.)

Can an author protect ideas, as such, before they are published?

Yes, to some extent. Copyright does not protect ideas, and once they are publicly disclosed they are in the public domain. But this does not mean that those ideas have no value before they are disclosed, or that an author is powerless to protect them from unauthorized use.

It is obvious that ideas can have enormous value; countless books, movies, TV shows and advertising campaigns owe much of their success to an underlying idea. Under certain circumstances, wholly apart from copyright, the law will protect the creators of such ideas from their misappropriation. For example, if a creator discloses an idea under circumstances where it is understood —or should have been understood—that it would be kept confidential or that the creator would be compensated if it was used following disclosure, the law may well treat those "understandings" as contracts and permit the creator to recover for their breach. In some cases, these contracts will be "implied" by the conduct of the parties; in others they will be "implied" by the law as construed by the courts.[130] It may also be possible, in appropriate cases, to recover for unauthorized use where there has been no disclosure at all—e.g., where the idea has literally been stolen from its creator—but there are few precedents to support such relief and the burden of proof on the plaintiff would be very high, since the courts recognize that the same or similar ideas can often be devised independently and that many people erroneously assume that an idea similar to theirs "must have been stolen."[131]

What can an author do to protect ideas before they are disclosed?

First, the creator should put the idea in writing, as fully as possible. This will ensure that the expression of the idea, at least, will be protected by copyright, and may also discourage others from trying to distinguish between the copyrighted expression and the uncopyrighted idea. Second, the creator should date the writing and take steps to establish proof of that date—by mailing a copy to him- or herself or another person and keeping the envelope sealed; by having the date notarized or otherwise confirmed by a trusted other person, such as an agent or lawyer; or by filing the writing with a group like the Authors League (if the creator is a member) that will be able to confirm the date of filing. This establishes when the creator had the idea, which may be crucial if the dispute involves who had the idea first. Third, the creator should be extremely careful to whom, and under what circumstances, the idea is disclosed. In fact, the idea should only be disclosed when it is understood that the creator is not gratuitously relinquishing it but expects to be compensated if it is used. If the creator signs a release waiving any such expectation—and such releases are frequently demanded—or if the creator makes the disclosure knowing that the recipient has no obligation to pay if the idea is used, then the creator may well be without legal recourse if the idea is used following that disclosure.

NOTES

1. U.S. CONST. ART. I., Sec. 8, Clause 8.
2. *See generally* 1 Nimmer, Copyright, Chapter 4 (1981).
3. 17 U.S.C. §301.
4. *See generally* 17 U.S.C. §106.
5. 17 U.S.C. §502.
6. 17 U.S.C. §509.
7. 17 U.S.C. §504(b).
8. 17 U.S.C. §§504(b), (c).
9. 17 U.S.C. §505.
10. 17 U.S.C. §506.
11. 17 U.S.C. §102(a).
12. *See generally* 35 U.S.C. §§101–03. Congress recognized this difference, the legislative history stating that the standard under the copyright (as

opposed to the patent) law "does not include requirements of novelty." H.Rep. 94–1476, 94th Cong., 2d Sess. 51, reprinted in [1976] U.S. Code Cong. & Ad. News 5659, 5664 [Hereinafter "H.Rep."].

13. *Alfred Bell & Co., Ltd. v. Catalda Fine Arts, Inc.*, 191 F.2d 99, 102–03 (2d Cir. 1951).

14. *Sheldon v. Metro-Goldwyn Pictures Corp.*, 81 F.2d 49, 54 (2d Cir. 1936), aff'd, 309 U.S. 390 (1940).

15. *Alfred Bell & Co., Ltd. v. Catalda Fine Arts, Inc.*, supra n.13.

16. *Alva Studies, Inc. v. Winninger*, 177 F.Supp. 265 (S.D. N.Y. 1959).

17. *Harcourt, Brace & World, Inc. v. Graphic Controls Corp.*, 329 F.Supp. 517 (S.D. N.Y. 1971).

18. 17 U.S.C. §101.

19. 17 U.S.C. §102(a).

20. 17 U.S.C. §101.

21. 17 U.S.C. §102(b).

22. *Dellar v. Samuel Goldwyn, Inc.*, 150 F.2d 612 (2d Cir. 1945); *see, e.g., Mazer v. Stein*, 347 U.S. 201 (1954); *Baker v. Seldon*, 101 U.S. 99 (1879); *Peter Pan Fabrics, Inc. v. Martin Weiner Corp.*, 274 F.2d 487, 489 (2d Cir. 1960).

23. *Nicholas v. Universal Pictures Corp.*, 45 F.2d 119, 121 (2d Cir. 1930), cert. denied, 282 U.S. 902 (1931).

24. Indeed, in *Warner Bros., Inc. v. ABC, Inc.*, 654 F.2d 204 (2d Cir. 1981), Warner Bros. contended that because a character in the defendant's show "The Greatest American Hero" also flew, had superhuman strength, did battle with villains, etc., the defendant had infringed Warner's copyright in the character of Superman. The court affirmed the trial court's refusal to grant a preliminary injunction on the claim.

25. U.S. Copyright Office, "Ideas, Plans, Methods or Systems," Circular 31 (1982).

26. *Miller v. Universal City Studios, Inc.*, 650 F.2d 1365, 1368–69 (5th Cir. 1981).

27. *Id.* at 1372.

28. *Hoehling v. Universal City Studios, Inc.*, 618 F.2d 972, 980 (2d Cir. 1980).

29. U.S. Copyright Office, "Copyright Protection Not Available for Names, Titles or Short Phrases," Circular R34 (1978).

30. 17 U.S.C. §§101, 105.

31. *Public Affairs Assocs., Inc. v. Rickover*, 268 F.Supp. 444 (D. D. C. 1967); *see generally Scherr v. Universal Match Corp.*, 417 F.2d 497 (2d Cir. 1969); *Public Affairs Assocs., Inc. v. Rickover*, 284 F.2d 262 (D.C. Cir. 1960), vacated for insufficient record, 369 U.S. 111 (1962).

32. H.Rep. at 59; U.S. Code Cong. & Ad. News at 5672.

33. *See Walt Disney Productions v. The Air Pirates*, 345 F.Supp. 108 (N.D. Cal. 1972), aff'd, 581 F.2d 751 (9th Cir. 1978), cert. denied, 439 U.S. 1132 (1979).

34. *E.g., Warner Bros. Pictures, Inc. v. CBS, Inc.*, 216 F.2d 945 (9th Cir. 1954), *cert. denied*, 348 U.S. 971 (1955); *cf. CBS v. DeCosta* [I], 377 F.2d 315 (1st Cir.), *cert. denied*, 389 U.S. 1007 (1967).

35. *Warner Bros. Pictures, Inc. v. CBS, Inc.*, *supra* n. 33.

36. *Nicholas v. Universal Pictures Corp.*, *supra* n. 23, at 121.

37. 17 U.S.C. §106.

38. 17 U.S.C. §101.

39. 17 U.S.C. §103(b).

40. 17 U.S.C. §101.

41. *Id.*

42. 17 U.S.C. §103(b).

43. 17 U.S.C. §106.

44. 17 U.S.C. §108.

45. 17 U.S.C. §109.

46. *See generally* 3 Nimmer, *supra* n. 2, §13.05.

47. 17 U.S.C. §107.

48. H.Rep. at 65; Code Cong. & Ad. News at 5678–79.

49. *Id.*

50. 17 U.S.C. §107.

51. *See Harper & Row Publishers, Inc. v. Nation Enterprises*, 557 F. Supp. 1067 (S.D.N.Y. 1983), which involved an article in *Nation* Magazine that contained extensive quotations from Former President Gerald Ford's about-to-be-published memoirs, to which the magazine obtained unauthorized access. The trial court rejected the magazine's claim that the article was reporting news and that its use of the quotations was therefore protected by the fair use doctrine. That decision has been appealed.

52. *Universal City Studios, Inc. v. Sony Corporation of America*, 659 F.2d 963, 974 (9th Cir. 1981), *quoting* 3 Nimmer, *supra* n. 2, § 13.05[E][4] [C] at 13–84. [Italics in original].

53. *Pillsbury Co. v. Milky Way Productions, Inc.*, 8 Med.L.Rptr. 1016 (N.D.Ga. 1981), at 1023–24.

54. *Benny v. Loews, Inc.*, 239 F.2d 532 (9th Cir. 1956), *aff'd by an equally divided court*, 356 U.S. 543 (1958).

55. *Walt Disney Productions v. The Air Pirates*, *supra* n. 33.

56. *Berlin v. E.C. Publications, Inc.*, 329 F.2d 541 (2d Cir.), *cert. denied*, 379 U.S. 822 (1964).

57. *Metro-Goldwyn-Mayer, Inc. v. Showcase Atlanta Cooperative Productions, Inc.*, 479 F.Supp. 351 (N.D. Ga. 1979).

58. *Compare Berlin v. E.C. Publications, Inc.*, *supra* n. 56 (fair use permits taking only as much of the copyrighted work as is necessary to conjure up the original) *with Elsmere Music, Inc. v. NBC, Inc.*, 482 F.Supp. 741 (S.D.N.Y.), *aff'd*, 623 F.2d, 252 (2d Cir. 1980) (the appellate court affirming in part because of a belief that "in today's work of often unrelieved solemnity, copyright law should be hospitable to the humor of parody").

59. 17 U.S.C. §201(a).
60. *See generally* Nimmer, *supra* n. 2, Chapter 4.
61. 17 U.S.C. §105.
62. 17 U.S.C. §101.
63. *See, e.g., Picture Music, Inc. v. Bourne, Inc.*, 314 F.Supp. 640 (S.D. N.Y. 1970), *aff'd*, 457 F.2d 1213 (2d Cir.), *cert. denied*, 409 U.S. 997 (1972).
64. 17 U.S.C. §101.
65. *Id.*
66. *Id.*
67. Nimmer, *supra* n. 2, pp. 5–25.
68. 17 U.S.C. §§201(a); 101.
69. H.Rep. at 120; U.S. Code Cong. & Ad. News at 5736.
70. *See* 17 U.S.C. §201 (d) (1).
71. *See generally* Latman, *The Copyright Law* 99–101 (5th ed. 1979).
72. 17 U.S.C. §204(a).
73. Latman, *supra* n. 71, at 101.
74. *See, e.g., Pushman v. New York Graphic Society, Inc.*, 25 N.Y.S.2d 32 (Sup.Ct. 1941), *aff'd*, 28 N.Y.S.2d 711 (1st Dept. 1941), *aff'd*, 287 N.Y. 302 (1942).
75. *E.g.*, N.Y. Gen.Bus.L. §219–g (McKinney 1982).
76. 17 U.S.C. §202.
77. *See* 17 U.S.C. §109(b).
78. 17 U.S.C. §302(a).
79. 17 U.S.C. §302(b).
80. 17 U.S.C. §303.
81. 17 U.S.C. §302(c).
82. *See generally* Latman, *supra* n. 71, at 71–91.
83. 17 U.S.C. §304(a) (b).
84. *See generally* H. Rep. at 142–43; U.S. Code Cong. & Ad. News at 5758–59.
85. 17 U.S.C. §305.
86. 17 U.S.C. §304(a).
87. *Fred Fisher Music Co., Inc. v. W. Witmark & Sons*, 318 U.S. 643 (1943).
88. *Compare* 17 U.S.C. §203 (termination of grants made after January 1, 1978) *with* 17 U.S.C. §304(c) (termination of grants made before January 1, 1978).
89. Ringer, "Finding Your Way Around in the New Copyright Law," *Publishers Weekly*, Dec. 13, 1976, p. 38.
90. *Id.*
91. *Id.*
92. 17 U.S.C. §401(a).
93. 17 U.S.C. §101.
94. 17 U.S.C. §401(b).

95. 17 U.S.C. §401(c).
96. H.Rep. at 146; U.S. Code Cong. & Ad. News at 5762.
97. 17 U.S.C. §405.
98. 17 U.S.C. §404(a).
99. *Id*.
100. 17 U.S.C. §201(c).
101. *See* 17 U.S.C. §408.
102. 17 U.S.C. §411.
103. *See* 17 U.S.C. §412.
104. *See* 17 U.S.C. §§408(b), 702.
105. Copyright Office Regs., §202.21, reprinted in Nimmer, *supra* n. 2, Appendix 3.
106. *Id*.
107. 17 U.S.C. §205(a).
108. 17 U.S.C. §205(c).
109. 17 U.S.C. §§203(a)(4) (A), 304(c)(4)(A).
110. 17 U.S.C. §501(a).
111. Nimmer, *supra* n. 2, §8.01[A].
112. *Id*. at §8.01[G].
113. 17 U.S.C. §502(a).
114. 17 U.S.C. §503.
115. 17 U.S.C. §504(b).
116. 17 U.S.C. §504(c).
117. 17 U.S.C. §505.
118. 17 U.S.C. §504(b).
119. 17 U.S.C. §504(c)(1).
120. 17 U.S.C. §504(c)(2).
121. 17 U.S.C. §506.
122. *See generally* R. Callmann, Unfair Competition Trademarks and Monopolies (1982).
123. 17 U.S.C. §301.
124. *Gilliam v. ABC, Inc.*, 538 F.2d 14 (2d Cir. 1976).
125. *Id*. at 21.
126. *Id*. at 24.
127. *Id*.
128. *Id*.
129. *Id*. In a recent case, a publisher that planned to publish a collection of public domain stories by the author Louis L'Amour was ordered to make clear on the book's cover and in its promotion that the author had nothing to do with the collections and that the stories were not new, and to redesign the proposed covers so as not to resemble the covers that appeared on the author's authorized books. The court stated that the publisher's proposed covers and promotion ''have a tendency or capacity to deceive the relevant industry and the public into believing that (the author) either authored or participated in or authorized these two

collections,'' which violated the author's rights under the federal Lanham Act and state unfair competition law, *L'Amour v. Carroll & Graf Publications, Inc.*, No. 83 Civ. 4658 (S.D.N.Y. 1983).

130. See generally Nimmer, *supra* n. 2, Chapter 16.

131. One theory of recovery in such cases might be for ''unjust enrichment.'' See *Bevan v. Columbia Broadcasting System, Inc.* 175 U.S.P.Q. 475 (S.D.N.Y. 1972).

III

Contracts Involving Authors and Artists

The author or artist who creates work solely for his or her own personal enjoyment or fulfillment—and has no interest in selling or otherwise disseminating the work—probably has no need to read this chapter. All others do, because almost any conceivable arrangement for the transfer, publication, or production of a creator's work involves one or more contracts. Indeed, it is probably true that the contracts entered into by authors and artists will prove at least as important to them as the quality or popularity of their work.

We will first review some of the basic legal principles applicable to all contracts, then examine some of the most common contractual relationships involving authors, and finally deal with the special legal problems and contractual relationships involving visual artists.

What is a contract?

A contract is a legally enforceable agreement, or understanding, reached between two or more parties about one or more subjects of interest to them. Contracts are often set forth in writing, but many valid and enforceable contracts are not. In fact, many contracts are not even expressed orally—they are simply understood or "implied" by the conduct of the parties or the established customs of their businesses.

Not every agreement or understanding constitutes what the law considers a binding contract. For example, an "agreement" between an author and a publisher that they do not desire to do business with each other would not be a contract. More significantly, a mere "agreement" or "understanding" between that author and publisher that they do desire to do business together does not constitute a binding contract. An agreement or understanding must satisfy certain basic legal requirements before it will constitute a binding legal contract.

What are the legal requirements of a binding contract?

If you ask most lawyers, you will get a technically correct but largely incomprehensible response including such terms as "offer," "acceptance," and "consideration."[1] They will tell you that every contract requires them. However, in real life it is often impossible, and almost always irrelevant, to isolate these three factors.

It is probably more useful to view contracts as agreements in which each party commits itself to do something that it was not otherwise obligated to do, in which that commitment is acceptable to the other party or parties, in which the law will enforce the commitments or compensate for their breach.[2] The commitments or promises constitute the offer, acceptance, and consideration that the law requires.

For example, if an author agrees to allow Publisher A to publish his book, but the publisher remains non-committal, no contract has been reached. If the publisher agrees to publish but the author remains non-committal, there is still no contract. Only if they agree on publication does a contract exist. Moreover, the major components of the agreement must be discussed and agreed upon before the contract will be deemed enforceable. If, for example, the monies to be paid the author are not included in the contract, the courts will almost certainly find it fatally incomplete and incapable of enforcement.

Who may enter into a contract?

Individuals and business entities—such as corporations and partnerships—can enter into binding contracts, unless the law declares that they do not have the "capacity" to do so.[3] People who are insane or otherwise declared "incompetent" do not have this capacity, and in many states neither do children under a certain age (18 or 21); their contracts have to be approved by a legal guardian or parent. A loosely formed organization such as a local block association or ad hoc committee lacks the capacity to enter into contracts in its own name unless it establishes a more formal structure, or unless members of the group join the contract as parties.

Is there any limit to how many parties can enter into a contract?

Except where the law decrees otherwise—as in the "contract" for marriage—the answer is no. Contracts involving authors and artists often have many parties, including several contributors to a work and several publishers. But most contracts are entered into between two parties. Note that the document of one "contract" can contain, in the eyes of the law, several contracts.

Are there contracts that the law will refuse to enforce?

Yes. Contracts to commit crimes or otherwise violate the law will not be enforced.[4] Contracts that violate what the courts find to be the prevailing "public policy"—even though not technically illegal—may also be refused enforcement. For example, in one case[5] an author had entered into a contract with a celebrity; they agreed that the celebrity's name would appear as the author of the book. When the celebrity changed his mind, the author sued to enforce the contract. But the court refused, holding that the purpose of the contract was to perpetrate a fraud on the public and that the contract was unenforceable. (The court was careful to distinguish this situation from the usual agreements among co-authors, collaborators, and even ghostwriters, the validity of which it did not question.)

Contracts that are entered into as a result of force or duress will not be enforced,[6] but mere "hard bargaining" will not free a contracting party. For example, if a publisher told an author that if he did not sign the publisher's proposed contract the publisher would destroy the author's only copy of the manuscript, that would be duress and would lead a court to declare the contract unenforceable. However, if the publisher knew it was the only firm interested in the book and offered the author a minuscule payment on a "take it or leave it" basis, such bargaining—however "unfair" or disadvantageous—would not be duress.

Otherwise, the parties to a contract are free to structure their agreement any way they please, no matter how unorthodox, difficult, or "unfair" their agreements may seem. In general, the law will not protect or rescue parties from foolish or horrendous contracts which meet the basic legal requirements.[7]

When must a contract be in writing to be enforceable?

Whenever the applicable law says so. For example, every state has enacted what is somewhat confusingly called a "statute of frauds."[8] Under these statutes, contracts that cannot by their own terms be fully performed within a single year must be in writing to be enforceable: A contract to hire a collaborator to work on a project for two years, or a contract to publish a book not sooner than a year after the contract is signed, has to be in writing. Most states also provide that contracts involving at least some specified amount of money must be in writing. In addition, the U.S. Copyright Act,[9] as well as various other state and federal laws, requires that specified agreements—such as the transfer of a copyright or the grant of an exclusive right in a copyrighted work[10]—must be in writing.

Even if the law does not require a contract to be written, it is almost always advisable. Memories are unreliable, and it may often be difficult—if not impossible—to reconstruct an agreement from the memories of the parties. More important, the exercise of reducing an agreement to writing usually forces the parties to focus on the terms of their agreement and to deal with the contingencies that may arise. This can only enhance the effectiveness and enforceability of the contract. To be enforceable, the written contract should contain all the major rights and obligations that comprise the agreement that has been reached.

Is a lawyer necessary for a binding written contract?

Almost always, no. Indeed, binding contracts can be quite informal, as in a letter or an exchange of letters among the parties; it is rare that the law requires that a particular form or particular formalities be used. But the more complicated the contract, and the more that is at stake, the more advisable it is to seek the assistance of a lawyer or similar person who is experienced in drafting such agreements. Such persons can usually anticipate potential problems and help ensure that the agreement is as clear and enforceable as possible.

Although many contracting parties, including most publishers and galleries, have standard forms that they insist be used in their agreements, the law does not require that any particular form be used. Those parties almost invariably are prepared to modify at least some of the terms of the forms while negotiating an agreement. No one should assume that because a proposed contract is set forth on a printed form it cannot or should not be challenged or changed. Sometimes, indeed, each party has his or her own printed form, and the parties end up using neither and creating a new form instead.

What happens if the parties to a contract disagree about what it provides, or if one party claims that the other has breached the contract?

Usually they try to resolve their differences by themselves, perhaps with the help of one or more third parties. This is almost always preferable to taking the matter to court. Contract litigation is usually time-consuming and expensive, and it can produce results that are unsatisfactory to all the parties.

One alternative, arbitration, is usually quicker and less expensive than litigation. The parties present their dispute to one or more (often three) arbitrators, who have the power to render a full and final resolution to the dispute. Parties to arbitration may, but are not required to, have lawyers. The advantages of arbitration are economy and efficiency. Disadvantages are that arbitrators are not bound by legal precedents and can render almost any decision they consider appropriate, and that a party unhappy with an arbitrator's decision cannot appeal it.

All the parties must agree before a dispute can be submitted to arbitration. (Occasionally, but not usually, "arbitration" clauses are included in a party's standard form contract.) As a general rule, the party who can least afford the costs of court litigation will desire arbitration, while the party who is better able to afford to litigate will not. Arbitration clauses are especially appropriate, and most common, in collaboration agreements and the like where quickness and economy are important.

How do the courts deal with vague or incomplete agreements?

Often, especially with oral or very casual contracts, the parties fail to anticipate possible contingencies or they leave a provision of the contract so vague that it is essentially meaningless. Suppose a collaborator gets sick and can't work for two months. The vague clause that refers to "incapacitation for a significant period of time" becomes important. If the parties cannot resolve their differences, the courts (or arbitrators) will resolve the differences for them.

The courts will first try to decipher the intentions of the parties.[11] They scour the terms of the agreement for clues. If at all possible they resolve the dispute from the terms of the agreement. But if that doesn't work, the courts will examine the surrounding circumstances, and, if necessary, they will consider the established "customs" or "practices" in the particular field and be inclined to assume that the parties intended to conform to these customs and practices.[12] Many oral contracts, or "handshake" contracts where the parties don't bother even to express their agreement out loud, will be constructed or "implied" by the courts using these techniques.

Not every contract can be salvaged this way. Sometimes a provision is so crucial to the agreement, and yet so indecipherable, that the courts will conclude that there never was an enforceable contract. For example, a publishing agreement that called upon the author to deliver the book "as soon as he was satisfied with it" would probably be found so vague as to be "illusory" and thus unenforceable. This shows how important it is for the parties to a contract to be as specific and objective as they can.

How do the courts enforce contracts?

In several ways. First, in appropriate cases, they can issue orders compelling parties to perform their obligations under the contract ("specific performance") and they can issue injunctions prohibiting parties from engaging in conduct in breach of the contract.[13] Such orders are only available, in general, where the remedy of money damages would not adequately compensate for the breach and where the comparative fairness of the situation (the "equities") justifies the granting of extraordinary relief.[14]

Most of the time, however, the courts will require the breaching party to compensate the non-breaching party for the consequences of the breach, usually with money.[15] Not every breach causes injury; if it doesn't, the non-breaching party is only entitled to a nominal award.[16] Even more important, not every breach causes *provable* injury. For example, if an author fails to deliver his manuscript as promised, or if the publisher fails to publish it as promised, it is likely that the non-breaching party will suffer some injury as a result; but before the courts allow recovery of money damages, the party claiming the injury will be required to prove (and not just speculate or surmise) that the injury was sustained and to offer a rational, credible way to calculate or estimate the damage. In the absence of such proof, the non-breaching party may not recover anything.[17]

Finally, depending on how serious the breach is, the courts can declare the contract terminated—or they can keep it in effect and compensate for the breach. For example, if a publisher is two weeks late in making royalty payments, or underpays royalties by a small amount, it is unlikely that a court will terminate the contract. But if the publisher refuses to make any royalty payments, or is found to have deliberately underpaid royalties by a substantial amount, the outcome may be different.[18]

A. The Author-Agent Contract

People tend to be good at what they're good at, and not so good at other things. Creative people are no exception. They may be very good at writing books, for example, but not very good at (and not very interested in) doing what is necessary to ensure that a book is published and otherwise disseminated on terms that are fair to the author. For this reason many authors enter into contracts with literary agents.

What does a literary agent do?

Many things. First, the agent will "represent"—i.e., attempt to sell—the author's work to appropriate publishers. Second, when a sale is made, the agent will handle the negotiation of the terms of the contract with the publisher. Third, the agent will oversee and collect all payments due the author, and attempt to ensure that the publisher is complying fully with all contractual obligations. Fourth, the agent will explore, and often handle, other markets for the author's book, such as a motion picture or television adaptation. And fifth, a good agent will give a client valuable advice and guidance about the client's work.[19]

What should the author-agent contract consist of?

As much of their specific agreement as possible, preferably in writing. For example, does the relationship apply only to one work of the author, or all the work? Does it cover the world, or only parts of it? Does it apply to all media, or only some? Does the agent have the authority to commit the author? What compensation is the agent entitled to? What expenses should the agent be reimbursed for? What happens if the relationship is terminated?

All these questions, and many more, should be discussed and agreed upon before the author and the agent enter into their contract. Questions that are not answered at the outset are likely to have to be answered later—at a time when one or both parties may be at a disadvantage.

Does the law impose requirements on the author-agent relationship?

Yes. The law considers the agent to be a "fiduciary" of the author, a person who holds a special position of trust and who therefore owes the author full loyalty and honesty.[20] In most contractual relationships the parties are said to be at "arm's length," but an agent owes a much higher personal duty to an author; the courts will therefore scrutinize the agent's conduct closely.

Because the relationship is fiduciary, the law provides that either party can terminate the relationship at will.[21] However, even after termination the agent may be entitled to compensation for services already performed. If the parties are unable to agree about the termination, the courts (or arbitrators) will resolve the question.

Many agents include in their contracts that their relationship with the author is an "agency coupled with an interest."[22] This gives the agent more rights: for example, the agency cannot be terminated at will. It is very doubtful that the mere declaration of an "agency coupled with an interest" suffices to make it one, since the law requires that such an agent have a financial interest in the subject of the agency, for example, a financial investment in the project, other than the right to receive commissions or other compensation. Author and agent should discuss such a clause if it is proposed and agree on what, if anything, it is supposed to mean.

B. Collaboration

Many creative efforts are collaborative. Sometimes the contributions are essentially equal—for example, two people working together to research and write a historical novel or biography—while at other times the contributions may be very different, as where one person provides research or expertise to a writer, or where one person rewrites or even ghostwrites the work of another. All these collaborations require contracts.

What should a collaboration contract consist of?

It should contain as much of the specific agreement as possible, preferably in writing, just like an author-agent contract. For example, exactly what is each collaborator promising to do? Are there deadlines? How will disagreements be resolved? Who will have the authority to enter into contracts, etc., for the work? Who will own the copyright and other literary property rights in the work? Who will own the physical property? How will expenses be shared? How will earnings be divided? How will credit for the work be determined? What happens if a collaborator fails to fulfill his or her obligations, or becomes incapacitated or dies? What about future works, especially works based on this one?

These important questions should be addressed and answered —in writing—at the beginning of the relationship. The entire project can be jeopardized—not to mention the emotional, professional, and financial well-being of the parties—if such questions are left to a time when it may be much harder to reach an amicable, good-faith agreement.

Does the law impose any provisions on the collaboration relationship?

Some, but not many. Perhaps the most important are the provisions in the U.S. Copyright Act on "joint works."

Section 101 of the Act defines a joint work as "a work prepared by two or more authors with the intention that their contributions be merged into inseparable or interdependent parts of a unitary whole."[23] It is not necessary, for a work to be considered a "joint work," that the collaborators work together, work simultaneously, or even know each other. The crucial element is whether each contributor prepares his or her contribution with the knowledge and intention that it will be merged with the contribution of others as "inseparable or interdependent parts of a unitary whole."

Almost all collaborations on a written work, or collaborations between an author and an artist or photographer where the intention is to create a unitary whole, qualify as a joint work for copyright purposes. The Copyright Act provides that "the authors [creators] of a joint work are co-owners of copyright in the work."[24] All the co-owners are presumed to own equal interests; each co-owner is free to make use of the work so long as he or she accounts to the other co-owners for the profits; and each is free to sell or otherwise convey his or her ownership interest and/or pass it on to heirs. The consent of all the owners is necessary to convey the entire copyright or to grant any exclusive right related to the work.

In the absence of an agreement providing otherwise, the collaborators' rights in the work will be as set forth in the Copyright Act. Many, if not most, collaboration relationships contemplate different arrangements, which makes it imperative to agree on the issues and reduce the agreement to a written contract.

C. The Author-Publisher Contract

Except for the rare author who is self-published,[25] anyone who expects his or her work to be published must eventually enter into one or more contracts with publishers—contracts which can be extremely important to the author.

Most major publishers of newspapers, magazines, and books have developed standard contract forms. However, as indicated above, authors should never assume that clauses in printed forms cannot be questioned or negotiated. They should feel free to question any point in a form agreement that they do not understand or agree with. Nevertheless, the use of forms probably gives the publisher an advantage in negotiations, since they put the author in the position of having to seek changes from the form, rather than having both parties start negotiations on an equal footing. As in any field, the success an author has in negotiating a contract largely depends on his or her bargaining power; some authors inevitably have much more power than others.

It is not our purpose to review in detail the usual contents of author-publisher agreements. For guidance, an author should consult his or her literary agent, if any, or the comprehensive and useful guides to author-publisher contracts prepared by the Author's Guild[26] and the P.E.N. American Center.[27] We will concentrate on the aspects of such contracts that have generated legal precedents or have the most direct legal significance for the author.

A publishing contract depends in large part on the nature of the work and the publisher. Free-lance articles written for newspapers or magazines involve significantly different considerations from books. Textbooks are covered by contracts that are substantially different from contracts for "trade" books (the kind sold in bookstores), and trade-book contracts vary depending on, for example, the nature, size, and expense of producing the book. Most of our discussion is concerned with the typical trade-book contract, but reference will be made to other kinds of written work.

What is the essential component of every author-publisher contract?

What is sometimes called the "grant of rights." As was discussed in Chapter II, the creator (author) of an article, short story, or book begins as the owner of the copyright in the work.[28] The author completely controls the destiny of the work. When the author and a publisher agree on publication the author agrees to grant certain rights in the work to the publisher. The contract should set forth the nature and extent of these rights, and of the rights the author is not granting to the publisher but "reserving" to him- or herself.

It is common for a publisher of magazine articles and stories to be granted very limited rights, usually the right to publish the work once in a magazine (and perhaps again in a collection or anthology drawn from the magazine).[29] But magazine publishers often seek much broader rights, even *all* the rights, and it is incumbent upon the author to negotiate about this.

Books are somewhat different. The publisher's standard contract usually states that the author grants all, or almost all, his rights in the book to the publisher, and that the publisher is obligated to pay the author specified royalties or other sums. Such a grant would include not only the right to publish the book in English in the United States, but the right to publish it in every language everywhere (and to authorize others to publish); the right to authorize others to base a movie, TV show or series, or stage play on the book; indeed, the right to authorize others to manufacture and sell T-shirts, toys, and other commercial items based on the book or characters in the book. (The rights in a book other than the right to publish it in book form are often called subsidiary rights.)

The author (and/or agent) may not wish to grant all rights to the publisher; instead, they may want to limit the grant to, say, the right to publish the book in the United States (and Canada), and limited subsidiary rights, including the right to authorize others to publish excerpts from the book and to sell the book through book clubs, with the author reserving "foreign" rights, motion picture rights, etc., and the right to dispose of the reserved rights as the author sees fit.

Most trade-book authors take particular interest today in the form in which their books will be published. Most trade books used to be published in hardcover; then—usually a year later—a paperback edition might be published. In recent years it has become increasingly common for books to be published only in paperback or for there to be simultaneous hardcover and "trade paperback" editions. A few authors with unusual bargaining power retain the paperback rights, granting only hardcover rights to their publisher. Other authors, who grant paperback rights to the hardcover publisher, reserve the right to approve the paperback publisher and/or the terms of the contract with the paperback publisher.

Also, many authors obtain or seek clauses that require the publisher to pay the author's share of major subsidiary rights income immediately upon receipt, at least where advance payments to the author have been "recouped" by the publisher, instead of holding the money until the next scheduled royalty payment.

The author needs to be as clear and certain as possible about what is and is not being granted to the publisher in the contract, and to understand and be satisfied with the payments the publisher is agreeing to, including royalty rates on book sales, author's share of major subsidiary rights income, and the advance (a payment that trade publishers usually, but not always, agree to pay before the book is written, much less published). An unclear contract can mean a later court case.

What are the author's obligations under a standard publishing contract?

The author's principal obligation in almost all book contracts and most magazine contracts is to deliver a manuscript that the publisher finds "acceptable" or "satisfactory." The most common formulation is that the manuscript must be "satisfactory to the publisher in form and content."

The full legal significance of such clauses is far from clear, and they have recently been the subject of several important court cases.[30] Traditionally, such clauses were interpreted by the courts to mean that the publisher had practically unlimited discretion to decide whether the manuscript as delivered was acceptable. If it wasn't, the contract would allow the publisher to declare the contract terminated and require the author to return any advance payments. And the publisher could base that determination solely on its own evaluation of the literary merits or even financial prospects of the book. It is not an overstatement to say that the author was almost completely at the mercy of the publisher's discretion. The only limitation was that the publisher must act in "good faith."

In 1982, however, a federal court in New York offered a more restrictive interpretation of the rights of the publisher.[31] The case involved a publishing agreement between Senator Barry Goldwater and Stephen Shadegg, who were to collaborate on a book of the Senator's memoirs, and Harcourt Brace Jovanovich, a major publisher. The contract had the standard "satisfactory to the publisher in form and content" requirement. After seeking but not obtaining editorial guidance from the publisher, the authors submitted their manuscript. The publisher found the manuscript unacceptable, formally rejected it, and demanded that the authors return a $65,000 advance. When the authors refused to return it, the publisher sued.

After a full trial, the court rejected the publisher's claim in its entirety. With respect to the "satisfactory" clause, the court stated:

> It is true that under the contract which was in force here between HBJ and the authors, the publisher has a very considerable discretion as to whether to refuse a manuscript on the ground that it is unsatisfactory to the publisher in form and content.
>
> It cannot be, however, that the publisher has absolutely unfettered license to act or not to act in any way it wishes and to accept or reject a book for any reason whatever. If this were the case, the publisher could simply make a contract and arbitrarily change its mind and that would be an illusory contract. It is no small thing for an author to enter into a contract with a publisher and be locked in with that publisher and prevented from marketing the book elsewhere.[32]

The court went on to describe the publisher's obligations under such clauses:

> It is clear, both as a matter of law and from the testimony in this case, that there is an implied obligation in a contract of this kind for the publisher to engage in appropriate editorial work with the author of a book. . . . It is clear that an author who is commissioned to do a work under a contract such as this generally needs editing to produce a successful book. . . .
> In a general way, it is clear that the editorial work which is required must consist of some reasonable degree of communication with the authors, an interchange with the authors about the specifics of what the publisher desires; about what specific faults are found; what items should be omitted or eliminated; what items

should be added; what organizational defects exist, and so forth. If faults are found in the writing style, it seems elementary that there should be discussion and illustrations of what those defects of style are. All of this is necessary in order to allow the author the reasonable opportunity to perform to the satisfaction of the publisher. If this editorial work is not done by the publisher, the result is that the author is misled and, in fact, is virtually prevented from performing under the contract.[33]

The court made it clear that its decision was based on the particular case before it, and it went on to observe:

There is no occasion in this decision to determine the full extent or the full definition of the editorial work which is required of a publisher under the contract. Here there was no editorial work. I emphasize, no editorial work. . . . In a given situation it could be that after a contract is entered into of the kind we have here, and after draft material is submitted, the material is so hopeless that editorial work might be fruitless. It is difficult to imagine such a situation occurring but I suppose it is conceivable. But this was far from the case here.[34]

Then the court summarized its conclusion:

I conclude that HBJ breached its contract with Shadegg and Goldwater by wilfully failing to engage in any rudimentary editorial work or effort. Consequently, HBJ cannot rely on the concept that the manuscript was unsatisfactory in form and content and can be rejected. HBJ had no right under its contract to reject that manuscript.[35]

Thus, at least in situations similar to the *Goldwater* case, the publishing company's discretion may be limited by its conduct. But no author wants to litigate the validity of a publisher's rejection of a manuscript. It is preferable to deal with the possibility of rejection when the contract is entered into.

Several approaches can be explored. First, the contract can require the publisher to give the author a written statement of defects found in the manuscript and a period of time (e.g., 30 or 60 days) within which to correct the defects. Second, the contract can have attached to it the outline, proposal, or sample materials the author had already shown the publisher, with a clause added that the book will be acceptable to the publisher if it is in substantial conformity with those materials. Third, the contract can incorporate a clause, proposed by the Authors Guild, stating that the manuscript must be "professionally competent and fit for publication," which the Guild considers an objective criterion compared to the subjectivity of the standard clause.[36] Fourth, the contract can include a provision for arbitration to determine whether the manuscript has been properly rejected. Fifth, the contract can provide that if the publisher rejects the book, the author is only obligated to repay the advance out of the first proceeds received from any other publisher for the book. (This is commonly called a first proceeds clause.) Finally, if the author is relying on a particular editor at the publishing company, and believes the book may be rejected if the editor leaves the company, a clause can state that the author may terminate the contract if the editor leaves the company before a decision is made on the book.

It may be difficult to get a publisher to agree to any of these clauses, but that does not mean the effort should not be made.

What are the publisher's obligations?

As indicated in the previous answer, one court has ruled that a publisher is obliged to provide editorial assistance to an author—especially if the author requests it.[37]

A publisher who accepts a manuscript almost certainly has the obligation to publish the book in good faith. (Some publishers' form contracts do not contain such an affirmative obligation; however, courts would probably construe such a contract as requiring the publisher to proceed with publication in good faith, since otherwise the contract would be "illusory.") Authors should be diligent to ensure that their contracts contain an affirmative duty to publish, preferably within a stated period (e.g., eighteen months after the book is accepted).

A 1983 federal court decision has elaborated somewhat on the publisher's duty to publish.[38] The author of an unflattering book about the Du Pont family sued his publisher (and the Du Pont company) because of the way the book was published and promoted, claiming that as a result of pressure from the company the publisher significantly restricted its activities in behalf of the book, thus breaching its contractual duty to publish. The publisher contended that it acted "fairly, reasonably and responsibly in publishing and promoting the book, and that all of its actions were taken for legitimate business reasons."[39]

The federal court of appeals reversed a lower court finding that the publisher breached the publishing contract, but it nevertheless declared that a publisher has an implied contractual duty "to make certain efforts in publishing a book it has accepted," which duty includes "a good faith effort to promote the book including a first printing and advertising budget adequate to give the book a reasonable chance of achieving market success in light of the subject matter and likely audience."[40] But once such "reasonable initial promotion activities" are made, "all that is required is a good faith business judgment."[41]

Thus authors have at least one legal precedent if they believe their publishers have failed to publish their books in good faith. But this does not mean that authors can tell their publishers how to publish their books or that the courts will second-guess the day-to-day decisions that every publisher makes. Publishers still have—and probably must have—great discretion to decide how much energy and resources to put into each book they publish and it seems likely that the courts will only interfere if they are persuaded that the publisher acted in bad faith or with no "sound business reason," something that is usually hard to prove.

Authors can attempt to ensure that their publishers publish their books vigorously. First, they should seek as large an advance payment of royalties as possible, since publishers often work harder to recoup a large investment—even with a book that disappoints them. Second, authors can try to include in their contracts specific obligations, for example, a specified number of copies in the first printing of the book, or spending a specified amount of money on promoting the book, perhaps including a promotional tour by the author. Such clauses will usually be difficult to obtain, but the effort should be made.

Finally, a publisher is obligated to report sales and other exploitation of the book periodically to the author and to pay the sums due according to that report. Most publishers' form contracts permit the publisher to withhold some royalties as a reserve against returns of books shipped to bookstores and the like; many authors and agents try to negotiate restrictions on these "reserves for returns." They also seek to require the publisher to report the number of copies printed, copies sold at particular discounts, copies returned, etc.—at least some publishers provide only the sketchiest information about this. It is common for the author to have the right, at the author's expense, to review the publisher's records on the author's work; such clauses usually provide that if errors to the author's detriment over a specified level (e.g., 5 percent) are found, the publisher must pay for the review. Authors should always try to have such clauses included in their publishing contracts.[42]

What happens if a lawsuit is brought because of something published?

First you cry. Then you quickly look up the provisions in your publishing agreement that deal with this contingency.

In most form contracts from publishers, especially book publishers, the author makes many "representations" and "warranties" to the publisher and agrees to "indemnify" the publisher if certain contingencies occur. The contracts have the author represent that nothing in the book is obscene or libelous, is otherwise illegal, invades anyone's right of privacy, infringes any copyright or other literary property right, will cause any injury, or violates anyone's legal rights. They provide that the author will fully indemnify and "hold harmless" the publishers from any expense, including its attorneys' fees and any damage award or settlement, incurred as a result of any claim asserted against the book, even if the claim is without merit. Under such clauses the author can be held responsible for the publisher's expenses even if the author did not in fact breach any representations to the publisher.

Understandably, many authors and agents consider these provisions grossly unfair, and more and more publishers have come to agree. This is especially true if the publishers have conducted, with the author's full cooperation, a legal review of the book and have declared the book legally suitable for publication. Then it seems difficult to justify requiring the author to serve as a backup insurer in case the publisher's evaluation is wrong.

To deal with this situation, first, authors and agents can seek to restrict the author's representations to the publisher so that they are made "to the best of his or her knowledge." Second, they can seek to limit the author's obligation to indemnify the publisher to amounts paid pursuant to final court judgments. Third, they can get the publisher to share equally the costs and payments before, and perhaps even including, a final judgment. Last and perhaps most important, they can get the publisher to extend its insurance coverage to cover the author for such claims, so that—except perhaps for a specified deductible—the author will be protected through the publisher.[43]

Such provisions—especially the insurance coverage—are not yet widespread, but the trend appears to be in their direction. Authors should make every effort to secure this kind of protection when they enter into contracts with publishers.

What about other works by the author?

Most book publishers' form contracts contain two clauses on other works by the author. First they provide, in very broad terms, that the author agrees not to publish any work that would "tend to compete with, or interfere with the sale of, the book" which is the subject of the contract. Second, they usually grant the publisher some form of "option" on the author's next book or books.

Many authors and agents are deeply troubled by standard "competitive works" clauses, because they are so vague that it is almost impossible to know what they mean. Courts have not interpreted them yet; it seems likely that if a case were brought the courts would construe the clause narrowly so as not to unduly constrict the ability of the author to continue to write and publish. Nevertheless, it is important for authors to attempt to narrow the scope of such clauses when the contract is entered into, perhaps by the deletion of such phrases as "tend to" and by the insertion of such words as "directly and significantly" before the word "compete." It may also be appropriate to limit the duration of the clause to a year or two after the book is first published.[44]

Option clauses are equally troublesome. Sometimes they provide that the author is required to submit his or her next book-length work to the publisher before submitting it to any other publisher and that the publisher has the option to publish the work on the terms of the present contract. Although such a provision may be grossly unfair to the author, it is probably enforceable; it should be resisted as strongly as possible.

Sometimes form contracts state that publishers have the option to publish the author's next work on "terms to be agreed upon." Such clauses, however, have been held by several courts to be mere "agreements to agree," and thus unenforceable.[45] They should still be resisted if proposed.

Finally, some form contracts state that the author agrees to give the publisher the first opportunity to consider and negotiate for the author's next book, and then perhaps the right to match any other publisher's offer for it. These clauses may well be enforceable; although they are not as harsh as the option "on the same terms," they restrict the freedom of the author to control his future work and should be resisted. In general, if the relationship between author and publisher has been good, probably no option clause is necessary; if it has not been good, no option clause is appropriate.[46]

What about sequels and revisions?

Publishers of some kinds of books, notably textbooks, usually seek the right to decide whether sequels or revised editions of the book should be published and to have them prepared by others if the author cannot or will not prepare them. Textbook authors should be especially concerned about such provisions and should attempt to protect their interests insofar as possible. For example, the contract can require the publisher to give the author the first opportunity to prepare further editions at a specified compensation, or at least the right to approve such editions if they are prepared by others. Also, textbook authors should seek to get compensation from future editions even if they do not prepare them. They can also seek the right to have their names removed from future editions over which they have no control.

Trade-book publishers usually do not have similar power, and authors should strongly resist any attempt to get it. Indeed, authors should remain free to control sequels and revised editions. Revised editions probably cannot be issued through other publishers because they would infringe on the exclusive rights to the book granted to the first publisher. Sequels, however, can be published through other publishers, unless the contract forbids it.

How long do publishing contracts remain in effect?

Most book-publishing agreements remain in effect for the full term of the copyright in the book, the life of the author plus 50 years.[47] However, there are several reasons why the contract may be terminated earlier.

First, most—but not all—book-publishing contracts contain "out-of-print" clauses. If the publisher allows the book to go out of print, which means that there are few or no copies still for sale, the author can demand that the publisher print additional copies within a specified time. If the publisher fails to, the author can terminate the contract and get back all rights previously granted to the publisher. Such clauses are most often very vague about when a book is out of print; frequently, they contain provisions that a book cannot be out of print if there are licenses in effect for the publication of the book by another publisher, even if no such books have been published. Authors and agents often strive to revise standard out-of-print clauses to be as specific, and as protective of the author's interests, as possible.[48]

Many standard publishing contracts state that if the publisher goes out of business, or becomes insolvent or files for bankruptcy, the contracts are terminated and all rights revert to the author. Although the legal validity of the bankruptcy provisions may be open to question,[49] authors should seek to incorporate in their contracts as much of this kind of protection as they can.

What is "vanity publishing"?

Vanity or subsidized publishing means that the author pays for the printing and publication of a book. Like the more traditional forms of book publishing, in which the publisher bears the costs of publication and is obliged to pay royalties to the author, this kind of publishing depends on the contract between the author and publisher. An author who pays the costs of publication needs to have a full understanding about the number of copies to be printed, manner and extent of distribution and promotion, etc., spelled out in a written agreement.[50] Otherwise, authors may find that their publishing contracts are more illusory than real and that they are the only customers for their books.

D. Contracts Involving Visual Artists

Although many of the legal rights of authors and artists are the same, the difference in work product has led to different legal problems and solutions. The writings of authors are intended to be reproduced and disseminated to as large an audience as possible, while original manuscripts usually have little value. The opposite is true of visual artists: the original has the most value, and the right to own and control the original is more important then the right to own and control reproductions.

We shall first discuss two important legal concepts—*droit moral* and *droit de suite*—and then the principal contractual relationships involving artists.

What is *droit moral*?

Droit moral is a French term, literally "moral right," which refers to the artist's right to maintain the integrity of work even after it has been sold.[51] This right, it has been said, is "perpetual, inalienable, and cannot be waived,"[52] and it has been further described as "non-property attributes of an intellectual and moral character which exist between a literary or artistic work and its author's personality; it is intended to protect his personality as well as his work."[53]

Droit moral is distinct from copyright. Copyright protects the artist's right to exploit a work—thus it protects an artist's property right. The right of *droit moral* is a personal right, protecting an artist's expression:

> [An artist] does more than bring into the world a unique object having only exploitive possibilities; he projects onto the work part of his personality and subjects it to the ravages of public use. There are possibilities of injury to the creator other than mere economic ones.[54]

There are three major components of moral right: the right of integrity of the work of art, the right of paternity, and the right of divulgation.[55] The right of integrity assumes that the work of art is an expression of the artist's personality and that distortion, dismemberment, or misrepresentation of the work can adversely affect the artist's identity, personality, and honor. In a celebrated case in France, the court ruled that the artist's *droit moral* prevented the owner of a refrigerator that had been decorated by Bernard Buffet from taking the refrigerator apart and selling its six panels separately.[56]

The right of paternity gives the artist the right to insist that his or her name be associated with the work.[57] Indeed, in France the right cannot be waived even by the artist. In one case where a painter had agreed to use a pseudonym in a contract commissioning works over a period of ten years, the court ruled that the artist could not be prohibited from using his real name in connection with the sale of the works.[58]

The right of divulgation gives the artist the absolute right to determine whether and when a work is complete and ready to be shown to the public.[59] Similar to the right of divulgation is the right to control the creation of a work. Thus, when Rosa Bonheur refused to paint a canvas pursuant to a contract, she was held liable for damages but the court refused to order specific performance.[60]

Has *droit moral* been adopted in the United States?

For the most part, America has not been receptive to this

right.[61] When it has been asserted, the courts have noted that it has not generally been recognized in the United States and suggested that if artists want its benefits, they should seek to secure them in the contracts they enter into.[62]

In 1983, however, the State of New York, declaring that "the physical state of a work of art is of enduring and crucial importance to the artist and the artist's reputation," enacted an "Artists' Authorship Rights Act"[63] that grants to artists significant *droit moral* protection. For example, the act provides that

> no person other than the artist or a person acting with the artist's consent shall knowingly publicly display or publish a work of fine art of that artist or a reproduction thereof in an altered, defaced, mutilated or modified form if the work is displayed, published or reproduced as being the work of the artist, or under circumstances under which it would reasonably be regarded as being the work of the artist, and damage to the artist's reputation could result therefrom.

The act also states that

> the artist shall retain at all times the right to claim authorship, or, for just and valid reason, to disclaim authorship of his or her work of fine art. The right to claim authorship shall include the right of the artist to have his or her name appear on or in connection with the work of fine art as the artist. The right to disclaim authorship shall include the right of the artist to prevent his or her name from appearing on or in connection with the work of fine art as the artist. Just and valid reason for disclaiming authorship shall include that the work of fine art has been altered, defaced, mutilated or modified other than by the artist, without the artist's consent, and damage to the artist's reputation could result or has resulted therefrom.

The act, which is limited to "works of fine arts knowingly publicly displayed, published or reproduced" in that state, enables an artist who believes these protections have been violated to sue for damages, including exemplary (punitive) damages "where appropriate," equitable (injunctive) relief, and reasonable attorney's and expert witness's fees. But it also provides that the court may require the artist to pay the defendant's attorney's and expert witness's fees "upon dismissal of any action on the grounds such action was frivolous and malicious." The entire New York act, which took effect on January 1, 1984, and which only applies to actions taken after that date, is reproduced at Appendix A.

It is much too early to know how these new rights will be interpreted and enforced, and whether they will in fact give artists meaningful new *droit moral* protection. Nevertheless, the enactment of such a law in a state as important to artists as New York can only be seen as a major advance for the rights of all artists. Indeed, it is likely that other states will follow New York's lead and enact similar—and perhaps even more extensive—*droit moral* legislation.[64] In the meantime, artists can apply other legal doctrines in order to secure some of the rights in *droit moral*.[65] In two cases involving motion pictures a right quite similar to that of integrity was found to protect filmmakers whose films were edited severely for television.[66] The question was whether the artist had contracted away "mutilation" rights. Protection similar to the right of integrity was also given the writers of the British show *Monty Python* when they claimed that a mutilated version of the work was misrepresented as theirs.[67] Other legal principles that may provide *droit moral*, in effect, are unfair competition[68] and defamation,[69] the latter arising if the attribution of a distorted version of a work to an artist damages his or her reputation.

The right to control the distribution and publication of a work is inherent in the artist's copyright in the unpublished work,[70] and possibly also under the right to privacy.[71] The right of paternity should, if possible, be contractually agreed upon insofar as it concerns the right of an artist to be associated with a work. Misattribution of authorship to a third party may be preventable before publication under copyright law, and thereafter under the doctrines of unfair competition [72] and libel.[73]

What is *droit de suite*?

Droit de suite has been loosely translated as the "art-proceeds" right.[74] It gives the artist the right to continue to receive payment each time a work is sold, especially if the work is resold at a price higher than what was originally paid. It is recognized in a number of European countries, with differences in kinds of sales covered (auction, dealer, private), in percentage of resale price to be paid the artist, in the length of time the right remains in effect, and in whether the price must exceed the original price.[75] Like *droit moral*, *droit de suite* has gained at least some acceptance in this country.

To what extent has *droit de suite* been recognized in the United States?

In 1977 California became the first state to enact a statute giving artists the right to receive royalties on the resale of their works.[76] The statute applies to sales of original paintings, sculpture, and drawings (not lithographs or prints) which take place during the artist's lifetime in California or in which the seller is a California resident. The artist receives 5 percent of the proceeds and dealers and agents are required to withhold that percentage from the purchase price and attempt to locate and pay the artist. If the artist cannot be found, the money goes into a state art fund. The statute does not apply to the initial sale, to a resale after an artist is dead, or to a resale where the gross price is less than the price paid by the seller or is less than $1000.

A similar bill, introduced in New York, engendered considerable debate.[77] Supporters argued that collectors and dealers make large profits on the sale of artwork which artists do not share; that this protection would benefit and provide an incentive for struggling young artists; and that since the artist is often responsible for the increased value of his earlier works, it is only fair that the artist participate in profits realized from their resale. Those opposed argued that collectors and dealers often lose money on the resale of artworks, particularly those by living artists; that the bill might force reductions in the prices paid to beginning artists; that dealers and collectors would purchase works of art outside New York to avoid the statutory payments to the artist; and that dealers and collectors are as much responsible for the artist's development as the artist is. They also argued that the bill would substantially complicate the sale of art by auction.[78]

Alternatively, it has been suggested that rather than re-enact California's *droit de suite* law, states tax the sale of art.[79] Proceeds would go into a central fund from which payments would be made to needy professional artists. This would assist the impoverished artist, would be deductible from the purchaser's other taxes, and, if the rate was small, would not materially interfere with the art market.

What is the standard contractual relationship between an artist and a gallery?[80]

There are two main kinds of artist-gallery relationship.[81] In the first the gallery purchases the work of the artist outright and sells it for its own benefit. This happens most often when an artist dies and the estate does not wish to continue to own the artist's works.

The relationship most common for living artists is that the gallery accepts an artist's work on consignment and acts as the artist's agent or representative. Laws have been passed in New York[82] and California[83] governing consignment of artworks to art dealers for exhibition and/or sale. They provide that unless artwork has been sold outright to a gallery or the artist has received full compensation, the work is deemed to be on consignment.

How does consignment operate?

Under the statutes the dealer is "deemed to be the agent of such artist," the work of fine art "is trust property in the hands of the consignee for the benefit of the consignor," and "any proceeds from the sale of such work of fine art are trust funds in the hands of the consignee for the benefit of the consignor."[84] The New York statute provides that

> a work of fine art initially received "on consignment" shall be deemed to remain trust property notwithstanding the subsequent purchase thereof by the consignee

73

directly or indirectly for his own account until the price is paid in full to the consignor. If such work is thereafter resold to a bona fide third party before the consignor has been paid in full, the proceeds of the resale are trust funds in the hands of the consignee for the benefit of the consignor to the extent necessary to pay any balance still due to the consignor and such trusteeship shall continue until the fiduciary obligation of the consignee with respect to such transaction is discharged in full.[85]

The statute also provides that "any provision of a contract or agreement whereby the consignor waives [most of the major provisions of the statute] is absolutely void."[86]

In states where no statute like New York's has been enacted, the consignment relationship is governed by the law of consigned goods generally.[87] The "fiduciary" and "trust" protections of the New York and California laws are not available, although it is generally believed that the artist/dealer relationship is always of principal/agent, with the agent assuming fiduciary responsibilities to the artist, especially where, as is often the case, there is a significant disparity of business acumen.[88] In such states an artwork is subject to the claims of the gallery's creditors,[89] unless (1) certain notices to the contrary are properly posted; (2) it can be established that the dealer is known by creditors to be substantially engaged in the business of selling the goods of others; and (3) a financial statement has been filed. Artists in these states who desire the kind of protection afforded by New York law will have to obtain it in their contracts with galleries.

If a gallery is acting as an artist's agent, what should their agreement consist of?

A gallery will usually insist on the exclusive right to represent the artist's work in a geographical territory. The artist should seek to exclude from exclusive coverage his or her studio sales, gifts, or barter of his or her work. The borders of the territory should be carefully spelled out. Also, the agreement should be clear about what works are covered: for example, does it apply only to already existing work, or does it include works created after the agreement is entered into? Is the agreement limited to a specific number of works per year, to all of the artist's output in a particular year, perhaps to the artist's work in one medium? Who chooses from the artist's work, the gallery or the artist? The agreement should always confirm the artist's ownership of the work and that the works are not subject to creditors' claims. It is most important that such questions be fully agreed upon when the contract is entered into.

The agreement should have a time limit; any period longer than three years is probably unwise from the artist's point of view. Many artists seek to impose an annual minimum sales requirement on the gallery as a condition of keeping the agreement in effect.

If the gallery has branches, the agreement should specify where the work will be displayed. Also, if the artist is relying on a particular person within the gallery to handle the work, the agreement should so specify.

The artist may seek the right to approve, or at least be consulted on, how and where in the gallery his or her works may be shown and whether some will be on permanent exhibition. The agreement can require a minimum number of exhibitions devoted to the artist during the term of the agreement, and can even specify the location, opening date, duration, and amount of space for the exhibitions. It can give the artist the right to be present and participate in the hanging, arranging, and lighting of exhibitions. It can specify whether the exhibition will be exclusive or whether other artists' work will also be shown. The artist may desire the right to withdraw from a group show if he or she does not approve of the other artists. It is important that the agreement specify who will bear the cost of exhibitions; otherwise, the artist may assume that the gallery will pay while the gallery assumes that the costs will be deducted eventually from the artist's return on sales. The cost and content of promotional and advertising material should also be dealt with in the agreement.

How does the gallery get paid?

Two methods are common. In the "net price" method the gallery's compensation is the difference between a fixed price agreed between gallery and artist and the actual price received by the gallery.[90] In the "commission" method the gallery gets a percentage of the sales price.[91] The problem with the net price method is that the gallery may profit unconscionably if the artist's work substantially increases in value after the price is fixed. Problems with the commission method include the allocation of prices if there are bulk sales and the risk that the gallery may conduct internal sales—i.e., sales to itself. Many artists seek to combine the two methods of payment or seek other remedies to these problems.[92]

How does the gallery price the artist's work?

If possible, the agreement should provide for consultation with the artist, if not the artist's prior approval. If prices have been agreed upon, the gallery may request discretionary authority to vary them by up to a certain percentage. The prices of the work should be reviewed periodically. The agreement may also deal with rental prices. Also, if the gallery extends credit, the agreement should specify whether the payment to the artist is to be based on the amount of the sale or on the money actually received by the gallery, the issue being whether the artist is to participate in the risks and delays inherent in the gallery's decision to grant credit.

What other provisions may the agreement include?

The agreement should contain provisions about record keeping. The artist should insist that records about his or her works be kept in a separate ledger and that the gallery keep separate receipts for each piece. Payment schedules should also be listed in the book. The artist should have the right to inspect the gallery's books and records periodically. The agreement should also provide for monthly or quarterly payments to the artist, accompanied by a statement. The agreement may also grant the artist the right to recapture the work from time to time without payment to the gallery, to exhibit or renovate it.

Every contract, especially a contract that excludes the artist's sales from his or her studio, should include a specific description of the work consigned and terms of payment. It should specify whether the artist or the gallery bears the risk of loss before delivery to the gallery, and the time and method of delivery.

Moreover, if the eventual purchaser will acquire the right to reproduce the work, the contract must expressly so provide; otherwise, the provisions of the U.S. Copyright Act of 1976,[93] as well as the laws of several states,[94] provide that reproduction rights do not go with the work but remain with the artist.

What about commissioned works?

Again, it is important to agree on this in writing. The subject matter of the work should be clearly described. Schedules for completion and payment should be spelled out: usually, payments are made at the beginning, on delivery of sketches, and on delivery of the final work. Since such a contract requires the artist's personal services, it is terminated by the artist's death or disability.[95] The agreement should make clear which rights in the unfinished work go to the commissioning party and which to the artist if the contract is terminated before completion. If the agreement provides that the work is to be completed to the satisfaction of the commissioning party, a matter that has been a continuing source of controversy,[96] it should set forth how such satisfaction shall be stated.

What if an artist is fortunate enough to have a showing at a museum?

There should be a full, written contract which spells out the rights and responsibilities of the museum and the artist. Matters to be considered include the museum's receipt of the work; condition and description of the work; whether the contract constitutes a loan of the work to the museum; how long the museum is entitled to keep the work; special precautions to be taken for the preservation and safety of the work, and who bears the responsibility for loss of the work; and who pays for insuring the work. The museum may seek an option to purchase; if so, the terms should be clearly set forth. If the method of installation is important, it should be specified, along with any requirements the artist deems important about framing or exhibiting the work. If prints are to be included in the museum's catalog, the artist can seek the right to approve the inclusion of each one. Many museums now seek the right to reproduce works of art which they have on exhibition: such a request should be most carefully considered by the artist.

What about an agreement between an artist and a publisher?

An artist enters into an agreement with a publisher when an existing work is to be reproduced in a book or magazine, when the artist creates graphic work for reproduction and distribution as an edition, and when the artist is asked to illustrate a book.

Many of the considerations discussed in section C apply to artists: the grant of rights, the manner of payment and accounting for it, representations and warranties, and so on.

If the artist is doing graphic work for reproduction and distribution as an edition, the agreement should specify the method of reproduction; the materials to be used—color, ink, paper, etc.; the size of the image; the size of the edition; perhaps even the printer. If only one or a few works are to be reproduced, the agreement can specify method of reproduction, size of publication, and time and place of publication.

As for illustrated books, it may be important to state whether the publisher or the artist has the right to the original work and who can exploit subsidiary rights in it, such as using the work commercially or as a graphic design. The agreement should spell out how many illustrations are necessary, their size and when they are due, and what colors will be used.

The artist should always seek the right to examine and approve proofs of the work before printing. The contract should make clear who owns the copyright in the artist's work and whether the artist is working as an "employee for hire" of the publisher.[97]

How have artists attempted to secure a continuing interest in the increase in the value of their work?

Although only California has a law giving artists the right to receive resale royalties, many artists have attempted to include such a right in the contracts they enter into.

Often, they have attempted to use the Artist's Reserved Rights to Transfer and Sale Agreement, a proposed form contract drafted in 1970 by Robert Projansky, a New York lawyer, and

Seth Siegelaub, an art dealer.[98] This "Projansky agreement" provides that when a work is resold, the artist is entitled to 15 percent of any increase in sales price. The agreement also provides the artist with

- a record of who owns each work at all times;
- the right to be notified when the work is to be exhibited so that the artist can advise upon or veto the proposed exhibition;
- the right to borrow the work for exhibition for two months every five years without payment to the owner;
- the right to be consulted if repairs are necessary;
- half of any rental income paid to the owner for the use of the work at exhibitions; and
- all reproduction rights in the work.

Financial participation in future sales continues for the life of the artist and of the artist's spouse, and for 21 years thereafter. The agreement also provides that if the work is destroyed by fire the artist is to receive 15 percent of the insurance proceeds.

How is the Projansky agreement designed to be used?

The artist is only a party to the first sale contract. To be binding on future purchasers, the agreement must be in the first sale, gift, or barter by the artist, and each owner must be required to incorporate it in every following transfer of the work. (It is not designed for use when works are loaned for exhibition or left with a dealer on consignment.) To ensure that successive owners use the agreement or at least are aware of it, it is necessary to affix a notice of the existence of the agreement somewhere on the work itself.

Since each owner uses the agreement in transferring the work to a successor, the agreement provides a ready record of the work's authenticity and chain of title, providing a benefit to the owners. It has been said that owners also benefit when a continuing relationship is created between owners and artist, providing assurance to each owner that the work is being used in harmony with the artist's intentions and recognizing that the artist maintains a moral relationship to the work even though the owner has possession and control of it.

Has the agreement been widely used?

Unfortunately, from the artist's point of view, the answer is no. Not only has it generated the same heated controversy that engulfed most proposed legislation in this area, it has encountered tremendous resistance from galleries and owners,[99] and doubts have been raised about its enforceability.[100]

An introduction to the agreement by co-author Siegelaub acknowledged the radical changes the agreement would cause in the art world. It nonetheless exhorted the artists to whom the agreement is addressed to be steadfast in their determination to use it. The introduction recognizes that to be effective the agreement must be used systematically by artists and that its acceptance depends upon the strength of the artists' will. The authors of the agreement have emphasized the importance of that effort:[101]

> We realize that this Agreement is essentially unprecedented in the art world and that it just may cause a little rumbling and trembling; on the other hand, the ills it remedies are universally acknowledged to exist and no other practical way has ever been devised to cure them.

Have there been attempts to devise similar contracts?

Yes. Several years after the Projansky agreement was introduced, another New York attorney, Charles Jurrist, developed a variation which in some respects is simpler and more practical.[102] The artist receives a more modest package of rights, and collectors receive safeguards designed to make the contract more palatable to them. Perhaps most significantly, the 15 percent royalty to the artist is only payable on the first resale of the work. This eliminates the requirement of ongoing contracts and consequently does not restrict the market for the work as much as the Projansky agreement does. However, it also denies the artist the right to participate in what may be the largest increases in the value of his or her work.

The Jurrist agreement too has not been widely adopted. It is still true that artists who desire to participate in the increased resale value of their work and to enjoy the other benefits of the Projansky and Jurrist agreements will have to continue to fight for their rights every time they enter into a contract for their work.

NOTES

1. *See, e.g.,* J. Calamari & J. Perillo, *The Law of Contracts* (1970) [hereinafter Calamari & Perillo]; 17 Am. Jur. 2d CONTRACTS §10 (1964) [hereinafter *Am. Jur.*].

2. For example, a contract is defined in the RESTATEMENT (SECOND) CONTRACTS §1 (1979) [hereinafter RESTATEMENT] as "a promise or set of promises for the breach of which the law gives a remedy, or the performance of which the law in some way recognizes as a duty."

3. *See generally Am. Jur.,* §16; RESTATEMENT, §§12–16.

4. Calamari & Perillo, *supra* n. 1, at 10; RESTATEMENT, §§178–85.

5. *Roddy-Eden v. Berle,* 108 N.Y.S.2d 597, 600; 202 Misc. 261, 264 (Sup.Ct. N.Y. Co. 1951).

6. *See generally Am. Jur.,* §§151–54; RESTATEMENT, §§174–77.

7. However, in a proposal that was somewhat controversial at the time it was first announced, Section 208 of the RESTATEMENT provides: "If a contract or term thereof is unconscionable at the time the contract is made a court may refuse to enforce the contract, or may enforce the remainder of the contract without the unconscionable term, or may so limit the application of any unconscionable term as to avoid any unconscionable result." Obviously, insofar as this proposal is concerned, the definition of "unconscionable" becomes crucial. In this connection, the drafters of the RESTATEMENT have commented as follows: "A bargain is not unconscionable merely because the parties to it are unequal in bargaining position, not even because the inequality results in an allocation of risks to the weaker party. But gross inequality of bargaining power, together with terms unreasonably favorable to the stronger party, may confirm indications that the transaction involved elements of deception or compulsion, or may show that the weaker party had no meaningful choice, no real alternative, or did not in fact assent or appear to assent to the unfair terms."

8. *See generally* RESTATEMENT, Chapter 5.

9. 17 U.S.C. §101 *et seq.*

10. *Id.* §204.

11. *See, e.g., Am. Jur.,* §§244–45; RESTATEMENT, Chapter 9.

12. *See, e.g.,* RESTATEMENT, §§219–223; Calamari & Perillo, *supra* n. 1, §52.

13. *See generally* RESTATEMENT, §§357–69.

14. *Id.* §§359–60.

15. *Id.* §§346–56.
16. *See* Calamari & Perillo, *supra* n. 1, §203.
17. For example, in *Freund v. Washington Sq. Press, Inc.*, 34 N.Y.2d 379 (1974), the plaintiff had delivered a manuscript in accordance with his agreement with the defendant publisher, which then failed to publish the work. The author sued for lost royalties, among other relief. The court refused to permit any award for the claimed lost royalties, saying that unless there was a "stable foundation for a reasonable estimate of what a book might earn," royalties could not be approximated. See also *Demaris v. G. P. Putnam's Sons*, 379 F.Supp. 294 (C.D. Cal. 1973); *Gilroy v. American Broadcasting Co.*, 58 A.D. 2d 533, 395 N.Y.S. 2d 658 (1st Dept. 1977). ("The proper measure of damages flowing from defendants' wrongful appropriation of plaintiff's literary property is the reasonable value thereof and opinion evidence of the value of the property is admissible.")
18. In *Frankel v. Stein & Day, Inc.*, 470 F.Supp. 209 (S.D. N.Y. 1979), the authors successfully sued for reversion of rights due to the publisher's failure to pay royalties. See also *Nolen v. Sam Fox Pub. Co.*, 499 F.2d 1394 (2d Cir. 1974).
19. There are two major organizations of literary agents, the Independent Literary Agents Association (ILAA) and the Society of Authors' Representatives (SAR). Authors interested in learning more about how agents function, or in obtaining lists of the agent members of those organizations, should contact ILAA at 21 W. 26th St., New York, NY 10010, and/or SAR at 225 W. 12th St., New York, NY 10011. In addition, agency contracts are discussed in Crawford, *The Writer's Legal Guide*, Chapter 6, Hawthorne Books, 1977.
20. *See* 3 Am. Jur., 2d AGENCY §199 (1964).
21. *Id.* §§37–50.
22. *Id.* §§62–67.
23. 17 U.S.C. §101.
24. *Id.* §201(a).
25. The legal aspects of self-publication are beyond the scope of this chapter. Interested authors should consult Henderson, ed., *The Publish-It-Yourself Handbook*, Pushcart Book Press, 1973, and Appelbaum & Evans, *How to Get Happily Published*, Harper & Row, 1978. The latter provides a wealth of pertinent and practical information.
26. The Authors Guild makes available a form contract prepared from the author's perspective, a guide for use along with it, and another, earlier published guide containing excellent explanations and comparisons of various clauses [hereinafter A.G. Guide]. It is available to Authors Guild members at the Guild's office, 234 W. 44th St., New York, NY 10036.
27. *P.E.N. Standards for Author's Access to Information from Book Publishers* [hereinafter P.E.N. Standards] was published in the Dec. 1980

82

issue of the P.E.N. newsletter. Reprints are available from P.E.N. at 47 Fifth Ave., New York, NY 10003.

28. *See* pp. 26–27.
29. The U.S. Copyright Act provides that in the absence of an express agreement providing otherwise, a magazine that acquires a free-lance article or work of visual art "is presumed to have acquired only the privilege of reproducing and distributing the contribution as part of that particular [issue of the magazine], any revision of that [issue], and any later [issue] in the same series." 17 U.S.C. §201(c).
30. *E.g., Harcourt Brace Jovanovich, Inc. v. Goldwater,* 8 Med. L. Reptr. 1217 (S.D.N.Y. 1982); *Stein and Day, Inc. v. Morgan,* 5 Med. L. Reptr. 1831 (Sup.Ct. N.Y. Co. 1979); *Random House, Inc. v. Gold,* 464 F. Supp. 1306 (S.D.N.Y.), *aff'd,* 607 F.2d 998 (2d Cir. 1979).
31. *Harcourt Brace Jovanovich, Inc. v. Goldwater, supra* n. 30.
32. *Id.* at 1221.
33. *Id.* at 1221–22.
34. *Id.* at 1222.
35. *Id.*
36. See *Supplement No. 3 of Recommended Trade Book Contract,* published by the Authors Guild, *supra* n. 26, which also appeared in the Jan.–Feb. 1981 issue of the *Authors Guild Bulletin.*
37. *Harcourt Brace Jovanovich, Inc. v. Goldwater, supra* n. 30.
38. *Zilg v. Prentice-Hall, Inc.,* No. 82-7335 (2d Cir. 1983).
39. John Koshel, an attorney for Prentice-Hall, quoted in "Author Wins Book Promotion Case," *National Law Journal,* May 10, 1982.
40. *Zilg v. Prentice-Hall, Inc., supra* n. 38, at 21.
41. *Id.* at 22.
42. An extensive discussion of publishers' royalty statements may be found in a three-part 1981 article by Richard Curtis in *Locus, the Newspaper of the Science Fiction Field,* reprinted in Curtis, *How to be Your Own Literary Agent,* Houghton Mifflin, 1983. See also *Supplement No. 4 of Recommended Trade Book Contract,* published by the Authors Guild, *supra* n. 26, which also appeared in the Sept.–Oct. 1981 issue of the *Authors Guild Bulletin;* and P.E.N. Standards, *supra* n. 27.
43. *See generally* Speiser, "Insuring Authors: A New Proposal," *Publishers Weekly,* May 7, 1982; Speiser, "Writing a New Page for Authors on Indemnification of Publishers," *National Law Journal,* Feb. 1, 1982; Pell, "Insuring Free Speech," *Nation,* Mar. 13, 1982.
44. *See, e.g., Supplement No. 1 of Recommended Trade Book Contract,* published by the Authors Guild, *supra* n. 26, which states in part: "Non-compete clauses should be deleted. If the publisher refuses, the clause should be tightened. There should be a reasonably short time period, after which it expires. The types of books to which it applies should be stated, specifically. Authors of textbooks should be particu-

larly careful that they limit the effect of the clause, so that the contract for one book on a subject does not prevent them from writing other texts on the subject for other age groups, or for different types of classes or schools.'' *See also Wolf v. Illustrated World Encyclopedia, Inc.*, 34 N.Y.2d 838 (1974), affirming 41 A.D.2d 191 (1st Dept. 1973).

45. *See, e.g., Harcourt Brace Jovanovich, Inc. v. Farrar, Straus & Giroux, Inc.*, 4 Med. L. Rptr. 2625 (Sup. Ct. N.Y. Co. 1979).

46. *See Supplement No. 1, supra* n. 44, which states in part: ''The best way to deal with an option clause is to delete it from the publisher's contract form. Many authors (even newcomers) and agents insist on this, and publishers do delete the clause. Some publishers accede because they recognize the clause is unfair; and that a harmonious relationship, and an author's continuing loyalty, cannot be coerced by this one-way provision.''

47. *See* pp. 27–28.

48. *See* Authors Guild Recommended Trade Book Contract *supra* n. 26, at 20.

49. Such a clause was upheld in *In re Little & Ives Co.*, 262 F. Supp. 719 (S.D.N.Y. 1966); but see 11 U.S.C. §365(e), in the revised Bankruptcy Act, which invalidates such clauses under certain circumstances.

50. For further discussion of this kind of publishing, with conflicting points of view, *see* Appelbaum & Evans, *How to Get Happily Published*, pp. 72–73, Harper & Row, 1978; Crawford, *The Writer's Legal Guide*, Chapter 8, Hawthorne Books, 1977; McDowell, ''More Authors Turn to Vanity Presses,'' *New York Times*, May 26, 1982

51. *See generally* R. Duffy, *Art Law: Representing Artists, Dealers, and Collectors*, 291 *et seq.* (1977); F. Feldman & S. Weil, *Art Works: Law, Policy, Practice*, 8 (1974).

52. Duffy, *supra* n. 52, at 292.

53. Sarraute, ''Current Theory of the Moral Right of Authors and Artists Under French Law,'' 16 *Am. J. Comp. L.* 465 (1968).

54. Roeder, ''The Doctrine of Moral Right: A Study in the Law of Artists, Authors and Creators,'' 53 *Harv. L. Rev.* 554, 557 (1940).

55. Merryman, ''The Refrigerator of Bernard Buffet,'' 27 Hastings L. J. 1023, 1027–28 (1976).

56. *Buffet v. Fersing*, [1962] Recueil Dalloz [D.Jur.] 570, 571 (Cour d'appel, Paris).

57. Merryman, *supra* n. 55, at 1027.

58. *Guille v. Colmant*, [1967] Recueil Dalloz-Sirey [D.S.Jur.] 284, [1967] Gazette du Palais [Gaz.Pal.] I.17 (Cour d'appel, Paris).

59. Merryman, *supra* n. 55, at 1028.

60. *Bonheur v. Pourchet*, Cour de Paris, D.P. 1865.2.201.

61. Indeed, Judge Jerome Frank once remarked that ''the phrase 'moral rights' seems to have frightened some [American] courts to such an

extent that some have unduly narrowed artists' rights." *Granz v. Harris*, 198 F.2d 585, 590 (2d Cir. 1952).

62. *See, e.g., Crimi v. Rutgers Presbyterian Church*, 194 Misc. 570, 89 N.Y.S.2d 813 (Sup.Ct. 1949).

63. Chap. 944, Laws of New York 1983. *See also* CAL. CIV. CODE §15–813 (West 1977).

64. Bills have been proposed in the U.S. Congress to provide artists with *droit moral* protection. *See, e.g.,* H.R. 8261, 95th Cong, 1st Sess. (1977).

65. *See generally* Duffy, *supra* n. 52, at 299–300, 302–4, 306–11.

66. *Preminger v. Columbia Pictures Corp.*, 49 Misc. 2d 363, 267 N.Y.S.2d 594 (S.Ct.N.Y.Co.), *aff'd*, 25 A.D.2d 830, 269 N.Y.S.2d 913 (1st Dept), *aff'd*, 18 N.Y.2d 659, 219 N.E.2d 436, 273 N.Y.S.2d 80 (1966); *Stevens v. NBC*, 148 U.S.P.Q. 755 (Super.Ct., L.A.Co. 1966).

67. *Gilliam v. ABC*, 538 F.2d 14 (2d Cir. 1976).

68. *See Granz v. Harris*, 198 F.2d 585 (2d Cir. 1952); *Prouty v. NBC*, 26 F.Supp. 265 (D. Mass. 1939).

69. *See Clevenger v. Baker Voorhis & Co.*, 8 N.Y.2d 187, 168 N.E.2d 643 (1960).

70. *See* 17 U.S.C. §106.

71. *Cf. Curtis Pub. Co. v. Neyland*, 65 F.2d 363 (2d Cir. 1933), *cert. denied*, 290 U.S. 661 (1933).

72. *See, e.g., Runger v. Lee*, 441 F.2d 579 (9th Cir. 1971).

73. *See, e.g., Gershwin v. Ethical Publishing Co.*, 166 Misc. 39, 1 N.Y.S.2d 904 (City Ct. 1937).

74. Price & Price, *The Rights of Artists: The Case of the Droit de Suite*, 31 *Art Journal* 144 (Winter 1971–72), reprinted in Feldman & Weil, *supra* n. 51, at 67.

75. *See generally* Duffy, *supra* n. 51, at 265 (France), 269 (Germany), 270 (Italy).

76. CAL. CIV. CODE §986 (West Supp. 1977).

77. *E.g.*, N.Y. Assy. 8171, 1977–78 Regular Session (1977).

78. The "pros and cons" of such legislation are discussed at length in Duffy, *supra* n. 51, at 276–81.

79. Duffy, *supra* n. 51, at 281–82.

80. *See also* the discussion in Associated Councils of the Arts, *The Visual Artist and the Law*, Praeger Publishers, 2d ed., 1974 [hereinafter Praeger]. Furthermore, there is an excellent (and seemingly exhaustive) checklist in Feldman & Weil, *supra* n. 51, at 499–504, of items which can be included in an artist/gallery contract.

81. Praeger, *supra* n. 80, at 20–21; Duffy, *supra* n. 51, at 380.

82. N.Y. GEN. BUS. L. §§219, 219–a (McKinney Supp. 1981).

83. CAL. CIV. CODE §§1738, 1738.5–9 (West Supp. 1977).

84. N.Y. GEN. BUS. L. §219–a.1(iii) (McKinney Supp. 1981); CAL. CIV. CODE §§1738.6, 1738.7 (West Supp. 1977).

85. N.Y. GEN. BUS. L. §219–a.1(b) (McKinney Supp. 1981).

86. *Id.*, §219–0.2.
87. *See* Duffy, *supra* n. 51, at 380–84.
88. *Id.*
89. U.C.C. §2–306(2).
90. *See* Duffy, *supra* n. 51, at 389–90.
91. *Id.*
92. *See* Praeger, *supra* n. 80, at 20–21.
93. 17 U.S.C. §202.
94. *See, e.g.*, N.Y. GEN. BUS. L., Art. 12–E, §224 (McKinney Supp. 1975).
95. *See, e.g.*, Calamari & Perillo, *supra* n. 1, at 307.
96. *See, e.g.*, the discussion in Calamari & Perillo, *id.* at 240.
97. *See* pp. 24–25.
98. The agreement is reprinted in, *inter alia,* Feldman & Weil, *supra* n. 51, at 81.
99. *Cf.* Duffy, *supra* n. 51, at 288–89.
100. *Id.* at 284–88.
101. Feldman & Weil, *supra* n. 51, at 90.
102. *See* Duffy, *supra* n. 51, at 282.

IV

Libel and Privacy

Most non-fiction writers—and an increasing number of fiction writers—are directly affected by the law of libel and privacy. Even visual artists can be confronted by claims in these areas. It is important that authors and artists understand the nature and extent of libel and privacy law and how to deal with potential claims.

What is the purpose of the law of libel?

As the Supreme Court recently put it, "[T]he legitimate state interest underlying the law of libel is the compensation of individuals for the harm inflicted on them by defamatory falsehoods. . . . The individual's right to the protection of his good name 'reflects no more than our basic concept of the essential dignity and worth of every human being—a concept at the root of any decent system of ordered liberty.' "[1]

Nevertheless, it has been argued—by no less than late Supreme Court Justices Hugo Black and William O. Douglas, among others—that any law of libel violates the freedoms of speech and press guaranteed by the First Amendment.[2] This view has not been accepted by any American court or legislature, and is not likely to be in the foreseeable future.

But this is not to say that the First Amendment is irrelevant to the law of libel and privacy. In 1964 the U.S. Supreme Court ruled for the first time that the traditional law of libel directly implicates the essential freedoms of speech and the press that are protected by the First Amendment;[3] since then the Court has substantially rewritten much of libel law to reconcile it with those precious First Amendment freedoms. The major changes imposed by the Supreme Court on the law of libel and privacy will be discussed later in this chapter.[4]

When will a statement give rise to a successful libel claim?

The answer varies with the nature of the statement, the speaker, the subject, the claimed injury, and other factors, including not incidentally the particular law that will apply.[5] In short, there is no short answer.

However, it is possible to list six requirements that must almost always be established before a statement can result in a successful libel suit: (1) The statement must be libelous (or defamatory). (2) It must be false. (3) It must be about ("of and concerning") the living person claiming to be libeled. (4) It must be "published." (5) It must be published with "fault." (6) It must cause actual injury to the plaintiff.

What is meant by libel?

Libel and slander together comprise what the law calls defamation. Libelous statements are in writing, or otherwise set down in concrete non-ephemeral form; slanderous statements are generally oral, and lack concreteness. It is unlikely that authors and artists will be confronted by claims of slander, so this chapter will be primarily concerned with libel.[6]

A statement, to be libelous, must tend "to harm the reputation of another as to lower him in the estimation of the community or to deter third persons from associating or dealing with him."[7] Or, expanded and formalized somewhat, it must be an

accusation . . . against the character of a person . . . which affects his reputation, in that it tends to hold him up to ridicule, contempt, shame, disgrace or obloquy, to degrade him in the estimation of the community, to induce an evil opinion of him in the minds of right thinking persons, to make him an object of reproach, to diminish his respectability or abridge his comforts, to change his position in society for the worse, to dishonor or discredit him in the estimation of the public, or his friends and acquaintances, or to deprive him of friendly intercourse in society, or cause him to be shunned or avoided.[8]

In short, it must be a charge that tends to injure a person's reputation. However, a great many statements that appear to provide the basis for a libel suit—or, as lawyers say, to be "actionable"—are protected by the law.

What kinds of statement may be found libelous?

There is no legal boundary since the libelousness of a statement depends on its relation to the reputation of an individual. It is conceivable that any statement about another, even one that appears to be laudatory, can be libelous. (See next question.)

The law has historically recognized four major categories of potentially defamatory statements; although the categories are not conclusive or all-encompassing, they are useful examples of the statements that most often are alleged to be libelous. They are imputations of (1) crime,[9] (2) a loathsome disease,[10] (3) incompetence or dishonesty in one's business or profession,[11] and (4) unchastity in a woman.[12] On the face of it, the false charge that a particular woman is "a syph-laden prostitute who regularly cheats her clients" could give rise to a claim of libel. However, as we shall see, even this statement might not result in a libel judgment. (A list of "red flag" words that frequently lead to libel claims is set forth at Appendix B to this book.)

If the libelous nature of a statement is apparent from the statement itself, it is considered libelous *"per se"* and the law will allow recovery of damages merely on proof that the subject's reputation has been injured as a result of the publication of the statement.[13] The issues of injury and damages are discussed more fully later in this chapter.

Can a statement that seems to be innocent be libelous?

Sometimes, if it is false, even a seemingly innocent statement can injure its subject's reputation. For example, the false statement that a woman was the guest of honor at a lavish dinner at the local Steak and Brew restaurant could be found libelous if it turned out that she is the president of the local branch of

"Vegetarian Tea-Totalers." Similarly, the false statement that John Smith is a "distinguished war hero" could be found libelous if Mr. Smith is an avowed lifelong pacifist.[14]

When, as here, the libelous nature of the statement is created by extrinsic facts—sometimes referred to as "libel *per quod*"—it is obviously much more difficult to guard against than is libel *per se*. For this reason, among others, the law in most states requires a person claiming to have been libeled by extrinsic facts to prove that he has sustained specific—"special"—damages as a result of the statement, not merely injury to his general reputation.[15] The issue of special damages is discussed more fully later in this chapter.

Can a true statement be libelous?

Probably not, although the law in some states, predating recent Supreme Court rulings, may suggest the contrary.[16] Under libel law as it existed before the Supreme Court revolutionized large parts of it during the last two decades, defamatory statements were presumed by the law to be false. The burden was on the libel defendant to prove that they were true, which was not always easy.

Since 1964, however, it is probably more accurate to state that the person claiming libel must prove that the statement is false. Moreover, it has long been the law that substantially true statements cannot give rise to successful claims of libel. The plaintiff must prove not merely that the statement is not completely true in every particular, but that it is substantially false in its material elements.[17]

Can a statement of opinion be libelous?

Generally not. The Supreme Court has reiterated in several recent cases that only a false statement of fact can give rise to a successful libel claim. This means a statement that is capable of being proved true or false. As the Court grandly put it, in an oft-quoted passage:

> Under the First Amendment there is no such thing
> as a false idea. However pernicious an opinion may

seem, we depend for its correction not on the conscience of judges and juries but on the competition of other ideas.[18]

If a statement is found to be opinion, it cannot be found libelous. But it is often very difficult to determine whether a particular statement is one of fact or opinion.[19] While the statement that "Senator Smith is a brilliant orator" is clearly one of opinion, what about the statement that the Senator is "a corrupt liar and post-crypto Nazi"? The courts have made it clear that the mere use of such phrases as "in my opinion" or "I believe" will not convert a statement of fact into one of opinion, and that purported statements of opinion will be treated as statements of fact if they suggest criminal activity. Thus, on both scores, a statement like "In my opinion, Jack Brown is a thief" will, in general, be treated as a statement of fact and not as a protected statement of opinion. However, a statement that literally seems to charge another with a crime will not be treated as a libelous statement of fact if the context makes clear that the charge could not have been taken literally. Such statements are discussed at pp. 112–13.

There are no clear guidelines to help writers determine whether a statement will be found to be opinion or fact.[20] As a leading authority on libel has put it:

> The determination of what is fact and what is opinion (or "comment") is made on the basis of the effect which the communication may reasonably be expected to have on its recipient. Although difficult to state in abstract terms, as a practical matter, the crucial differences between statement of fact and opinion depends upon whether ordinary persons hearing or reading the matter complained of would be likely to understand it as an expression of the speaker's or writer's opinion, or as a statement of existing fact. The opinion may ostensibly be in the form of a factual statement if it is clear from the context that the maker did not intend to assert another objective fact but only his personal comment upon the facts he had stated—and vice versa.[21]

Who can sue for libel?

Only those who are alive at the time of publication can sue for libel. The law considers that the interest in one's reputation that the law of libel is designed to protect no longer applies when a person dies; as a result, it is generally impossible to libel the dead.[22]

Corporations, partnerships, associations, and the like have legitimate interests in their reputations, but, usually, far more limited interests than those of living people. Such entities can sue for alleged libels which affect their financial credit or standing in their own fields, or which cast aspersions on their honesty.[23]

Must a person be named to be able to sue for libel?

No, but the plaintiff must prove that the alleged libel refers to him or her—in the words of the law, that it is "of and concerning" him or her. Obviously, a named person meets this requirement. (Several persons may have the name of the person named in an alleged libel, and it has happened that a person other than the one intended to be referred to has successfully sued.)[24]

Without being named, a person can sometimes prove that the libel is "of and concerning" him or her. For example, a libelous reference to "the only dentist in town" will be found to apply to the person who meets that description; a reference to "a Main Street dentist" will be found to apply to the dentist who can prove that he or she is the only dentist on Main Street.[25]

Can members of groups sue for libelous statements about their groups?

Generally, no. The courts have consistently held that a libelous statement about a large group—e.g., "All Lithuanians are child molesters" or "All Republicans cheat on their taxes"— does not refer to each member of that group in such a way to be "of and concerning" him or her.

Nevertheless, it may be possible for a group member to sue successfully for libel. If the context of the statement indicates that the plaintiff was its intended target—e.g., if the statement "All lawyers are thieves" is made in an article about one lawyer—then the plaintiff may be found to have been libeled by the general statement.[26] Similarly, the courts have been willing to find group members to have been libeled if the group is small enough to justify the conclusion that the members were effectively referred to.[27] In probably the most famous case involving such a claim, the court upheld the right of 15 of the 25 salesmen at the Neiman-Marcus store in Dallas to sue for libel based on the statement that "most of [the store's] sales staff are fairies," but denied the right of several of the store's 382 saleswomen to sue because the group was too large.[28] As a leading authority has concluded, while "it is not possible to set definite limits as to the size of the group or class . . . the cases in which recovery has been allowed usually have involved numbers of 25 or fewer."[29]

Must a statement be published to give rise to a successful libel claim?

Yes. The most libelous statement imaginable cannot give rise to a successful libel claim if it remains in the author's manuscript—or diary—and is not "published" to anybody else. The traditional rule is that a statement is published in this sense if it is shown to a person other than the subject of the libel. A handwritten letter from A to B, in which B is seriously libeled, does not enable B to sue A for libel—unless, for example, A dictated the letter to his secretary.[30] (B's damages, if any, may be smaller in this case than in the case of mass publication. See pp. 117–18.)

What about someone (not the originator) who repeats or reports a libelous statement?

The traditional rule is that anyone who repeats, republishes, or distributes a libelous statement made by another can be held legally responsible,[31] but this has been significantly modified in the last two decades.

First, the law now requires that a plaintiff prove that a libelous statement was published with some degree of "fault," which means at least that it was published negligently. It is conceivable, and in some cases probable, that the repeater of a libelous statement will be found to have acted reasonably—even if the original speaker has not—and cannot be held liable.

Second, some courts have extended a special protection

from liability to repeaters of some libelous statements in neutral and accurate reporting on newsworthy subjects—even if the writer knows the statement is false or has serious doubts about its truth. As a federal court of appeals put it in the leading case:

> At stake in this case is a fundamental principle. Succinctly stated, when a responsible, prominent organization like the National Audubon Society makes serious charges against a public figure, the First Amendment protects the accurate and disinterested reporting of those charges, regardless of their reporter's private view regarding their validity. . . . What is newsworthy about such accusations is that they were made. We do not believe that the press may be required under the First Amendment to suppress newsworthy statements merely because it has serious doubts regarding their truth. Nor must the press take up cudgels against dubious charges in order to publish them without fear of liability for defamation. . . . The public interest in being fully informed about controversies that often rage around sensitive issues demands that the press be afforded the freedom to report such charges without assuming responsibility for them.[32]

It should be emphasized that other courts have refused to adopt the "neutral reporting" privilege, and that the Supreme Court has not yet addressed it.[33]

Third, legal protection has been established for the accurate (or "fair") repetition of libelous statements made during official governmental proceedings, such as trials, legislative hearings, or debates. This "qualified privilege" is discussed more fully on pages 95-96.

When is a libelous statement insulated from legal liability?

Whenever the law—the courts and/or the legislative branch of government—decides that the public interest requires that certain otherwise libelous statements be protected. Then the libelous statements are said to be cloaked with a privilege.

How many kinds of privilege does the law provide?

Two. An absolute privilege completely protects a libelous statement from legal action, regardless of circumstances, motive, or the injury that the statement causes. Qualified privilege cloaks a libelous statement with a legal immunity that can be overcome by showing that the maker of the statement "abused" the privilege. The burden generally is on the plaintiff to prove this.

What kinds of statements are protected by an absolute privilege?

Statements made in the course of official governmental activities may be so protected. This includes pertinent statements by the judicial branch of government: by attorneys, parties, witnesses, or jurors.[34] In general, statements by federal and state legislators are also protected, although this is not as clearly true of lesser legislative bodies.[35] In the executive branch, statements made by high federal and state officials are generally protected—again, this is less clear for lower level officials and units of government.[36]

Outside the government, otherwise libelous statements made by one spouse to the other are generally protected by an absolute privilege, as are statements that are made with the consent of their subjects.[37]

Absolute privilege applies only to a statement made in a privileged setting, and is generally not available if the statement is repeated outside the setting—whether the repetition is by the original speaker or someone else.[38] Such repetitions may, however, be protected by a qualified (conditional) privilege.

When are statements protected by a qualified privilege?

Basically, when it is considered more important to encourage (and protect) the making of statements which may be false and libelous than to allow victims of such statements to recover damages for libel. A qualified privilege generally only applies if the statement is made in good faith, consistently with the purposes that gave rise to the privilege.[39] Examples include statements to proper authorities accusing another person of a crime or other improper conduct (unethical conduct by a doctor or lawyer, physical abuse by a policeman) and statements made by credit-reporting agencies and private detectives to clients.[40]

Of special interest to writers is the qualified privilege that protects ''fair'' reports of governmental statements (which themselves are protected by an absolute privilege).[41] As one legal authority has summarized it, ''The publication of defamatory matter concerning another in a report of an official action or proceeding or of a meeting open to the public that deals with a matter of public concern is privileged if the report is accurate and complete or a fair abridgement of the occurrence reported.[42] A fair report in a book or newspaper article that Tom Brown testified during the trial of his suit against his partner Bill Jackson that Jackson embezzled money from the firm, cheated clients, and was always drunk is privileged even if the testimony is false *and* if Brown and the writer knew or suspected it was false. But if the report is not ''fair''—if the charges are taken out of context, are erroneously reported, or are reported to be true—then the author and publisher can be successfully sued for libel.[43]

How has the Supreme Court changed the law of libel?

Dramatically. Before 1964 a libelous statement was presumed to be false. The plaintiff was virtually assured of victory once he established that a libelous statement had been published about him, unless the maker of the statement could prove that the statement was true, was protected by a privilege, or caused the plaintiff no injury.

Against that background, one L. B. Sullivan, an elected commissioner of Montgomery, Alabama, sued the *New York Times* and four black Alabama clergymen because of what he considered libelous references to him (even though he wasn't named) in a full-page advertisement in a 1960 issue, signed by a number of civil rights leaders (including the four Alabama defendants), that sought support for the civil rights movement in the South. Applying the traditional law of libel, a Montgomery jury awarded Sullivan $500,000 in damages—the full amount requested—and the award was upheld by the Alabama appellate courts.

A unanimous Supreme Court found that the traditional libel

rules violate the protections for speech and press in the First Amendment. The Court set aside the jury's award and declared that a public official like Sullivan could not recover for allegedly libelous criticisms of his official conduct such as were contained in the *Times* ad.[44]

In reaching that conclusion, the Court—speaking through Justice William J. Brennan, Jr.—observed that "freedom of expression upon public questions is secured by the First Amendment" and that this constitutional safeguard "was fashioned to assure unfettered interchange of ideas for the bringing about of political and social changes desired by the people."[45] As a result, Brennan wrote, "[w]e consider this case against the background of a profound national commitment to the principle that debate on public issues should be uninhibited, robust, and wide-open, and that it may well include vehement, caustic, and sometimes unpleasantly sharp attacks on government and public officials."[46] He continued:

> The present advertisement, as an expression of griev-
> ance and protest on one of the major public issues of
> our time, would seem clearly to qualify for the constitu-
> tional protection. The question is whether it forfeits
> that protection by the falsity of some of its factual
> statements and by its alleged defamation of respondent.[47]

The Court stated that some factual error is "inevitable in free debate," and that such error "must be protected if the freedoms of expression are to have the 'breathing space' that they 'need . . . to survive.' "[48] It added that the defamatory nature of such criticism of public officials does not alter this: "Criticism of . . . official conduct does not lose its constitutional protection merely because it is effective criticism and hence diminishes their official reputations."[49] It was not enough that the Alabama libel law allowed the defense of truth:

> A rule compelling the critic of official conduct to
> guarantee the truth of all his factual assertions—and to
> do so on pain of libel judgments virtually unlimited in
> amount—leads to . . . "self-censorship." Allowance

of the defense of truth, with the burden of proving it on the defendant, does not mean that only false speech will be deterred. . . . Under such a rule, would-be critics of official conduct may be deterred from voicing their criticism, even though it is believed to be true and even though it is in fact true, because of doubt whether it can be proved in court or fear of the expense of having to do so. . . . The rule thus dampens the vigor and limits the variety of public debate. It is inconsistent with the First and Fourteenth Amendments.[50]

In what may be the most important sentence in the law of libel, the Court rewrote a significant part of that law: *"The constitutional guarantees require, we think, a federal rule that prohibits a public official from recovering damages for a defamatory falsehood relating to his official conduct unless he proves that the statement was made with 'actual malice'—that is, with knowledge that it was false or with reckless disregard of whether it was false or not."*[51] From then on, at least as far as public official libel plaintiffs were concerned, the rules of the game were different indeed.

What does "actual malice" mean?

The term "actual malice" as used by the Supreme Court is confusing and does not mean what most people might think it means. As one federal judge has put it, " 'Actual malice' is . . . a term of art having nothing to do with actual malice."[52]

In the *New York Times* case the Court indicated that "actual malice" means that a statement alleged to be libelous was made "with knowledge that it was false or with reckless disregard of whether it was false or not." Later, the Court elaborated, indicating that "actual malice" required a "high degree of awareness of [the statement's] probable falsity;"[53] "either deliberate falsification or reckless publication 'despite the publisher's awareness of probable falsity;' "[54] "sufficient evidence to permit the conclusion that the defendant *in fact* entertained serious doubts as to the truth of his publication;"[55] and "subjective awareness of probable falsity."[56] (Emphasis added.)

It is clear that negligence—which simply means acting in an

"unreasonable" way—is not actual malice. Misremembering the facts underlying an event, or failing to confirm the substance of a story, or relying on a source that turns out to be unreliable, which may constitute negligence, does not qualify as actual malice in the absence of proof that the author "entertained serious doubts as to the truth of his publication."[57] And proof of malice in its commonsense (as well as common law) meaning— "hatred, ill will or enmity or a wanton desire to injure"—does not in itself prove "actual malice."[58]

How has actual malice been established in libel actions?

It is difficult to establish that an author or publisher published matter the truth of which he or she seriously doubted. The threshold of proof is high in order to protect freedom of expression. Still, libel plaintiffs have been known to establish actual malice— for example, in the widely publicized action brought by Carol Burnett against the *National Enquirer*, which resulted in a $1.6 million jury verdict against the *Enquirer*,[59] which verdict was subsequently reduced to $200,000. The falsity of the article, which strongly implied that Carol Burnett was drunk and rowdy, and caused a disturbance with Henry Kissinger in a Washington, D.C., restaurant, was not in dispute. And there was, according to the trial and appeals courts, sufficient proof that the *Enquirer*'s gossip columnist had serious doubts about the truth of the publication. Indeed, according to the trial court, "[t]here is a high degree of probability that [the editor] fabricated part of the publication [relating to Henry Kissinger]."[60] Moreover, in attempting to verify the story received from a "free-lance tipster," there was uncontradicted evidence that the editor was warned of the tipster's unreliability and that witnesses at the scene gave the editor information that substantially contradicted the tipster's story. The story was nonetheless published without removing the false and potentially defamatory information.

In what situations has actual malice *failed* to be established?

In most cases plaintiffs have failed to meet this demanding standard. Among allegations that have failed to prove actual malice are these:

- publication of "emotionally tinged" documents;[61]
- insufficient checking or verification of the details of a news story;[62]
- negligence combined with hostility toward the plaintiff;[63]
- mere ill will toward the plaintiff;[64] and
- political or editorial bias.[65]

How has "reckless disregard" been defined under *Times v. Sullivan*?

Besides "knowledge of falsity," the *New York Times* standard provides for recovery in case of "reckless disregard of the truth or falsity" of a defamatory statement.[66] Obviously, reckless disregard is a looser concept than actual knowledge of falsity. "Reckless" means that the publisher entertained serious doubts and then, without further checking or adequate verification, published the material while continuing to harbor doubts.

Under the Supreme Court's decisions, a finding of "recklessness" depends on the publisher's subjective state of mind and not an objective determination of whether a reasonably prudent person would have published the material. However, mere "professions of good faith" will not necessarily defeat liability "when the publisher's allegations are so inherently improbable that only a reckless man would have put them in circulation. Likewise, recklessness may be found where there are obvious reasons to doubt the veracity of the informant or the accuracy of his reports."[67] Two recent cases seem to suggest that a court can substitute an objective assessment of the circumstances of the publication.[68] Such an approach could seriously erode the protections of the "actual malice" test, especially if it can be applied to an author or publisher who did not in fact harbor subjective doubts about the published material.

Who qualifies as a "public official"?

In the *Times* case, an elected city commissioner was held to be a public official. Later, the Supreme Court has found a mayor, a former public recreation area supervisor, a county attorney, an elected clerk of a county court, a police chief, a deputy sheriff, and a candidate for public office to be public officials. However, the Court has emphasized that while it has "not provided precise boundaries for the category of 'public official,' it cannot be thought to include all public employees."[69]

In the important *Gertz* case (discussed below), the Court had no difficulty finding that being a lawyer—and hence an "officer of the court"—and membership on committees appointed by a big-city mayor do not make a libel plaintiff a public official. A recent California case held that a public school teacher, in her libel case against a fraternal lodge for its criticism of her choice of reading material for her course, was not a public official. However, other cases have found teachers to be public officials.[70]

For whatever guidance it provides, the Supreme Court has said that "the 'public official' designation applies at the very least to those among the hierarchy of government employees who have, or appear to the public to have, substantial responsibility for or control over the conduct of government affairs."[71]

The Court has ruled that the protection of allegedly libelous statements about public officials applies to statements made after the official has left office. But the Court added, without further elaboration, that there may be cases in which the plaintiff "is so far removed from a former position of authority that comment on the manner in which he performed his responsibilities no longer has the interest necessary to justify the New York Times rule."[72]

Are all statements about public officials protected by the "actual malice" standard?

Not necessarily. The Court has held that the protection of the *New York Times* case only applies to statements about official conduct. However, the Court has also stated:

> The New York Times rule is not rendered inapplicable merely because an official's private reputation, as well as his public reputation, is harmed. The public-official rule protects the paramount public interest in a free flow of information to the people concerning public officials, their servants. To this end, anything which might touch on an official's fitness for office is relevant.[73]

Moreover, the Court has declared that "a charge of criminal conduct, no matter how remote in time or place, can never be irrelevant to an official's or a candidate's fitness for office" when one is applying the "actual malice" requirement.[74]

O.K., but what about libel plaintiffs who are not public officials?

We knew you'd ask. In 1967, three years after the *Times* case was decided, the Court extended the protection of its new rule to allegedly libelous statements made about people who were not public officials but were "public figures": a college football coach and an outspoken retired army general.[75] In 1971 the Court also seemed to extend the new rule to allegedly libelous statements about people who were neither public officials nor public figures—i.e., "private figures"—where the statements concerned matters "of public or general interest."[76] However, in 1974 the Court withdrew this protection and rewrote further most of our law of libel.

What happened in 1974?

In *Gertz v. Welch*[77] the Court declared that libel plaintiffs who were not public officials or public figures should not be required to meet the stringent *New York Times* test in order to recover for libelous statements made about them—even if the statements concerned matters of public or general interest. However, the Court also ruled that the First Amendment would not tolerate a return to the pre-1964 law, where a defamatory statement was presumed to be false and to have caused injury to the subject's reputation. Instead, the Court created a new set of ground rules for libel cases brought by private persons, while leaving intact its rules for public officials and public figures.

What was the *Gertz* case about?

The plaintiff, Elmer Gertz, was a practicing lawyer in Chicago who had "long been active in community and professional affairs. He had served as an officer of local civic groups and of various professional organizations, and he has published several books and articles on legal subjects." As a private lawyer, he was retained by the family of a youth who was killed by a Chicago

102

policeman in connection with the family's lawsuit for damages against the policeman. The defendant, Robert Welch, Inc., was the publisher of *American Opinion,* a monthly outlet for the views of the John Birch Society. In an article that purported to demonstrate that the prosecution of the policeman was a "frame-up" and part of a Communist campaign to discredit local law enforcement agencies, Gertz was portrayed as an architect of the frame-up (whose police file took "a big, Irish cop to lift"), a former official of the "Marxist League for Industrial Democracy, originally known as the Intercollegiate Socialist Society, which has advocated the violent seizure of our government," as well as a "Leninist" and a "Communist-fronter," among other charges.

Gertz sued for libel. The trial court and the appellate court concluded that Gertz was neither a public official nor a public figure, but they ruled that the actual malice test still applied because the defendant's statements about Gertz involved a matter of public interest. They found that Gertz could not show that the defendant had published the statements with actual malice, and as a result they held that he could not recover for the libelous statements.[78]

What did the Supreme Court do?

A lot. On appeal, it reversed the lower-court rulings and ordered a new trial to be held in accordance with new rules.

The Court agreed that Gertz was not a public official or a public figure. But the Court did not agree that the actual malice standard applies to statements about private figures that involve matters of public interest. The Court declined to go back to the pre-1964 libel law, however. It made important rulings on the definition of a public figure, on the law governing private figure libel suits, and on what kinds of damages a libel plaintiff can recover.

If not "actual malice," then what standard applies to private figure libel suits?

The Supreme Court held that the First Amendment does not require the stringent "actual malice" test applicable to public officials and public figures when private figures like Gertz sue, because such "private individuals are not only more vulnerable to injury than public officials and public figures; they are also more deserving of recovery.''[79]

The Court adopted what it considered a middle ground between pre-1964 law and recent rulings, that ''so long as they do not impose liability without fault, the States may define for themselves the appropriate standard of liability for a publisher or broadcaster of defamatory falsehood injurious to a private individual.''[80] The Court ruled that a private figure must prove at least that the defendant was negligent in making a statement, and that the states were free to impose more stringent requirements, including, if they desired, the actual malice test.[81] (The standards of the various states are set forth in Appendix C.)

How did the Court deal with the public figure issue?
On whether Gertz was a public figure, the Court stated:

That designation may rest on either of two alternative bases. In some instances an individual may achieve such pervasive fame or notoriety that he becomes a public figure for all purposes and in all contexts. More commonly, an individual voluntarily injects himself or is drawn into a particular public controversy and thereby becomes a public figure for a limited range of issues. In either case such persons assume special prominence in the resolution of public questions.[82]

The Court continued:

Although [Gertz] was consequently well known in some circles, he had achieved no general fame or notoriety in the community. None of the prospective jurors called at the trial had ever heard of [Gertz] prior to this litigation, and respondent offered no proof that this response was atypical of the local population. We would not lightly assume that a citizen's participation in community and professional affairs rendered him a public figure for all purposes. Absent clear evidence of general fame or notoriety in the community, and pervasive involvement in the affairs of society, an individual should not be deemed a public personality for all aspects of his life. It is preferable to reduce the public figure question to a more meaningful context by looking to the nature and extent of an individual's participation in the particular controversy giving rise to the defamation.[83]

After applying that analysis, the Court concluded: "In this context it is plain that [Gertz] was not a public figure. . . . He plainly did not thrust himself into the vortex of this public issue, nor did he engage the public's attention in an attempt to influence its outcome."[84]

The law now recognizes two kinds of public figures—first, the person who is a "public figure for all purposes and in all contexts," and second and "more commonly," the person who "voluntarily injects himself or is drawn into a particular public controversy and thereby becomes a public figure for a limited range of issues."[85]

What became of the *Gertz* case?

A new trial was finally held in 1981. The jury found for Gertz and awarded him $100,000 in compensatory damages and $300,000 in punitive damages. In 1982 the verdict was affirmed by the federal appellate court in Chicago. Ironically, even at the second trial Gertz was required by the trial judge to prove actual malice on the part of the defendant, since the judge found that such proof was necessary to defeat the defendant's qualified "fair report" privilege.[86]

Who qualifies as an "all-purpose" public figure?

Although the Supreme Court indicated in the *Gertz* case that all-purpose public figures were relatively rare, the lower courts have found a wide variety of individuals and entities who so qualify, including Johnny Carson,[87] the Holy Spirit Association,[88] Ralph Nader,[89] and William F. Buckley.[90] In a number of other libel cases plaintiffs who are less famous nationally but prominent in their localities have been found to be pervasive public figures.[91] Nevertheless, most libel plaintiffs will not qualify as all-purpose public figures.

Who qualifies as a "vortex" public figure?

Besides those who "thrust" themselves "into the vortex" of public issues, the Court in *Gertz* allowed that persons could become public figures through no choice of their own. As the Court put it:

> Hypothetically, it may be possible for someone to become a public figure through no purposeful action of his own, but the instances of truly involuntary public figures must be exceedingly rare.[92]

In a number of cases since *Gertz* the Supreme Court has proved reluctant to find libel plaintiffs to be even vortex public figures.

In *Time, Inc. v. Firestone*[93] a socialite sued *Time* magazine for libel arising from its account of her divorce litigation. Although the woman had given a number of press conferences, had felt it necessary to employ a clipping service, had her divorce reported in over 100 Florida publications, and was involved in a trial which, according to the judge, included evidence of sexual escapades "which would have made Dr. Freud's hair curl,"[94] the Supreme Court said she did not qualify as a public figure: since she had no choice but to use the courts in connection with her divorce, such use did not make her a vortex public figure in connection with accounts of the divorce.[95]

The Court reached similar results in two 1979 cases. In *Hutchinson v. Proxmire*[96] a scientist, who received public funds to conduct research on monkeys and behavior patterns found himself the recipient of Senator William Proxmire's "Golden Fleece" award. When the scientist sued for libel, the defendants claimed he was a public figure. Not so, said the Court; the receipt of public funds, the publication of scholarly articles, and limited access to the media was not enough.[97]

The plaintiff in *Wolston v. Reader's Digest Assn.*[98] had failed to appear at grand jury proceedings investigating Soviet intelligence activities in the United States in 1958, although he had been subpoenaed. He later pleaded guilty to contempt, in large part because his pregnant wife became hysterical on the witness stand during his contempt trial. At the time he was mentioned or discussed in at least 15 news stories. Some 13 years later he was listed in a book as "a Soviet agent convicted of contempt charges following espionage indictments." The Court said that he was not a public figure even in 1958 since he "was dragged unwillingly into the controversy."[99] His failure to respond to the grand jury subpoena, the Court found, resulted not from a desire to draw attention to himself or to influence the public on an issue but from his ill health.

Summarizing the gist of the Court's ruling, and casting serious doubt on the likelihood of a person ever being found an involuntary public figure, Justice Harry Blackmun observed:

> The Court seems to hold . . . that a person becomes a limited-issue public figure only if he literally or figuratively "mounts a rostrum" to advocate a particular view.[100]

Justice Blackmun would have limited the inquiry to whether the plaintiff was a public figure when the book was published, which he would have answered in the negative, but the Court as a whole did not address the "passage of time" issue in determining the plaintiff's public figure status.[101]

In spite of these rulings, lower courts have not hesitated to find a wide variety of libel plaintiffs to be vortex public figures, including a worldwide religious movement claiming 5 million adherents,[102] a high-school student senate president,[103] a former secretary in an urban renewal agency,[104] the president of a major oil company,[105] a prisoner spokesman for other inmates,[106] the major witness in the 1932 Scottsboro rape case,[107] and a law school dean.[108] However, Miss Wyoming of the Miss America pageant,[109] the son of the president of a major oil company,[110] an apartment house manager interviewed in a television documentary,[111] an unsalaried police informant,[112] and a country club tennis pro were all found not to be vortex public figures.[113]

Can fiction and satire be libelous?

Yes. Some of the largest and most controversial libel judgments in recent years have involved works of fiction and satire—

107

which, because of the difference in their nature, will be discussed separately.

In most fiction, by definition the characters and events are "fictitious": they are created by their author and are not supposed be literal, accurate portrayals of actual people and events. Nevertheless, the courts have held that a person who believes he is depicted and libeled in a work of fiction can sue.[114]

A person claiming to have been libeled by a work of fiction (or any other work) must establish that the alleged libel was "of and concerning" him or her. (See pages 92-93.) Although the characters in most works of fiction have different names and appearance from their models in real life, if any, it is possible for a plaintiff to persuade judge and jury that the fictional portrayal is of and concerning him or her, and is libelous.

A recent, controversial case provides a good example. A principal character in the defendant's novel *Touching* was a psychologist named Simon Herford who, among other things, conducted nude marathon therapy groups. The author had attended a nude therapy session conducted by a real Dr. Paul Bindrim. Although the novel's therapist had a different name, physical description, and professional background, Dr. Bindrim claimed to recognize himself in the book and, supported by a few colleagues who testified that they recognized Bindrim in the novel, sued for libel. Although the court ruled that Dr. Bindrim was a public figure and had to prove actual malice, the jury and the California appellate court upheld a substantial libel judgment in Bindrim's favor.[115]

The court's use in *Bindrim* of the actual malice test, which looks to the author's knowledge of falsity, seems anomalous, since fiction by definition is "false." Also dubious was the court's reliance on the testimony of a few of Bindrim's colleagues in concluding that the fictional portrayal was "of and concerning" Bindrim. What is needed in such cases is an effective alternative standard by which to determine whether a claim of libel-by-fiction succeeds or fails. Several courts since *Bindrim* have grappled with the problem, and in so doing have alleviated much of the concern among authors and publishers about the implications of the *Bindrim* decision.

In *Lyons v. New American Library, Inc.*, a novel based

upon the notorious "Son of Sam" murders referred in passing to an unnamed sheriff in a manner suggesting incompetence and perverted sexual proclivities. A sheriff from the same county sued, but an appellate court held that he could not prove the statements referred to him because the book was clearly labeled fiction and because it described incidents in which he had never participated.[116]

In *Springer v. The Viking Press,* a female character in a novel dealing with the Vatican was portrayed as a prostitute who engaged in abnormal sexual activity. A former friend of the author, whose first name was the same as the character's, sued for libel. An appellate court ruled that a person who knew the plaintiff and who had read the book could not reasonably conclude that the plaintiff was the fictional character, since the similarities between the two were "superficial" while the dissimilarities in both manner of living and outlook were "profound." For a plaintiff to recover in such cases, the court declared, "statements made about a character in a fictional work . . . must be so closely akin to the real person claiming to be defamed that a reader of the book, knowing the real person, would have no difficulty linking the two. Superficial similarities are insufficient as is a common first name."[117]

In *Pring v. Penthouse International, Ltd.,* a multi-million dollar libel judgment arising out of a satire of the Miss America pageant was overturned by a federal appeals court because the plaintiff failed to prove that the publication contained statements of fact about her. Several similarities between the article's Miss Wyoming and the plaintiff, a former Miss Wyoming, which similarities were claimed by the author to be coincidental, persuaded the court that the story was "of and concerning" the plaintiff. However, the court further held that "the story must be reasonably understood as describing actual facts about the plaintiff or her actual conduct." And because the allegedly defamatory events "about" plaintiff were physically impossible and could not reasonably be believed, the court held that those descriptions must be considered statements of opinion and not fact and therefore incapable of being libelous.[118]

Whether the author (and publisher) intended the fictional references to be taken as a reference to the real-life plaintiff, or acted in reckless disregard of whether they could reasonably be so taken, appears to provide an appropriate test that balances the interests of plaintiffs and the rights of authors and publishers, but despite these recent decisions this test has not yet become the law.[119] The traditional rules of libel, which were designed to deal with non-fiction, continue to be applied to fiction, and until special rules for fiction are adopted writers and publishers of fiction are advised to recognize their potential liabilities and to take steps before publication to avoid these problems. Disclaimers, changes in details that might suggest real persons, and care to avoid inclusion of derogatory false matter that is unnecessary to the artistic integrity of the work, while not guarantees of non-liability, are mechanisms that can and should be given consideration in appropriate cases.

What about satire?

In satire, real people are placed in fanciful, exaggerated contexts to make a satirical point. There is no question in satire, as there is in fiction, of who is described; instead, the question is whether the exaggerated statements qualify as libel.

Two cases illustrate the problem. In late 1968 after the election of President Nixon, then Los Angeles Mayor Sam Yorty, who supported Nixon, let it be known that he was available for a Cabinet appointment. Paul Conrad, a political cartoonist for the *Los Angeles Times,* set forth his view of such an appointment in a cartoon picturing Yorty behind his desk on the telephone while a number of attendants in white coats entered his office. In the caption Yorty says over the phone, "I've got to go now . . . I've been appointed Secretary of Defense and the Secret Service men are here."

Not amused, Yorty sued for libel, claiming that the cartoon accused him of being mentally unstable.[120]

In the second case, as part of its review of the highlights of the year, a Boston magazine rated a local sportscaster "worst" and said he was "the only newscaster in town who is enrolled in a course for remedial speaking." He too sued for libel.[121]

The courts ruled in both cases that the claims of libel could not be sustained. In the Boston case, the Massachusetts Supreme Court declared:

We conclude that a reader would not reasonably understand the statement that Myers ''is enrolled in a course for remedial speaking'' to be an assertion of fact. Taken in context, it can reasonably be understood to suggest that Myers should have been so enrolled. Even the latter statement may be hyperbolic. The author may have meant only that Myers' sports news reading needed improvement. On either of these interpretations, the challenged publication states a critical judgment, an opinion.[122]

However, in another recent case the trial court ruled that whether a satiric reference to the plaintiff was a protected form of humor or a grievous libel had to be determined by a jury after a full-fledged trial:

Humor, then, may well be a defense to a suit in libel, but the mere assertion that a statement was meant to be funny does not automatically absolve the utterer. Humor is intensely subjective. Blank looks or even active loathing may be engendered by a statement or cartoon that evokes howls of laughter from another. What is amusing or funny in the eyes of one person may be cruel and tasteless to someone else. There is always a thin line between laughter and tears. . . .

Thus, the writer resorting to parody must be wary, for his shafts may miss the mark, and be cruel without purpose, inflicting real hurt where only laughter was intended. . . .

It is difficult for a court to impose its own opinions as to the intent and impact of a purportedly humorous work. . . .

Just as questions of what is truth, what is reasonable, or what is obscene are left to the collective judgment of a group of laymen serving on a jury, so the question of whether a particular statement is nonactionable humor or compensable libel should appropriately be left to the judgment of a jury.[123]

As in fiction, legal tests looking toward falsity—like the actual malice test—are essentially useless in cases of libel-by-satire, since satire is intentionally exaggerated and in that sense is "false." Here too a new legal test is required, but has not been fully developed. One appropriate standard might be generally to consider satire as constitutionally protected expression of opinion which by definition can be neither true nor false.[124] Only in those rare cases when satire could not be considered to be opinion because of seemingly factual assertions should a court determine whether the author and publisher intended the satire to be taken as fact, or whether they acted recklessly about whether it could reasonably be so taken. Until such a test is adopted, the courts may continue to apply a falsity standard in cases where falsity is just about the only issue not in dispute.

Can epithets and hyperbole be libelous?

Generally, no—unless they can reasonably be taken as literal statements of fact.

A few cases will illustrate the point. In *Curtis Publishing Co. v. Birdsong*[125] the plaintiff had been referred to as one of "those bastards." A federal court of appeals rejected his claim of libel, declaring:

> [I]t is perfectly apparent that these words were used as mere epithets, as terms of abuse and opprobrium. As such they had no real meaning except to indicate that the individual who used them was under a strong emotional feeling of dislike toward those about whom he used them. Not being intended or understood as statements of fact they are impossible of proof or disproof. Indeed such words of vituperation and abuse reflect more on the character of the user than they do on that of the individual to whom they are intended to refer. It has long been settled that such words are not of themselves actionable as libelous.[126]

In *Greenbelt Cooperative Pub. Assn., Inc. v. Bresler*,[127] the plaintiff's bargaining position in a dispute with the local government was characterized as "blackmail." The Supreme Court rejected the claim of libel, stating:

> It is simply impossible to believe that a reader who reached the word "blackmail" in either article would not have understood exactly what was meant: it was Bresler's public and wholly legal negotiating proposals that were being criticized. No reader could have thought that either the speakers at the meetings or the newspaper articles reporting their words were charging Bresler with the commission of a criminal offense. On the contrary, even the most careless reader must have perceived that the word was no more than rhetorical hyperbole, a vigorous epithet used by those who considered Bresler's negotiating position extremely unreasonable. Indeed, the record is completely devoid of evidence that anyone in the city of Greenbelt or anywhere else thought Bresler had been charged with a crime.[128]

But not every epithet is necessarily immune from a claim of libel. In a recent case, for example, a federal court of appeals stated that calling a scientist a "liar" because of his perceived misuse of statistics would be a statement of opinion and hence not libelous, but reference to him as a "paid liar" would not be similarly protected.[129] As a leading contemporary authority on libel has put it, "The context in which particular statements are used thus is the key to determining whether they are accusations actionable in libel or slander, or merely epithets which, as a matter of law, are not."[130]

Can works of visual art be libelous?

Yes, although there have been comparatively few cases. In one famous case an optical illusion in which the plaintiff's genitals appeared to be exposed resulted in a recovery for libel.[131] A more recent case involved a painting entitled "The Mugging of the Muse," in which several masked figures were portrayed mugging a female form while cherubs and the like hovered nearby. The plaintiffs, whose faces appeared on the masks, claimed that the painting accused them of being violent criminals, while the artist's claim was that his painting was an allegorical statement of his opinion that the plaintiffs were enemies of art. A jury sustained the plaintiffs' claims, and the trial judge upheld that verdict. But an appellate court reversed the judgment. The court accepted the jury's finding that the artist intended to and did portray the plaintiffs in the painting, and it assumed that a work of art can be libelous. Nonetheless it held that the libel claim could not be sustained, since the painting was clearly allegorical and as such should be considered a non-actionable statement of opinion.[132]

But the point remains that a person can successfully sue for libel by a work of visual art, provided that he or she satisfies all the legal requirements discussed in this chapter.

Where can an author be sued for libel?

In theory at least, libel injury may occur wherever defamatory matter is circulated to persons who know the libel plaintiff and can be influenced by the matter. A statement published or broadcast in the mass media can cause injury almost anywhere. The "jurisdictional" question becomes whether circulation of the libel within a given forum has caused injury within the forum and whether the publisher's or author's contacts with the forum are sufficient to permit assertion of jurisdiction. It is generally held that circulation of a libel within a forum causes injury within the forum. Once actionable injury is established, the question becomes to what extent and on what basis a forum can legitimately reach out to assert jurisdiction over a non-resident of the forum. The limits of such jurisdiction are found in constitutional concepts of due process and the First Amendment.

Due process here amounts to little more than an analysis of whether it is fair to require publishers and authors to defend an action in a forum where their contacts, if any, may not be great.[133] At least minimal contacts are required, such as doing business in the jurisdiction (not a consideration for most authors), or substantial circulation of the material, substantial solicitation of advertising, or news gathering within the jurisdiction.[134]

Due process may be satisfied, even if other contacts are insufficient, if it was foreseeable that the publication would have a major impact in a forum. A major piece of investigative journalism about individuals' activities in forum X may create jurisdiction in that forum.[135] Of course, usually other contacts with the forum, such as news gathering, will have occurred.

First Amendment considerations have been held to be relevant, on occasion, in determining whether jurisdiction should be exercised. As has been noted:

> The expense of unnecessarily defending libel suits in foreign jurisdictions is of particular First Amendment concern. At the least, the existence of a special protection for the circulation of ideas and information can weigh in the total calculus of whether the maintenance of suit offends "fair play and substantial justice."[136]

Unfortunately, few courts have adopted a special First Amendment rule on jurisdiction in defamation actions, although some cases have recognized First Amendment considerations.[137]

If an author or artist is sued in an out-of-state forum and cannot defeat jurisdiction, there is the opportunity at least to "remove" the case to a federal court within the foreign jurisdiction, which may provide a more neutral and hospitable forum for the litigation, or to seek a change of venue to a more convenient forum or in the interests of justice.[138]

How do headlines, captions and photographs present potential libel problems for the author or artist?

It is beyond the scope of this book to deal with libel and related problems in news reporting and news publication. For more complete coverage the reader is referred to Joel Gora's excellent *The Rights of Reporters* (1974), another in the ACLU Handbook Series. But even authors who are not reporters should know that a libel claim may be based not only upon the author's work, but from its presentation in published form. If, for example, headlines, captions, or photographs are added, these can form the basis—alone or together with the author's material—of a libel or privacy action. In fact, in some jurisdictions defamatory matter in a caption or headline is actionable even if the rest of the story explains away, or supports, the defamatory allegations.[139] In most jurisdictions, however, headlines and captions are read with the rest of the publication and will be actionable based on the meaning of the overall story; however, if headlines are particularly prominent and so unrelated as to separately damage the plaintiff's reputation, they may be separately actionable.[140] Accordingly, as far as possible, authors and artists should review material in its final form before publication, or (if possible) secure an indemnification for matter added by the publisher.

Is retraction a meaningful protection from a libel claim?

Not always. Especially in the context of book and even magazine publication, retraction protection is often not practically or legally available, or will be of only limited assistance in defeating or limiting a libel claim. Nonetheless, an author or artist should be aware of this option.

As a matter of common (rather than statutory) law, retraction is often recognized as evidence of an innocent or nonactionable intent. It can assure the availability of a claim of privilege or at least limit recoverable damages. The law often prevents recovery of punitive damages, for example, if a retraction has been made; an effective retraction may also limit the actual harm caused by the initial publication.

There are retraction statutes in 33 states.[141] They differ widely, but most of them relate mainly or entirely to newspapers, broadcasters, and other "hot news" media. Most book publishers and many magazines could not meet their requirements, since time limits for retraction typically range from 48 hours to three weeks.[142] The statute may also require prominent publication (say, on the front page) in the same or larger type size than the item retracted, etc.—requirements that cannot be met by a book publisher. Still, an offer of a retraction in the form of a letter to the plaintiff, a public announcement, or a correction in a subsequent edition of a book can be made in appropriate circumstances; even if the retraction is technically not in compliance with the rules, it may not be entirely irrelevant in ensuing libel litigation.

What legal remedies are available to a successful libel plaintiff?

Essentially, only money damages. The Supreme Court has made it clear that because of the special threat to the freedoms protected by the First Amendment represented by direct government intrusion into the workings of the press, the government may neither issue injunctions against the dissemination of libelous statements[143] nor order a publisher to publish a retraction (or to make space available for rebuttal) if the publisher does not wish to.[144]

What kinds of damages can be awarded in libel actions?

Special damages, general or compensatory damages, and punitive damages.

Special damages are out-of-pocket losses that the plaintiff can prove were sustained as a result of the libel, for example, loss of a job, fellowship, or scholarship, or incurred psychiatric or medical expenses.[145]

General damages compensate the plaintiff for injuries that are not susceptible to precise calculation: in particular, injury to the plaintiff's reputation.[146] Before the Supreme Court's decisions in the *New York Times* and *Gertz* cases, the law was that once a plaintiff established libel, damage would be presumed without proof. In *Gertz*, however, the Court ruled that presumed damages are inconsistent with the First Amendment. A libel plaintiff (at least in cases involving writers, publishers, or other media) can only recover for proved "actual injury," although the Court went on to observe:

> Suffice it to say that actual injury is not limited to out-of-pocket loss. Indeed, the more customary types of actual harm inflicted by defamatory falsehood include impairment of reputation and standing in the community, personal humiliation, and mental anguish and suffering.[147]

In the *Firestone* case, the Supreme Court seemed to indicate that an award of compensatory damages could constitutionally be sustained in the absence of proof of injury to reputation,[148] but some state courts, including New York appellate courts, have held as a matter of state law that a libel plaintiff cannot recover damages without proving injury to reputation.[149]

Punitive damages are designed not to compensate the plaintiff but to punish the defendant for egregious conduct and to serve as a deterrent. In the *Gertz* case the Supreme Court disapproved the general availability of punitive damages. It held that they can only be awarded if the plaintiff proves that the defendant acted with "actual malice"—i.e., with knowledge that the statement was false or with reckless disregard of its truth or falsity.[150] The Court left open whether punitive damages should be abolished in libel cases; a small number of state courts have done so, while the majority continue to allow them. No million dollar libel award has yet to be finally affirmed on appeal.[151]

The fact remains that a significant number of large awards, several in millions of dollars, have been made since *Gertz*. However, most of those verdicts are being appealed, and a number have been reduced or set aside. No million dollar libel award has yet to be finally affirmed on appeal.[152]

What does the law mean by "privacy"?

There are probably few words that have as many—and as diverse—legal meanings. For example, "privacy" has come to mean the right of individuals to decide for themselves—i.e., without government interference—whether to use contraception, or whether to have an abortion.[153] The word also refers to the Fourth Amendment right to be free from "unreasonable searches and seizures" by the government. Federal and state privacy statutes are designed to protect the confidentiality of the government (and private) records that are maintained on just about all of us.

The word "privacy" has also—somewhat unfortunately and confusingly—come to refer to four categories of lawsuits—most of them against a writer and a publisher or producer—for allegedly invading or violating the "right of privacy."[154] Those four categories are often referred to as "false light," "private facts," "appropriation," and "intrusion."[155]

What is a "false light" invasion of privacy?

It is similar to a libel. The main difference is that while the law of libel is designed to vindicate the subject's reputation, the "false light" claim is designed to remedy injured feelings. A "false light" invasion involves "publicity placing a person in a 'false light' in a manner which would be highly offensive

to a reasonable person or 'a person of ordinary sensibilities.' "[156]
The elements have been succinctly summarized as follows:

> The statement must be made public, it must be about
> the plaintiff, it must be unprivileged, and it must be
> false. The element of falsity must be proved by the
> plaintiff and the falsity shown must be substantial and
> material.[157]

What are some "false light" invasions?

The Supreme Court has considered two "false light" cases,
which provide useful examples. *Time, Inc. v. Hill*[158] arose from
an article in *Life* magazine mentioning the opening of a new play
about a family that was held hostage by three escaped convicts; it
indicated that the play was an account of the experiences of a
named family some years earlier. The family sued, claiming that
its experience was different from that portrayed in the play and
that the *Life* article placed the family in a false and embarrassing
light.

In 1967 the Supreme Court, by a narrow 5–4 vote, held that
"[t]he factual reporting of newsworthy persons and events is in
the public interest and is protected"[159] and that falsity is not
enough to defeat that protection. Echoing its landmark *New York
Times* libel decision of three years before, the Court declared that
"the constitutional protection for speech and press preclude
[recovery for invasion of privacy] to redress false reports of
matters of public interest in the absence of proof that the defendant published the report with knowledge of its falsity or in
reckless disregard of the truth."[160]

In *Cantrell v. Forest City Publishing Co.*[161] a woman and
her son sued the publisher and reporter of a newspaper article on
the impact on their family of the father's death some months
before in a publicized bridge collapse. The article purported to
reflect face-to-face interviews with the family, but the reporter
had had no direct contact with them. The Supreme Court found
that there was sufficient evidence to support a finding that the
paper and reporter were guilty of "actual malice"—i.e., knowledge of falsity or reckless disregard of truth or falsity—so that a
"false light" recovery could be justified.[162]

Cantrell was decided after the Court in *Gertz* ruled that private figures need not prove actual malice in libel cases. However, since proof of actual malice had been established, the Court did not address whether a "false light" plaintiff is still required by the First Amendment to satisfy the actual malice test in connection with discussions of matters of "public interest," which is what the Court announced in the *Hill* case. Some lower courts and commentators have speculated that the *Hill* decision no longer applies to "private figure false light" cases,[163] but the answer will have to await word from the Supreme Court.

What is a "private facts" invasion of privacy?
It has been defined as follows:

One who gives publicity to a matter concerning the private life of another is subject to liability to the other for invasion of his privacy if the matter publicized is of a kind that

- (a) would be highly offensive to a reasonable person and
- (b) is not of legitimate concern to the public.[164]

Unlike libel and "false light" claims, which are made against false statements, here the fact that the statements are true is at the heart of the claimed invasion.

Because a "private facts" invasion must be "not of legitimate concern to the public," and because the courts have given broad application to this "newsworthiness" aspect, it is rare that such claims against authors and publishers have prevailed.[165] Most successful cases have been brought against non-media defendants, such as employers, bankers, and doctors, who improperly disclosed embarrassing private facts about the plaintiffs.[166]

There have been exceptions, however, usually with plaintiffs who were once notorious but have since receded into anonymity. In a celebrated 1931 case a woman who had been a prostitute and a defendant in a sensational murder case changed her life-style, married, and dropped out of sight. Several years later a movie based on her earlier life was released. The California courts upheld her "private facts" claim of invasion of privacy.[167] In a 1971 case[168] an article about hijacking in the *Reader's Digest* mentioned that the plaintiff had stolen a trunk in Kentucky and engaged in a gun battle with the police. The article did not indicate that the events had occurred 11 years earlier, after which the plaintiff had moved to California, started a family, and become a respected member of the community. The California courts upheld his claim, stating that while they approved complete reporting about current and past criminal activity, "the identity of the *actor* in reports of long past crimes usually has little public purpose."[169]

Still, many other cases have ruled that "Where are they now?" features about once notorious or famous people are "newsworthy" and thus protected.[170] In general, courts will be more sympathetic to plaintiffs' claims if their earlier notoriety was involuntary than if it was of their own choosing.

What is an "appropriation" invasion of privacy?

Much of it is not really a matter of privacy, but of the appropriation of a person's—often, a celebrity's—name or likeness for commercial benefit without consent or remuneration. Aspects of this branch of privacy law are often referred to as "the right of publicity."[171] Non-celebrities have this right too, but their claims seem more closely related to "privacy" than "publicity" concerns.[172]

The Supreme Court has found that misappropriation or right of publicity claims do not inherently violate First Amendment rights. In the leading case, a performer whose act consisted of being shot from a gun prevailed in a suit against a television station that broadcast his act—which took all of 15 seconds—without consent or compensation.[173] The broadcaster had asserted, to no avail, that the performance was newsworthy and therefore protected by the First Amendment.

Occasionally this branch of privacy law is applied (or misapplied) to editorial rather than commercial uses of a person's name or likeness. However, the law seems clear that "appropriation" invasion of privacy protection does not apply to communications about matters of legitimate public interest, as will be found in most non-fiction newspaper or magazine articles

121

and books. For example, in a recent case,[174] the plaintiff's photograph was prominently displayed on the cover of the *New York Times*'s Sunday magazine to illustrate an article on "the black middle class." He was not named or otherwise referred to in the article and he disagreed with portions of it. He sued for invasion of privacy, but the court rejected the suit, holding that the publication of his picture was a legitimate editorial use that did not violate any right of privacy recognized in that state. Similarly, other courts have found that "fleeting" or "incidental" references to real people in works of fiction—or fictionalized nonfiction—do not violate those people's privacy or publicity rights.[175]

More difficult problems are presented where real people are portrayed—other than fleetingly—in substantially fictionalized contexts, including so-called "docudramas." Fictionalized dialogue and events in a biography of a baseball star resulted in a privacy judgment in the star's favor,[176] and some courts have held that satiric performances, parodies, and imitations can violate the right of publicity even when there is substantial independent editorial content in the material.[177]

Elizabeth Taylor has recently sued to enjoin the showing of an allegedly ficionalized TV movie of her life. The outcome of that case may shed light on the law's limits relating to such works.

What is an "intrusion" invasion of privacy?

It has been defined as follows:

> One who intentionally intrudes, physically or otherwise, upon the solitude or seclusion of another or his private affairs or concerns, is subject to liability to the other for invasion of his privacy, if the intrusion would be highly offensive to a reasonable person.[178]

In essence this means wrongful conduct, rather than published work, by writers and media representatives: for example, breaking and entering,[179] surreptitious surveillance,[180] unauthorized physical presence,[181] and the kind of harassing pursuit that some writers and photographers have been known to engage in.

For example, photographer Ron Galella was found to have

violated the right of privacy of Jacqueline Kennedy Onassis by the manner of his pursuit of photographs of her.[182] Reporters who place a hidden camera and microphone in a private place,[183] or who enter a public restaurant[184]—or hospital room[185]—with cameras rolling and without permission, have been found to be in violation of the "intrusion" privacy right. As a leading commentator has observed, "(C)rimes and torts committed in news gathering do not ordinarily receive special protection under the First Amendment."[186]

What can a writer or artist do to minimize the risk of a libel or privacy suit?

The first rule, of course, is to be careful and accurate. But, as even the Supreme Court has repeatedly recognized, errors are inevitable, as are libel and privacy suits arising out of these errors. Even complete accuracy does not guarantee that no lawsuits will be brought, since some plaintiffs will have a different understanding of the truth while others will bring suit for reasons other than the expectation of winning, such as using the suit as a dramatic way to deny the charges against them or as a way to harass and intimidate the writer or publisher of the charges.

Responsible writers should retain the notes and tapes they have compiled in preparing their work, so as to be able to demonstrate in any future litigation that they acted reasonably and without negligence or reckless disregard of the truth. (However, if the notes would disclose a confidential source, there is the countervailing risk that they will have to be produced in litigation.)

If the subject matter of a writer's work suggests the potential of a libel or privacy claim—for example, if it accuses its subject of criminal or otherwise improper or unpopular activities—then many writers, and most major publishers and radio and TV stations, will have the work reviewed by a libel specialist: usually, but not necessarily, a lawyer. The specialist should be able to isolate aspects of the work that can lead to legal liability and to suggest ways to minimize exposure—for example, by deft rephrasing or careful editing—and/or to best prepare for the potential legal claim. (This is sometimes referred to as "libel vetting.")

Especially if a writer's publisher does not provide such review, the writer concerned about lawsuits should consider getting such review on his or her own.

Who can be sued in a libel or privacy case?

The original writer or creator is always directly answerable, much as the driver of a delivery truck is answerable for any accident. The employer of the writer, if any, is also answerable, like the employer of a driver. The publisher/broadcaster of the work may also be answerable, even if the writer is a free-lance contributor; and individual editors, producers, and collaborators who participate in the creation of a work may also be held answerable.[187]

It occasionally happens that a plaintiff sues the printer of a work, its distributor and/or retailer, even the advertisers who have sponsored it. However, because of the Supreme Court's decision in the *Gertz* case requiring plaintiffs to prove that libelous statements have been published with fault on the part of the defendant, it seems unlikely that tangential defendants will be found liable.[188]

Who bears the costs of a libel or privacy case?

It depends on what we mean by "costs," and on the relationship among the people and entities involved in the publication.

"Costs" has at least three meanings. First, there are the physical and emotional costs inevitably incurred in litigation. Second, there are the out-of-pocket costs of defending a lawsuit: lawyers' fees, investigators' expenses, and the like. And third, there may be an award of damages to the plaintiff.

Writers or artists who are sued for libel or invasion of privacy bear most of the emotional and physical costs. Their work gave rise to the suit, and their reputations—and careers—may be directly affected. They are most likely to be intimidated and frightened by a lawsuit—this includes fear of major financial loss—and least likely to be experienced and sophisticated in dealing with lawsuits. Publishers or other media outlets are probably more experienced in such matters and can take the suit in stride as an unavoidable part of their business.

As for out-of-pocket costs, much depends on the relationship between writer and publisher. A newspaper or broadcaster will almost always assume—at no cost to the writer—full responsibility for legal defense. And most of the time a magazine or book publisher will assume the initial costs of a joint defense with a non-employee writer, including providing lawyers to represent both. But this does not mean that such protection must be provided or that the publisher will not ultimately seek a contribution toward costs from the writer.

Finally, the original writer is almost always held responsible for some or all of any damages awarded to the plaintiff—at least in the absence of culpable conduct on the part of the publisher. The writer, too, may be technically obliged to reimburse the publisher for damages the publisher has paid to the plaintiff.

In practice, however, the writer and publisher will often agree on sharing the ultimate liability. The publisher can usually much better afford the payment of damages, and it is increasingly common for publishers to be covered by insurance for them. Such coverage is increasingly common for writers, primarily through coverage obtained by the publisher.[189]

Many of these issues can be dealt with in the contract that is entered into between the writer and publisher (see Chapter III, section C).

NOTES

1. *Gertz v. Robert Welch, Inc.*, 418 U.S. 323, 341 (1974), quoting Justice Potter Stewart's concurring opinion in *Rosenblatt v. Baer*, 383 U.S. 75, 92 (1966).
2. Justices Black and Douglas expressed their view in a number of concurring and dissenting opinions, including *New York Times v. Sullivan*, 376 U.S. 254 (1964), *Garrison v. Louisiana*, 379 U.S. 64 (1964), and *Curtis Publishing Co. v. Butts*, 388 U.S. 130 (1967). In the *Butts* case, the two Justices succinctly stated that "it is time for this Court . . . to adopt the rule to the effect that the First Amendment was intended to leave the press free from the harassment of libel judgments." 388 U.S. at 172. *See also* Hentoff, *The First Freedom* ,Delacorte, 1981.
3. *New York Times v. Sullivan*, 376 U.S. 254 (1964). This case represents what has been called the "constitutionalization" of libel law. Before 1964 allegedly libelous statements were generally considered outside

the protection of the First Amendment. *See Chaplinsky v. New Hampshire*, 315 U.S. 568 (1942), where the Court stated (in dictum) that libelous statements deserve no constitutional protection because they are "no essential part of any exposition of ideas and are of slight social value."

4. Legal commentators have written extensively on the *New York Times* case and its effect on libel law. Among the most informative and readable are Kalven, "The New York Times Case: A Note on 'The Central Meaning' of the First Amendment," 1964 *Sup. Ct. Rev.* 191 (1965); Eaton, "The American Law of Defamation Through Gertz v. Robert Welch, Inc. and Beyond: An Analytical Primer," 61 *Va. L. Rev.* 1349 (1975); Hill, "Defamation and Privacy Under the First Amendment," 76 *Colum. L. Rev.* 1205 (1976); and Sack, *Libel, Slander, and Related Problems*, PLI, 1980, Chapter I [hereinafter Sack]. The Sack book is probably the most comprehensive and useful work available today on the law of libel, and the authors of this book gratefully acknowledge that it was invaluable to them in the preparation of this chapter.

5. Defamation law is traditionally a creature of state law. While defamation law from state to state follows predictable patterns, specific legal rules will vary, sometimes markedly, depending upon the particular state and issue. Although federal constitutional law has significantly changed some state rules in response to First Amendment requirements, the Supreme Court continues to allow the states significant latitude to define their defamation laws within broad constitutional parameters. For a comprehensive comparison of current law state by state, *see LDRC 50-State Survey 1982: Current Developments in Media Libel and Invasion of Privacy Law*, Libel Defense Resource Center, 1982, Henry R. Kaufman, ed. (hereinafter LDRC survey). The LDRC 50-State Survey will be updated annually.

6. The basic distinctions, if any, between libel and slander vary from state to state. In general, a slander claim is more difficult to maintain. Some states limit slander claims to specific, narrowly limited types of defamation, akin to the *per se* categories in libel (*see infra* nn. 9–12). Many states require proof of "special damages" (*See* p. 117). In some states the statute of limitations for slander is very short. All these distinctions assume that oral defamation is less widely disseminated and therefore less harmful. (*See* Sack at 43–45). Slander claims are rare for the average author: they can arise out of oral statements made during research or investigation before publication, press conferences, interviews or talk shows after publication, or broadcasts or performances of the work.

7. RESTATEMENT (SECOND) OF TORTS §559 [hereinafter RESTATEMENT] (1977). This "model" legal code, prepared by legal scholars, has been very influential in the development of libel law. *See also Prosser on Torts*, §111 at 739 (4th ed. 1979).

Libel and Privacy

8. Seelman, *The Law of Libel and Slander in the State of New York*, p. 8, ¶18 (1933) [quoted in Eldredge, *The Law of Defamation*, p. 32, §7 (1978)].

9. RESTATEMENT §571, comment g, lists murder, rape, treason, and operating a bawdy house as examples of crimes which if falsely alleged may give rise to a libel action. Most states require that the crime be one of "moral turpitude," so that false allegations of minor offenses such as parking violations would not be considered libelous.

10. *See Solly v. Brown*, 220 Ky. 576, 295 S.W. 890 (1927) (statement that plaintiff "is eat up with the clap" found to be defamatory *per se*); *Simpson v. Press Publishing Co.*, 33 Misc. 228, 67 N.Y.S. 401 (1900) ("To falsely say of one that he has leprosy is slander *per se*"). The imputation must be to a disease which would be likely to result in excluding the plaintiff from society. *See, e.g., Chuy v. Philadelphia Eagles Football Club*, 595 F.2d 1265 (3d Cir. 1979), where a statement by the physician for a professional football team that a player was suffering from polycythemia vera was found not to be defamatory because the disease is not "loathsome." "The decided cases concerned with loathsome disease have limited the term to sexually communicable venereal disease and leprosy. Polycythemia vera is a disease of unknown cause characterized by increased concentration of hemoglobin and a great absolute increase in red cells attended by an enlargement of the spleen. It is neither contagious nor attributed in any way to socially repugnant conduct." 595 F.2d at 1281. For an interesting glimpse into the origins of this aspect of libel law *see Austin v. White*, Cro. Eliz. 214, 78 Eng. Rep. 470 (1590) ("Thou wert laid of the French pox" syphilis mound slanderous).

11. Examples of statements that have been found defamatory *per se* include charges that a lawyer or physician is unqualified, *e.g., McGuire v. Jankiewicz*, 8 Ill. App.3d 319, 290 N.E.2d 675 (1972) ("you could not have chosen a worse attorney"); that a businessman is dishonest or bankrupt, *e.g., Ridgeway State Bank v. Bird*, 185 Wis. 418, 202 N.W. 170 (1925) (statement that bank was insolvent); and that a clergyman is a drunkard, *e.g., M'Millan v. Birch*, 1 Binn. 178 (Pa. 1806) (statement that the plaintiff, a minister, was "a liar, a drunkard, and preacher of the devil").

12. RESTATEMENT §574 treats an imputation of unchastity or serious sexual misconduct to either sex as defamatory *per se. But see Moricoli v. Schwartz*, 46 Ill. App.3d 481, 361 N.E.2d 74 (1977), where the court held that alleging that a male was a homosexual was not slanderous *per se*. In the light of contemporary social mores, which seem largely to accept the fact that many people are sexually active before marriage, it may be questioned whether the imputation of unchastity continues to be defamatory *per se*.

13. Distinctions between defamation *per se* and *per quod* are discussed to some extent in this chapter, but since they are among the most complex elements of defamation law, not all aspects are considered. For a more complete treatment *see* Sack at 94–112; *infra* n. 15.

14. *See Morrison v. Ritchie & Co.*, [1901–02] Sess. Cas. 645 (Scot. 2d Div.), 39 Scot. L. R. 432 (1902), where an erroneous but seemingly innocent, in fact laudatory, announcement of the birth of twins was found libelous because the "parents" had been married only one month.

15. *See* Eldredge, "The Spurious Rule of Libel Per Quod," 79 *Harv. L. Rev.* 733 (1966); Prosser, "More Libel Per Quod," 79 *Harv. L. Rev.* 1629 (1966). According to the RESTATEMENT §569, explanatory note (tent. draft no. 11, 1965), some 30 states require proof of special damages in libel *per quod* cases. The other jurisdictions make no distinction between libel *per se* and libel *per quod* and thus only require proof of harm to reputation.

16. In those states truth is not a complete defense to a claim of libel; the statement must not only be true but be published with "good motives" or for "justifiable ends." *See, e.g.*, MASS. GEN. LAWS ANN., Chapter 231, §92 (1974) (statement must be true and published with good motive); KANSAS CONST. BILL OF RIGHTS §11 (statement must be published for justifiable ends.) At least in cases involving public figures, the Supreme Court has stated that the Constitution requires truth to be an absolute defense. *Cox Broadcasting Corp. v. Cohn*, 420 U.S. 469, 489–90 (1975). However, the Court in *Cox* refused to address whether the absolute defense of truth is required in libel actions brought by private figures. Truthful statements may also be the basis for certain invasion of privacy claims. *See* pp. 120-21.

17. For example, a newspaper report that a juvenile was arrested for a crime instead of for delinquency was not considered a false statement in *Piracci v. Hearst Corp.*, 263 F. Supp. 511 (D. Md. 1966), *aff'd*, 371 F.2d 1016 (4th Cir. 1967). Some courts have interpreted the substantial truth concept quite broadly. In *Picard v. Brennan*, 307 A.2d 833 (Me. 1973), the court found that stating that a person who had resigned was fired was substantially true since the truth would not have affected the reader differently from the statement complained of. *But see Denny v. Mertz*, 84 Wis.2d 654, 267 N.W.2d 304 (1978), where what was essentially the same statement was found to be defamatory.

18. *Gertz v. Robert Welch, Inc.*, 418 U.S. 323, 339–40 (1974).

19. *See, e.g., Goldwater v. Ginzburg*, 261 F.Supp. 784 (S.D. N.Y. 1966), *aff'd*, 414 F.2d 324 (2d Cir. 1969), *cert. denied*, 396 U.S. 1049 (1970), where the court stated that the distinction between fact and opinion "has proved to be a most unsatisfactory and unreliable one." 261 F.Supp. at 786. One commentator has gone even further to state that the distinction is "clumsy because its basic assump-

tion is an illusion." *McCormick on Evidence*, §11 at 23 (2d ed. 1972).

20. Calling someone a Nazi or Communist has been found to be a statement of fact in some cases and a statement of opinion in others. *Compare Potts v. Dies*, 132 F.2d 734 (D.C. Cir. 1942), *cert. denied*, 319 U.S. 762 (1943) (accusing plaintiff of pro-Nazi sentiments held to be an expression of opinion), with *Holy Spirit Ass'n v. Sequoia Elsevier Publishing Co.*, 75 A.D.2d 523 (1st Dept. 1980) (statement that religion was "Nazi-style" found to be a statement of fact). *See also Buckley v. Littell*, 539 F.2d 882 (2d Cir. 1976), *cert. denied*, 429 U.S. 1062 (1977), where the court found that a reference to William F. Buckley as a "fellow traveler" of "fascism" was a statement of opinion and not of fact, but that a further statement that "like Westbrook Pegler, who lied day after day in his column about Quentin Reynolds and goaded him into a lawsuit, Buckley could be taken to court by any one of several people who had enough money to hire competent legal counsel and nothing else to do" was a statement of fact and not opinion, and was libelous. *See also* the discussion of epithets and hyperbole on pp. 112-13.

21. Sack at 157; *see Rinaldi v. Holt, Rinehart & Winston, Inc.*, 42 N.Y. 2d 369 *cert. denied*, 434 U.S. 969 (1977) where a statement that a judge was "incompetent," based upon disclosed facts or examples, was held to be a constitutionally-protected statement of opinion, while a statement that he was "probably corrupt" was held to be an unprivileged factual statement because it strongly suggested to the ordinary reader undisclosed factual "undertones of conspiracy and illegality."

22. *See, e.g., Kelley v. Johnson Publishing Co.*, 160 Cal. App.2d 718, 325 P.2d 659 (1958). In most states if a person is libeled and later dies, the cause of action for libel dies with the person. *See Gruschus v. Curtis Publishing Co.*, 342 F.2d 775 (10th Cir. 1965). In a few states the dead person's survivors can continue a suit that was commenced before the plaintiff's death. *See Moyer v. Phillips*, 462 Pa. 395, 341 A.2d 441 (1975); *MacDonald v. Time, Inc.*, 9 Med. L. Rptr. 1025 (D.N.J. 1983).

23. *See, e.g., Continental Nut Co. v. Robert L. Berner Co.*, 345 F.2d 395 (7th Cir. 1965) (corporation can only be libeled by statements that attack its financial or business practices). Municipal corporations may not sue for libel. *See* Sack at 124–25.

24. *See, e.g., Washington Post Co. v. Kennedy*, 3 F.2d 207 (D.C. Cir. 1925), where a newspaper article about an accused forger was found to libel a person with the same name. The article identified the forger as a 40-year-old Washington attorney named Harry Kennedy. The successful plaintiff in the libel action was the only Washington attorney named Harry Kennedy. Even though the *Post* did not intend the story to refer to the plaintiff, he was able to prevail because his friends and acquain-

tances thought the article was about him. However, as Sack notes, these results may now be different in light of the Supreme Court's requirement —at least in cases against the media—that allegedly libelous statements be published with "fault." Sack at 120. *See* pp. 103-04.

25. *But see Allen v. Gordon*, 86 A.D.2d 514, 446 N.Y.S.2d 48 (1st Dept.), *aff'd*, 56 N.Y.2d 780, 542 N.Y.S.2d 25 (1982), where it was held that the portrayal of a Manhattan psychiatrist named Dr. Allen in a non-fiction book was not "of and concerning" the only Manhattan psychiatrist named Allen. On the other hand, a fictional account of a "nude marathon therapist" which did not name the plaintiff and which, indeed, attempted to change the character's name, description, and circumstances in order to avoid identification, was held to be of and concerning the plaintiff and therefore actionable. *Bindrim v. Mitchell*, 92 Cal. App.3d 61, 155 Cal. Rptr. 29, *cert. denied*, 444 U.S. 984 (1979). *See* pp. 107-08.

26. *See* RESTATEMENT §564A, which states: "One who publishes defamatory matter concerning a group or class of persons is subject to liability to an individual member of it, *but only if*, (a) the group or class is so small that the matter can reasonably be understood to refer to the member, or (b) the circumstances of publication reasonably give rise to the conclusion that there is particular reference to the member."

27. *See, e.g., Farrell v. Triangle Publications, Inc.*, 399 Pa. 102, 159 A.2d 734 (1960) (statement referring generally to the 13 town commissioners found to be "of and concerning" an individual commissioner); *Kirkman v. Westchester Newspapers, Inc.*, 287 N.Y. 373, 39 N.E.2d 919 (1942) (statement that "union officials are feathering their nests" found to be "of and concerning" one of 16 union officials). Cases that have not allowed individual members of a group to recover for defamatory statements about the group include *Granger v. Time, Inc.*, 568 P.2d 535 (Mont. 1977) (statement that "arson has become common" in Butte, Montana, because "people who are unable to sell their devalued buildings burn them for the insurance" found not to be of and concerning a Butte businessman who lost his building to fire, since the statement could apply to over 200 people), and *Kentucky Fried Chicken, Inc. v. Sanders*, 563 S.W.2d 8 (Ky. 1978) (article criticizing the quality of food served at Kentucky Fried Chicken found not to be of and concerning one particular franchise because there are more than 5000 franchises nationwide).

28. *Neiman-Marcus v. Lait*, 13 F.R.D. 311 (S.D.N.Y. 1952). Even though the book stated that all of the saleswomen at Neiman-Marcus were "call girls," the court denied the women a right to sue because their class was too large. *But see also Owens v. Clark*, 154 Okla. 108, 6 P.2d 755 (1931), where an Oklahoma Supreme Court judge was unable to recover for defamatory statements made about "certain members of the [Oklahoma] Supreme Court," which had nine members.

29. RESTATEMENT §564A, comment b. *But see Brady v. Ottaway Newspapers, Inc.*, 84 A.D. 2d 226, 445 N.Y.S. 2d 786 (2d Dept. 1981), where 25 members of a group of "at least 53 unindicted police officers" were permitted to press their libel claim, 445 N.Y.S. 2d at 794.

30. *See, e.g., Ostrowe v. Lee*, 256 N.Y. 36, 175 N.E. 505 (1931), where the dictation of a letter to a stenographer was held to be "publication."

31. *See* RESTATEMENT §578.

32. *Edwards v. National Audubon Society*, 556 F.2d 113, 120 (2d Cir.), *cert. denied sub nom. Edwards v. New York Times Co.*, 434 U.S. 1002 (1977). *See also Krauss v. Champaign News Gazette, Inc.*, 59 Ill. App. 3d 745, 375 N.E.2d 1362 (1978).

33. *See, e.g., Dickey v. CBS, Inc.*, 583 F.2d 1221, 1225 (3d Cir. 1978), where the Circuit Court rejected the "neutral reportage" concept. The highest state court in Kentucky rejected the concept in *McCall v. Courier-Journal*, 623 S.W. 2d 882 (Ky. 1981), and New York's highest court has affirmed a lower court opinion declining to recognize it. *Hogan v. Herald Co.*, 8 Med. L. Rptr. 2567 (N.Y. 1982).

34. *See* RESTATEMENT §585, comment e. The extent of the privilege is illustrated in *Nadeau v. Texas Co.*, 104 Mont. 558, 69 P.2d 586 (1937), where the Chief Judge of the Montana Súpreme Court wrote a "scandalous, scurrilous and defamatory" opinion about a defendant and his counsel. The opinion was so defamatory that the other justices of the court disclaimed responsibility for it. In fact, they ordered that the opinion "not [be] published in the reports of the decisions of this court." The court, however, denied libel relief to the subjects of the attack because of the judge's absolute privilege.

35. Members of Congress are not liable for defamatory statements made in relation to legislative activity. Article I, §6 of the Constitution states that "any Speech or Debate in either House . . . shall not be questioned in any other Place." (Most states have constitutional or statutory provisions giving similar protection to state legislators.) In *Hutchinson v. Proxmire*, 443 U.S. 111 (1979), the Supreme Court interpreted the clause to protect all statements directly relating to the legislative process, but it excluded from the absolute privilege the dissemination of statements by a member of Congress through newsletters or press releases. In a press release Senator Proxmire had given a "Golden Fleece Award" to the National Science Foundation and other agencies for granting federal funds to Hutchinson, a research scientist who was examining the emotional behavioral patterns of certain animals. The Supreme Court held that Proxmire's press releases were not protected by the speech and debate clause of the U.S. Constitution because they were not part of the Senate's "deliberative process."

36. *See, e.g., Barr v. Matteo*, 360 U.S. 564 (1959), where the Supreme Court held that statements made by federal executive officials while

acting in their executive positions were absolutely protected from defamation claims. Defamatory statements made by members of local legislative bodies or agencies are absolutely privileged in some states and enjoy only a qualified privilege in others. *Compare, e.g., Hartman v. Buerger,* 71 Wis. 393, 238 N.W.2d 505 (1976) (statements made by a town clerk held absolutely privileged), with *Cohen v. Bowdoin,* 288 A.2d 106 (Me. 1972) (member of the board of selectmen in a Maine town was granted only a qualified privilege for accusing the plaintiff of lying at a town meeting).

37. The scope of a person's consent often presents problems. For example, in *Burton v. Crowell Publishing Co.,* 82 F.2d 154 (2d Cir. 1936), the court held that the plaintiff's consent to use of a photograph of him did not include consent to use of a particular photo which he found defamatory. Problems also arise in the area of implied consent. For example, in *Genglar v. Phelps,* 92 N.M. 465, 589 P.2d 1056 (App. 1978), the court held that the plaintiff by filling out a job application consented to having defamatory statements made about her by her present employer to her prospective employer.

38. *See Hutchinson v. Proxmire,* 443 U.S. 111, 127–28 (1979), where the Supreme Court stated that "precedents abundantly support the conclusion that a Member may be held liable for republishing defamatory statements originally made in either House." *See also Williams v. Williams,* 23 N.Y.2d 592, 298 N.Y.S.2d 473 (1969) (court proceedings).

39. The concept of qualified privilege was first set forth in an English case, *Toogood v. Spyring,* 1 C.M.&R. 181, 193, 149 Eng. Rep. 1044, 1050 (Ex. 1834). Toogood, a repairman, was sent to the defendant's farm to make repairs. A defamatory statement was circulated by the defendant to the effect that instead of fixing anything Toogood broke into the defendant's wine cellar. The court held that the statement was privileged, stating: "[A]n action lies for the malicious publication of [false statements] . . . unless it is fairly made by a person in the discharge of some public or private duty . . . or in the conduct of his own affairs. . . . In such cases . . . the law . . . affords a qualified defense depending upon the absence of actual malice. If fairly warranted by any reasonable occasion or exigency, and honestly made, such communications are protected for the common convenience and welfare of society."

40. *See, e.g., Marchesi v. Franchino,* 283 Md. 131, 387 A.2d 1129 (1978) (a statement to a supervisor complaining of improper sexual advances by a co-worker was held privileged); *Anderson v. Dun & Bradstreet Co.,* 543 F.2d 732 (10th Cir. 1976) (report of a credit-reporting agency protected by a qualified privilege). *But see Johnson v. Bradstreet Co.,* 77 Ga. 172 (1886) (qualified privilege not extended to a credit-reporting agency). The privilege extended to a credit-reporting agency may be overcome by showing that its investigation was conducted recklessly. *See, e.g., Brown v. Skaggs-Albertson's Properties, Inc.,* 563 F.2d 983

(10th Cir. 1977), where the court held that the owner of a grocery chain could be sued for libel because he stated to a check verification agency that the plaintiff had "bounced" two checks when in fact the checks were returned because the plaintiff had failed to endorse them. The court found that the defendant was liable and awarded the plaintiff $20,000 compensatory damages and $10,000 punitive damages.

41. In recent cases in some jurisdictions the fair report privilege has been extended even more broadly to cover other kinds of official proceedings and even official files and documents. *See, e.g., Medico v. Time, Inc.,* 643 F.2d 134 (3d Cir.), *cert. denied,* 454 U.S. 836 (1981). But see *Bufalino v. The Associated Press,* 692 F.2d 266 (2d Cir. 1982), *cert denied,* 51 U.S.L.W. 3872 (1983) (author must actually have relied on the records or reports in preparing the material in question.)

42. RESTATEMENT §611.

43. Sack explains the rationale for the "fair report" privilege as follows: "The privilege finds persuasive support in the general social and political interest in permitting citizens to learn . . . about the operations of their courts and other governmental agencies . . ." Sack at 317. Authors and publishers are sometimes given a great deal of leeway in reporting official proceedings. *See, e.g., Binder v. Triangle Publications, Inc.,* 442 Pa. 319, 275 A.2d 53 (1971) (the phrase "bizarre love triangle" was held to be a fair and accurate report of testimony in a murder trial because the plaintiff had many lovers who lived with her and her husband from time to time). In other cases, however, courts have been remarkably strict in second-guessing the accuracy of reports of such proceedings. *See, e.g., Time, Inc. v. Firestone,* 424 U.S. 448 (1976).

44. *New York Times v. Sullivan,* 376 U.S. 254 (1964).

45. *Id.* at 269 quoting *Roth v. United States,* 354 U.S. 476, 484 (1956).

46. *Id.* at 270.

47. *Id.* at 271.

48. *Id.* at 271–72, quoting *NAACP v. Button,* 371 U.S. 415, 433 (1962).

49. *Id.* at 273.

50. *Id.* at 279.

51. *Id.* at 279–80.

52. *Reliance Insurance Co. v. Barron's,* 442 F.Supp. 1341, 1350 (S.D. N.Y. 1977) (Brieant, J.).

53. *Garrison v. Louisiana,* 379 U.S. 64, 74 (1964).

54. *St. Amant v. Thompson,* 390 U.S. 727, 731 (1967) (Justice White quoting in part Justice Harlan's opinion in *Curtis Publishing Co. v. Butts, supra* n.2).

55. *Id.* at 731.

56. *Gertz v. Robert Welch, Inc.,* 418 U.S. 323, 335 n. 6 (1974), citing *St. Amant v. Thompson, supra* n. 54. The Supreme Court's definition of "actual malice" has been said to focus on the defendant's subjective

attitude toward the truth rather than on the defendant's attitude toward the plaintiff. This test has led to problems in other aspects of libel law. For example, in *Herbert v. Lando*, 441 U.S. 153 (1979), the Court dealt with the permissible scope of pre-trial discovery in public official/public figure libel cases. The plaintiff was a military officer who sued the producers of TV's "60 Minutes" because of an unflattering report. Herbert claimed that the producers deliberately edited the report so as to distort the truth insofar as he was concerned. The Court found that since he was required to prove "actual malice," he should be permitted to inquire into the decision-making process of the editors of "60 Minutes."

57. See *St. Amant v. Thompson, supra* n. 54, at 731 (1968).

58. *Garrison v. Louisiana*, 379 U.S. 64, 73–74 (1964). *See also Beckley Newspapers Corp. v. Hanks*, 389 U.S. 81, 82 (1967), and *Greenbelt Cooperative Publishing Ass'n, Inc. v. Bresler*, 398 U.S. 6, 10–11 (1970), where the Supreme Court again rejected the common law meaning of "malice" in "actual malice" cases.

59. 7 Med. L. Rptr. 1321 (Cal Super. L.A. Co. 1981) modified on appeal, 9 Med. L. Rptr. 1921 (Cal. Ct. App. 1983).

60. 7 Med. L. Rptr. at 1321.

61. *Gallman v. Carnes*, 254 Ark. 987, 497 S.W.2d 47 (1973).

62. *Corbett v. Register Publishing Co.*, 33 Conn. Supp. 4, 356 A.2d 472 (1975); *Times Publishing Co. v. Huffstetler*, 409 So.2d 112 (Fla.2d DCA 1982); *Peisner v. Detroit Free Press*, 82 Mich. App. 153, 266 N.W.2d 693 (1978); *Pasculli v. Jersey Journal*, 7 Med. L. Rptr. 2574 (N.J. App. Div. 1981).

63. *Rebozo v. Washington Post Co.*, 637 F.2d 375 (5th Cir.), *cert. denied*, 454 U.S. 964 (1981).

64. *Marchiano v. Sandman*, 178 N.J. Super. 171, 174 (App. Div. 1981); *Moore v. Bailey*, 628 S.W.2d 431 (Tenn. App. 1981).

65. *Nader v. deToledano*, 408 A.2d 31 (D.D.C. 1979), *cert. denied*, 444 U.S. 1078 (1980); *Stripling v. Literary Guild*, 5 Med. L. Rptr. 1958 (W.D. Tex. 1979).

66. *See, e.g., Gertz v. Robert Welch, Inc.*, 680 F.2d 527 (7th Cir. 1982), *cert. denied*, 51 U.S.L.W. 3613 (1983).

67. *St. Amant v. Thompson, supra* n. 54, at 732 (1968).

68. *Gertz v. Robert Welch, Inc., supra* n. 66; *Fitzgerald v. Penthouse International, Ltd.*, 691 F. 2d 666 (4th Cir. 1982).

69. *Hutchinson v. Proxmire*, 443 U.S. 111, 119 n. 8 (1979). *See also Rosenblatt v. Baer*, 383 U.S. 75, 84–85 (1965).

70. *Compare Franklin v. Lodge No. 1108*, 97 Cal. App.3d 915 (1979), *with Sewell v. Brookbank*, 119 Ariz. 422, 425, 581 P.2d 267, 270 (Ariz. Ct. App. 1978), where the court stated that "as far as the law of defamation is concerned, teachers are 'public officials.'" *See also Basarich v. Rodeghero*, 24 Ill. App.3d 889, 321 N.E.2d 739 (1974).

71. *Rosenblatt v. Baer, supra* n. 69, at 85 (1966).
72. *Id.* at 87 n. 14. *Compare Hart v. Playboy Enterprises, Inc.*, 5 Med. L. Rptr. 1811 (D. Kan. 1979) (passage of six years did not render a federal narcotics agent a private figure) *with Jones v. Himstead*, 7 Med. L. Rptr. 2433 (Mass. Super. 1981) (former state senator who had not run for elective office since 1974 was found not to be a public official or public figure).
73. *Garrison v. Louisiana*, 379 U.S. 64, 77 (1964).
74. *Monitor Patriot Co. v. Roy*, 401 U.S. 265, 277 (1971). *See also Rinaldi v. Holt, Rinehart & Winston, Inc.*, 42 N.Y.2d 369, *cert. denied*, 434 U.S. 969 (1977).
75. *Curtis Publishing Co. v. Butts*, 388 U.S. 130 (1967); *Associated Press v. Walker*, 388 U.S. 130 (1967).
76. *Rosenbloom v. Metromedia, Inc.*, 403 U.S. 29 (1971). A Philadelphia man was called "a main distributor of obscene material" and a "smut distributor" by a local radio station following his arrest for selling nudist magazines. He was later acquitted of the charge because his magazines were found not to be obscene. The distributor sued the radio station for libel and won $25,000 actual damages and $250,000 punitive damages after a trial. The Third Circuit Court of Appeals reversed the lower court, stating that because the plaintiff was involved in a matter of public concern he was required to prove "actual malice" on the part of the radio station. The Supreme Court affirmed that decision. However, the members of the Supreme Court could not agree on a rationale for that decision; the Justices wrote five separate opinions, none of which spoke for more than three of them.
77. 418 U.S. 323 (1974).
78. The two lower courts were clearly following Justice Brennan's opinion in *Rosenbloom*, where he stated that the actual malice standard applied to all reports of "events of public or general concern." *Rosenbloom* at 52.
79. 418 U.S. at 345.
80. *Id.* at 347.
81. Of the 24 states that had decided the issue by the end of 1982, only four retained the actual malice standard for private figure plaintiffs—Alaska, Colorado, Indiana and Michigan. New York adopted a standard less demanding than actual malice but more rigorous than mere negligence. *See Chapadeau v. Utica Observer-Dispatch, Inc.*, 38 N.Y.2d 196, 199, 379 N.Y.S.2d 61 (1975), where the highest state court stated the New York "fault" standard as follows: "[W]here the content of the article is arguably within the sphere of legitimate public concern . . . the party defamed may recover [if he or she establishes], by a preponderance of the evidence, that the publisher acted in a grossly irresponsible manner without due consideration for the standards of information gathering and dissemination ordinarily followed by responsible parties." The New York standard for private figure libel plaintiffs, adopted in response to

Gertz, is more protective of libel defendants than *Gertz* requires. All of the remaining states that have ruled have chosen to adopt the minimum standard permitted by *Gertz:* mere negligence. The other states have not ruled definitely on the matter. (See Appendix C.)

82. 418 U.S. at 351.
83. *Id.* at 351–52.
84. *Id.* at 352.
85. *Id.* at 351.
86. *Gertz v. Robert Welch, Inc.*, 680 F.2d 527, 1769 (7th Cir. 1982), *cert. denied*, 51 U.S.L.W. 3613 (1983). This ruling was questioned by the appellate court, but since Gertz sought and was awarded punitive damages, he was required to prove actual malice in any event. See p.118.
87. *Carson v. Allied News Co.*, 529 F.2d 206 (7th Cir. 1976).
88. *Holy Spirit Association v. Sequoya Elsevier Publishing Co.*, 75 A.D.2d 523 (1st Dept. 1980).
89. *Nader v. deToledano* (D.C. Super 1977), *aff'd in part, rev'd in part on other grounds*, 408 A.2d 31 (D.D.C. 1979), *cert. denied*, 444 U.S. 1078 (1980).
90. *Buckley v. Littell*, 539 F.2d 882 (2d Cir. 1976), *cert. denied*, 429 U.S. 1062 (1977).
91. *See, e.g., Clements v. Gannett Co.*, 83 A.D.2d 988 (4th Dept. 1981) (where a man who was very active in local civic affairs was declared a "public figure for all purposes").
92. *Gertz v. Robert Welch, Inc.*, 418 U.S. 323, 345 (1974).
93. 424 U.S. 448 (1976).
94. *Id.* at 450.
95. *Id.* at 453–54.
96. 443 U.S. 111 (1979).
97. *Id.* at 116.
98. 443 U.S. 157 (1979).
99. *Id.* at 166.
100. *Id.* at 169 (concurring opinion).
101. Justice Blackmun argued in *Wolston* that the passage of time affects whether a person is a "public" or "private" figure because "the defamed party's access to the means of counterargument" may diminish with time. *Id.* at 170–71.
102. *Church of Scientology v. Siegelman*, 475 F.Supp. 950 (S.D. N.Y. 1979).
103. *Henderson v. Van Buren Public School*, 4 Med. L. Rptr. 1741 (E.D. Mich. 1978).
104. *Anderson v. Low Rent Housing Commission of Muscatine*, 304 N.W.2d 239 (Iowa 1981).
105. *Tavoulareas v. Washington Post Company*, 8 Med. L. Rptr. 2262 (D.D.C. 1982). A jury verdict in favor of the public figure plaintiff for $2.05 million was subsequently set aside in its entirety by the trial judge. 9 Med. L. Rptr. 1553 (D.D.C. 1983).

106. *Ali v. Daily News*, 8 Med. L. Rptr. 1844 (D.V.I. 1982).

107. *Street v. National Broadcasting Co.*, 645 F.2d 1227 (6th Cir.), *cert. dism.*, 454 U.S. 1095 (1981).

108. *Torgerson v. Minneapolis Star and Tribune*, 7 Med. L. Rptr. 1805 (Minn. D.C. 1981).

109. *Pring v. Penthouse*, 7 Med. L. Rptr. 1101 (D.C. Wyo. 1981), *rev'd*, 8 Med. L. Rptr. 2409 (10th Cir. 1982), *cert. denied*, 51 U.S.L.W. 3902 (1983).

110. *Tavoulareas v. Washington Post Company*, *supra* n. 105.

111. *Cantrell v. American Broadcasting Co.*, 8 Med. L. Rptr. 1239 (N.D. Ill. 1982).

112. *Jenoff v. Hearst Corp.*, 7 Med. L. Rptr. 1081 (4th Cir. 1981).

113. *From v. Tallahassee Democrat*, 7 Med. L. Rptr. 1811 (Fla.D.Ct.App. 1981).

114. *See generally* Silver, "Libel, The 'Higher Truths' of Art, and the First Amendment," 126 *U. Pa. L. Rev.* 1065 (1978) [hereinafter Silver].

115. *Bindrim v. Mitchell*, 92 Cal. App.3d 61, 155 Cal. Rptr. 29, *cert. denied*, 444 U.S. 984 (1979). Bindrim was awarded $50,000 compensatory damages and $25,000 punitive damages.

116. 432 N.Y.S.2d 536, 78 A.D.2d 723 (3d Dept. 1980). The court also found that one of the allegedly defamatory statements was rhetorical hyperbole and therefore a protected expression of opinion even if it had referred to the plaintiff.

117. 8 Med. L. Rptr. 2613 (1st Dept. 1982). The court also dismissed separate claims for "*prima facie*" tort, invasion of privacy, punitive damages and attorneys' fees. The plaintiff has appealed to the state's highest court.

118. 8 Med. L. Rptr. 2409 (10th Cir. 1982), *cert denied*, 51 U.S.L.W. 3902 (1983).

119. *See* Silver at 1069.

120. *Yorty v. Chandler*, 13 Cal. App.3d 467, 91 Cal. Rptr. 709 (1970). The court rejected Yorty's libel claim because it found the cartoon to be privileged as an expression of editorial opinion.

121. *Myers v. Boston Magazine, Inc.*, 6 Med. L. Rptr. 1241 (1980).

122. *Id.* at 1243.

123. *Salomone v. Macmillan Publishing Co., Inc.*, 97 Misc.2d 346, 350–52 (N.Y.Co. 1978), *rev'd on other grounds*, 77 A.D.2d 501, 429 N.Y.S.2d 441 (1st Dept. 1980).

124. *See* Silver at 1069 and Sack at 241–43.

125. 360 F.2d 344 (5th Cir. 1966).

126. *Id.* at 348.

127. 398 U.S. 6 (1970).

128. *Id.* at 14.

129. *See Edwards v. National Audubon Society*, 556 F.2d 113 (2d Cir.), *cert. denied sub nom. Edwards v. New York Times Co.*, 434 U.S. 1002 (1977).

130. Sack at 62.

131. *Burton v. Crowell Publishing Co.*, 82 F.2d 154 (2d Cir. 1936).
132. *Silberman v. Georges*, 8 Med. L. Rptr. 2647 (1st Dept. 1982). Th court suggested that the libel claim would also fail for failure to prov defamatory meaning, fault, or injury.
133. According to Sack at 515, "there is a substantial body of case law prohibiting jurisdiction in cases in which there exists only 'minima circulation' within the forum state." For example, circulation of 3 copies of a Georgia newspaper in Illinois was held insufficient, *Gonzale v. Atlanta Constitution*, 4 Med. L. Rptr. 2146 (N.D. Ill. 1979), while circulation of 2000 copies of the *New York Post* in Connecticut was hel sufficient, *Buckley v. New York Post Corp.*, 373 F.2d 175 (2d Cir. 1967)
134. Solicitation of a "small amount" of advertising, and "sporadi newsgathering," is generally held insufficient. See *Buckley v. Nev York Times Co.*, 338 F.2d 470 (5th Cir. 1964); *Church of Scientolog of California v. Adams*, 584 F.2d 893 (9th Cir. 1978) (almost 3 percen of advertising revenues held insufficient).
135. *See, e.g., Anselmi v. Denver Post, Inc.*, 552 F.2d 316 (10th Cir.), *cert denied sub nom. Times Mirror Co. v. Anselmi*, 432 U.S. 911 (1977 (California newspaper properly sued in Wyoming regarding article o alleged crime activities in Wyoming); *Edwards v. Associated Press* 512 F.2d 258 (5th Cir. 1975) (wire service could be sued in Mississipp over story originating in Louisiana about Mississippi events).
136. Sack at 523.
137. *See, e.g., New York Times Co. v. Connor*, 365 F.2d 567 (5th Cir 1966). In 1983 the Supreme Court agreed to hear two cases involving due process and First Amendment limits on jurisdiction over author and publishers in libel cases, and its decisions will likely have a dramatic impact on those issues. See *Keeton v. Hustler Magazine*, Inc. 682 F. 2d 33 (1st Cir. 1982), *cert. granted*, 51 U.S.L.W. 3662 (1983) *Calder v. Jones*, 138 Cal. App. 128, 187 Cal. Rptr. 825 (Cal. Ct. App 1982), *prob. juris. noted*, 51 U.S.L.W. 3756 (1983).
138. *See, e.g., Westmoreland v. CBS*, 8 Med. L. Rptr. 2493 (D.S.C. 1982 (transferring a suit by retired General Westmoreland against CBS and various CBS employees from South Carolina, where Westmorelan lived, to New York City).
139. *See, e.g., Hodges v. Oklahoma Journal Pub. Co.*, 4 Med. L. Rptr 2492 (Okl. App. 1979). According to Sack the following jurisdic tions do, or may, follow this onerous rule on liability for headlines Alaska, Delaware, Louisiana, Maine, Missouri, Nevada, New York Pennsylvania, Virginia, Tennessee, Texas, and Washington.
140. *See* cases cited in Sack at 56–57.
141. For a list of retraction statutes (with text) see Sack at 589–619 (Appendix IV).
142. Books, and sometimes "periodicals," are often not included in the lis of covered publications. Generally the statutes are interpreted narrowly

and would not be construed to cover media not listed. *See, e.g., Burnett v. National Enquirer*, 7 Med. L. Rptr. 1321 (Cal. Super. L.A. Co. 1981), *modified on other grounds*, 9 Med. L. Rptr. 1921 (Cal. Ct. App. 1983).

143. *See Near v. Minnesota*, 283 U.S. 697 (1931), and a case of more recent vintage, *Reliance Insurance Co. v. Barron's*, 428 F. Supp. 200, 205 (S.D.N.Y. 1977). The Supreme Court has stated that any "prior restraint" of the press is "presumptively unconstitutional." *See, e.g., New York Times Co. v. United States*, 403 U.S. 713 (1971). Moreover, long before the First Amendment implications were fully recognized courts declined to enjoin alleged libel on grounds of general equity. *See, e.g., Brandreth v. Lance*, 8 Paige N.Y. Chanc. 24 (1839). *See generally* Sack at 361–63.

144. *See Miami Herald Publishing Co. v. Tornillo*, 418 U.S. 241 (1974), where the Supreme Court struck down as unconstitutional a Florida statute that required newspapers to publish replies by political candidates to published criticisms. Referring to that statute, the Court stated that "it has yet to be demonstrated how governmental regulation of this [editorial] process can be exercised consistent with First Amendment guarantees of a free press as they have evolved to this time." *Id.* at 258. Sack states that the "broad language" quoted above "appears to foreclose statutory forced retractions in the context of libel cases." Sack at 363.

145. *See* RESTATEMENT §575, comment b. *See also Danias v. Fakis*, 261 A.2d 529 (Del. Super. 1969).

146. *See, e.g., Burnett v. National Enquirer, supra* n. 142.

147. *Gertz v. Robert Welch, Inc.*, 418 U.S. 323, 350 (1974).

148. *Time, Inc. v. Firestone*, 424 U.S. 448 (1976).

149. *Salomone v. Macmillan Publishing Co., Inc.* 77 A.D.2d 501, 429 N.Y.S.2d 441 (1st Dept. 1980); *see, also, e.g., France v. St. Clare's Hospital*, 82 A.D.2d 1, 441 N.Y.S.2d 71 (1st Dept. 1981); *Gobin v. Globe Publishing Co.*, 8 Med. L. Rptr. 2191 (Kan. 1982).

150. "In short, the private defamation plaintiff who establishes liability under a less demanding standard than stated by *New York Times* [i.e., actual malice] may recover only such damages as are sufficient to compensate him for actual injury." 418 U.S. at 350.

151. States that have abolished, on First Amendment grounds, punitive damages in libel actions include Massachusetts, Montana, and Oregon. Jurisdictions that do not permit punitive damages in any civil action are Louisiana, Nebraska, New Hampshire, Puerto Rico, and Washington. See LRDC Survey 600–03, 615.

152. The Libel Defense Resource Center reports seventeen million-dollar libel awards since 1976. Of these, at the end of 1983, not one has been affirmed on appeal. One case was reported settled for $1.4 million because the newspaper defendant was not fully insured and literally

could not afford to purchase the bond required to cover the jury's $9.2 million judgment in order to pursue an effective appeal. *Green v. Alton Telegraph Printing Co.*, 8 Med. L. Rptr. 1345 (Ill. App. 5th Dist. 1982). See LRDC Bulletin No. 4 (Part 1), August 15, 1982; LRDC Bulletin No. 5, Nov. 15, 1982; No. 6, March 15, 1983; No. 7, July 15, 1983.

153. *See Griswold v. Connecticut*, 381 U.S. 479 (1965) (contraception); *Roe v. Wade*, 410 U.S. 113 (1973) (abortion).

154. The genesis for a legally recognized "right of privacy" in civil actions against publishers or authors was a law review article written almost a century ago by Samuel Warren and Louis D. Brandeis, who was subsequently a Justice of the U.S. Supreme Court. The article, appropriately entitled "The Right to Privacy," appeared in 4 *Harv. L. Rev.* 193 (1890). The authors made clear the focus of their "privacy" concerns: "The press is overstepping in every direction the obvious bounds of propriety and of decency. Gossip is no longer the resource of the idle and of the vicious, but has become a trade, which is pursued with industry as well as effrontery. To satisfy a prurient taste the details of sexual relations are spread broadcast in the columns of the daily papers. To occupy the indolent, column upon column is filled with idle gossip, which can only be procured by intrusion upon the domestic circle. The intensity and complexity of life, attendant upon advancing civilization, have rendered necessary some retreat from the world, and man, under the refining influence of culture, has become more sensitive to publicity, so that solitude and privacy have become more essential to the individual; but modern enterprise and invention have, through invasions upon his privacy, subjected him to mental pain and distress, far greater than could be inflicted by mere bodily injury." *Id.* at 196. For an interesting glimpse into the genesis of the article see Sack at 387–89.

155. The four categories, which are now widely recognized, were first defined by Professor Prosser. See W. Prosser, *Handbook on the Law of Torts*, §117 (4th ed. 1971).

156. Sack at 394, *quoting* RESTATEMENT §652 E.

157. Sack at 394 (citations omitted).

158. 385 U.S. 374 (1967).

159. *Id.* at 383, quoting *Spahn v. Julian Messner, Inc.*, 18 N.Y.2d 324, 328 (1966).

160. *Id.* at 387–88.

161. 419 U.S. 245 (1974).

162. *Id.* at 252–53.

163. *See, e.g., Rinsley v. Brandt*, 446 F.Supp. 850 (D. Kan. 1977) (the court held that *Gertz* overruled the *Hill* decision and that only public figures must prove actual malice in "false light" privacy cases); *Dresbach v. Doubleday*, 518 F.Supp. 1285 (D. D.C. 1981) (a "private person" who was placed in a false light in a book about his brother, who was convicted of murdering their parents—a matter of legitimate public

concern—need only prove that the author's negligence resulted in the inaccuracies in the book).

164. RESTATEMENT §652 D.

165. *See, e.g., Meeropol v. Nizer,* 560 F.2d 1061 (2d Cir. 1977), *cert. denied,* 434 U.S. 1013 (1978) (the children of Julius and Ethel Rosenberg cannot prevail in a suit challenging disclosures made about them in a book concerning their parents' trial and electrocution); *Friedan v. Friedan,* 414 F.Supp. 77 (S.D. N.Y. 1976) (feminist Betty Friedan's former husband fails in a privacy claim concerning a magazine article about his ex-wife in which he was described and pictured). One leading commentator has observed that "the concept of newsworthiness has largely swallowed up the tort." Hill, "Defamation and Privacy under the First Amendment," 76 *Colum. L. Rev.* 1205, 1253 (1976). *But see Forsher v. Bugliosi,* 26 Cal.3d 792, 163 Cal Rptr. 628, 608 P.2d 716 (1980), where the plaintiff, who was named in a book about the Manson "family" murders, *Helter Skelter,* in connection with the murder of a defense attorney, was allowed to pursue a "private facts" case because his name had never appeared in the public record and because he was never charged with any crime in connection with the murder. *See also Campbell v. Seabury Press,* 614 F.2d 395 (5th Cir. 1980); *Gilbert v. Medical Economics,* 665 F.2d 305 (10th Cir. 1981); *Dresbach v. Doubleday,* 518 F.Supp. 1285 (D.D.C. 1981).

166. *See, e.g., Horne v. Patton,* 291 Ala. 701, 287 So.2d 824 (1973) (doctor's disclosure of private medical facts to plaintiff's employer); *Beaumont v. Brown,* 401 Mich. 80, 257 N.W.2d 522 (1977) (employer's letter to the Army disclosing private facts about the plaintiff).

167. *Melvin v. Reid,* 112 Cal. App. 285, 297 P. 91 (1931). The court held that although the retelling of the plaintiff's story was newsworthy, the film violated her right of privacy when it delved into her present situation and linked it to her past.

168. *Briscoe v. Reader's Digest Ass'n,* 4 Cal.3d 529, 93 Cal. Rptr. 866, 483 P.2d 34 (1971).

169. 4 Cal.3d at 537.

170. *See, e.g., Sidis v. F-R. Publishing Corp.,* 113 F.2d 806 (2d Cir.), *cert. denied,* 311 U.S. 711 (1940), where the court rejected the privacy claim of a former child prodigy who had not been in the public eye for over 25 years because it was a matter of public concern to see how he had developed his early genius.

171. For a fuller discussion of the right of publicity *see* Gordon, "Right of Property in Name, Likeness, Personality and History," 55 *Nw. U. L. Rev.* 553 (1960); Felcher & Rubin, "Privacy, Publicity and the Portrayal of Real People by the Media," 88 *Yale L. J.* 1577 (1979); Pilpel, "The Right of Publicity," 27 *Bull. Copy. Soc.* 249 (1980). The term "right of publicity" was first used in this context by Judge Jerome Frank in *Haelan Laboratories, Inc. v. Topps Chewing Gum, Inc.,* 202 F.2d 866 (2d Cir.), *cert. denied,* 346 U.S. 816 (1953).

172. In *Roberson v. Rochester Folding Box Co.*, 171 N.Y. 538, 64 N.E. 442 (1902), the New York Court of Appeals refused to recognize a common law claim for commercial misappropriation. As a result, within a year, the New York legislature passed a ''right of privacy'' statute which was limited to creating a cause of action for such misappropriation. N.Y. Civil Rights Law §§50 and 51. Similar statutes have been enacted in several other states.

173. *Zacchini v. Scripps-Howard Broadcasting Co.*, 433 U.S. 562 (1977).

174. *Arrington v. New York Times Co.*, 55 N.Y.2d 433, 449 N.Y.S.2d 941, 434 N.E.2d 1319 (1982), *cert. denied*, 51 U.S.L.W. 3533 (1983). The court also rejected a non-statutory ''false light'' claim and a claim for invasion of constitutional privacy rights.

175. *See, e.g.*, *Meeropol v. Nizer*, *supra* n.165; *Bauman v. Anson*, 6 Med. L. Rptr. 1487 (Sup. Ct. N.Y. Co. 1980).

176. *Spahn v. Julian Messner, Inc.*, 21 N.Y.2d 124 (1967), *app. dism'd*, 393 U.S. 1046 (1969).

177. *See, e.g.*, *Groucho Marx Productions, Inc. v. Day and Night Company*, 523 F. Supp. 485 (S.D. N.Y. 1981), *rvs'd on other grounds*, 689 F.2d 31 (2d Cir. 1982) (but questioning the lower court's First Amendment holding); *Estate of Presley v. Russen*, 513 F.Supp. 1339 (D.N.J. 1981).

178. RESTATEMENT, §652B.

179. *See, e.g.*, *Pearson v. Dodd*, 410 F.2d 710 (D.C. Cir.), *cert. denied*, 395 U.S. 947 (1969).

180. *See, e.g.*, *Dietemann v. Time, Inc.*, 449 F.2d 245 (9th Cir. 1971) (hidden camera); *Nader v. General Motors Corp.*, 25 N.Y.2d 560 (1970) (wiretapping and eavesdropping).

181. *See, e.g.*, *Florida Pub. Co. v. Fletcher*, 340 So.2d 914 (Fla. 1976), *cert. denied*, 431 U.S. 930 (1977).

182. *Galella v. Onassis*, 487 F.2d 986 (2d Cir. 1973).

183. *See Dietemann v. Time, Inc.*, *supra* n. 173.

184. *See LeMistral v. Columbia Broadcasting Syst.*, 61 A.D.2d 491 (1st Dept. 1978).

185. *See Barber v. Time, Inc.*, 348 Mo. 1199, 159 S.W.2d 291 (1942).

186. Sack at 443.

187. For a complex but important recent discussion of the potential defamation liability of the persons and entities in the publishing process—original newspaper publisher vs. paperback (re)publisher; original reporters vs. paperback editor, etc.—*see Karaduman v. Newsday*, 51 N.Y.2d 531 (1980).

188. *See, e.g.*, *Maynard v. Port Publications, Inc.*, 98 Wis.2d 555, 297, N.W.2d 500 (1980).

189. For a review of the availability of such insurance coverage for authors see *Media Insurance: Protecting Against High Judgments, Punitive Damages and Defense Costs* 461-91, Practicing Law Institute 1983.

V

Obscenity

The issue of obscenity has confounded the law for centuries. In the United States it has resulted in a clash between advocates of the greatest possible First Amendment freedom and those who believe that society has the power and duty to suppress at least some sexual expression in the name of public morality.[1]

In a sense, the forces of suppression appear to have prevailed. Despite the sexual liberation that characterizes much of our society today, the First Amendment, at least as interpreted by a narrow majority of Supreme Court Justices, has been held to permit the enactment and enforcement of state and federal criminal and civil laws against sexually explicit expression, even though suppression of any form of expression is fundamentally inconsistent with the full exercise of First Amendment freedoms. In addition, censorship almost inevitably has a "chilling effect" upon other forms of expression, which are not obscene but which could nonetheless be prosecuted (and persecuted) in the mistaken belief that they are.

In another sense it seems clear that authors and artists today have much more freedom of sexual expression than at any time since the early 19th century. Although obscenity laws have been held constitutional, they are permitted to operate only within narrow guidelines. Those limitations, together with the increasing acceptance by large segments of the public of sexually explicit expression and the lack of enthusiasm on the part of most law enforcement agencies toward enforcing obscenity laws, has led to unprecedented freedom. When obscenity laws are enforced it is generally against the most extreme and distasteful sexual materials—child pornography, for example, or pictorial magazines devoted to explicit and often perverse or violent sexual conduct. The era when literary classics such as *Ulysses* or *Lady Chatterley's Lover,* or even *Fanny Hill* or the works of the Marquis de Sade, could effectively be banned and their authors and publishers prosecuted has passed and probably will not come again.

Nonetheless, obscenity laws remain on the books and cannot be ignored by the author or artist whose work includes sexual subjects. This chapter will review the origins of today's obscenity law and how it is structured and enforced. It will also discuss those areas, however limited, where authors and artists continue to be vulnerable to legal action.

Do "obscenity" and "pornography" mean the same thing?

They have somewhat different but related dictionary definitions.[2] "Obscenity" is the term used most frequently by the law, and it is the term that will be used in this chapter.

For these purposes, "obscenity" refers to the kind of sexually explicit expression or materials that the Supreme Court has declared not protected by the First Amendment. Courts and legislatures have repeatedly—and almost entirely unsuccessfully—attempted to distinguish the obscene from the non-obscene in terms of definitions. But there is no one meaningful legal definition of obscenity today; indeed, the inability of the law effectively to define and limit the legal concept of obscenity is a major reason why the continued existence of any obscenity law seriously infringes First Amendment rights.

Why don't obscenity laws violate the First Amendment?

The First Amendment declares that Congress may pass *no law* abridging freedom of speech or of the press. However, obscenity laws plainly do abridge such freedoms. Since writings and visual creations that contain sexual themes or explicit sexual depictions seem to be expression entitled to the protections promised by the First Amendment, what has happened?

The short answer is that the Supreme Court—the ultimate

arbiter of what the Constitution means—has never held that the First Amendment is anywhere near as absolute as it appears. Instead, the Court has proclaimed that certain categories of expression are beyond the protection of the First Amendment, including libel, incitement to riot, and, of course, "obscenity."[3] According to prevailing majorities of the Supreme Court over the past three decades, since obscenity is "without redeeming social value," it is not entitled to First Amendment protection.

How can you distinguish between the "obscene" and the "non-obscene"?

This task is made even more difficult by the fact that legal judgments about obscenity involve matters of morality and taste, which are inherently subjective. The elaborate legal formulations of the Supreme Court cannot mask the fundamental impossibility of providing meaningful guidance to authors and artists who wish to deal with sexual themes. What follows is a review of today's legal structure, which attempts to define what in a very real sense cannot be defined, with a brief look at the background and history of obscenity law.

Are there different kinds of obscenity laws?

Yes; criminal and civil laws deal with obscenity. Criminal laws typically make it a criminal offense to publish, sell, lend, or otherwise disseminate materials that are found to be legally obscene. Exhibition of obscene matter, particularly of motion pictures, may be prohibited, and the production—i.e., the printing or manufacturing—of obscene materials may be proscribed. Some criminal statutes are limited to "commercial" dissemination; others are not. Authors and artists generally fall within the realm of commercial distribution, which does not depend on whether a profit has been made. Mere possession with the intent to disseminate may be considered a criminal offense.[4] However, private possession of obscene materials for personal use is recognized as constitutionally protected.[5] Advertising obscenity is also an offense under some statutes, regardless of whether the advertisement itself is obscene. But with increasing First Amendment protection for "commercial speech"—including advertising—these provisions may be constitutionally suspect.[6]

Besides these offenses, which generally involve dissemination or advertising to adults, there are special statutes dealing with distributing or displaying matter that is said to be "harmful to minors"[7] and with creating or disseminating so-called "child pornography," a category of sexually explicit materials subject to a different set of legal standards that were only recently established by the Supreme Court.[8]

Criminal obscenity offenses range from minor misdemeanors to serious felonies, depending upon the state or locality and the circumstances of the offense. Penalties range from fines to jail terms of up to several years.

What kind of civil obscenity laws are there?

Many kinds. And while they do not threaten incarceration, they do provide a range of burdensome sanctions which can have an impact on rights of free expression equal to and at times greater than criminal penalties. They can also place a significant economic burden on the individuals and business interests that are subject to them.[9] Civil obscenity laws and sanctions include:

- injunctions against publication, dissemination, or exhibition of materials found to be obscene;
- injunctions closing business enterprises which produce, distribute, sell, or display material found to be obscene. Such padlock or nuisance abatement laws can result in the seizure, forfeiture, or destruction of allegedly obscene materials;
- licensing schemes providing for prior review and possible censorship of materials to be exhibited or disseminated;
- civil proceedings to determine obscenity before possible criminal prosecution;
- statutes regulating the display of, and access to, sexually explicit matter, particularly to children or unconsenting adults, often with criminal penalties for their violation; and
- local zoning ordinances intended to limit, concentrate, or disperse sex-oriented businesses.

What levels of government can enact and prosecute obscenity laws?

All levels: federal, state, and local. Their laws may overlap or may be mutually exclusive. The U.S. Constitution, which governs the lawmaking power at all levels of government, has been interpreted by the Supreme Court to permit states and localities to deal with obscenity, but it has also imposed significant limits on this power.[10] Today's constitutional standards even accept the existence of inconsistent laws, by which materials are deemed non-obscene in one locality and obscene in another.[11]

The Constitution permits state and local obscenity laws, but it certainly does not require them. Nonetheless, almost all of the states, and many local governments, have obscenity laws.[12] These laws are often similar, but there are differences—sometimes significant ones—from state to state and within single states. Some states have adopted "statewide standards" or have precluded or pre-empted local control over obscenity. Although control of obscenity is essentially a local or state matter, there are important federal laws dealing with obscenity. The asserted justification for such laws is to control interstate distribution of obscenity and prevent circumvention of local and state obscenity laws.

Can an idea be obscene?

No. The law today does not permit prosecution of so-called thematic obscenity. The Supreme Court has ruled that the First Amendment protects ideas from attack under the guise of obscenity regulation, and has struck down as unconstitutional convictions based upon ideas advocated in a work even if the work was itself sexually explicit. It struck down one New York statute that permitted censorship of a movie deemed "sacrilegious"[13] and another under which a license for the motion picture version of *Lady Chatterley's Lover* was denied because it presented adultery as appropriate behavior.[14] In the latter case the Supreme Court declared:

> What New York has done, therefore, is to prevent the exhibition of a motion picture because that picture advocates an idea—that adultery under certain circumstances may be proper behavior. Yet the First Amendment's basic guarantee is of freedom to advocate ideas.

147

The State, quite simply, has thus struck at the very heart of constitutionally protected liberty.

It is contended that the State's action was justified because the motion picture attractively portrays a relationship which is contrary to the moral standards, the religious precepts, and the legal code of its citizenry. This argument misconceives what it is that the Constitution protects. Its guarantee is not confined to the expression of ideas that are conventional or shared by a majority. It protects advocacy of the opinion that adultery may sometimes be proper, no less than advocacy of socialism or the single tax. And in the realm of ideas it protects expression which is eloquent no less than that which is unconvincing.[15]

What are the historical origins of our obscenity laws?

It may be a surprise that the suppression of explicit sexual materials is little more than a hundred years old. Although governmental censorship has existed throughout recorded history, it has mostly been directed toward political and religious heresy rather than obscenity. In Greek and Roman times, and indeed until a few centuries ago, sexual explicitness was widely accepted in popular literature, drama, and ballads. Bawdy stories often became vehicles for the presentation of religious themes. Governmental and religious censors—who plainly had no qualms about suppressing other speech that displeased them—apparently saw no need to bother with even the most licentious matter.[16]

In 16th-century England, with the advent of the printing press, the first system of book licensing was established. Here too, licensing was directed toward books dealing with sedition and heresy, and, indeed, its principal purpose was not censorship but the protection of English printers and bookbinders from foreign competition.

During the second half of the century Puritanism became increasingly widespread, and the Puritans sought to purge England of everything they considered obscene. The tolerant attitude toward sexual materials that had marked almost every age began to change. And, except for a brief period following the Restoration in 1660, the Puritan influence has continued to be felt.

Even the Puritan concern for the "intollerable corruption of common lyfe and manners, which pestilently invadeth the myndes of many that delight to heare or read the said wantone woorkes" failed to specify what ought to be condemned. Books and pamphlets that would be considered hard-core pornography today circulated freely in England; if they lacked anti-religious content they apparently violated no law.[17]

No obscenity legislation was enacted in England until 1824, and the first laws only prohibited exposing an obscene book or print in public places.[18] By 1857, however, what was called Lord Campbell's Act generally prohibited the dissemination of obscene materials in England.[19]

How did obscenity law develop in the United States?

Although explicit sexual materials were very much in circulation throughout the American colonies, only Massachusetts had any law addressed to them,[20] and it was not until 1821—110 years after its enactment—that anyone was prosecuted for violating the statute.[21] This does not mean that there was no censorship. The American colonies were closely governed by the British sovereign and his appointees, and the British law of libel and slander, which made it a crime to criticize the government, was enforced.[22]

Against this background of governmental suppression of speech and press the American colonies won their independence, and, in 1789, adopted the Constitution—which was not ratified until the framers added the Bill of Rights, which made clear that certain precious individual freedoms, such as freedom of press, speech, religion, and assembly, could not be abridged by the newly created government.[23]

In 1821 Vermont became the first state in the new Union to pass an anti-obscenity statute,[24] and many other states soon followed. The first federal anti-obscenity statute, passed in 1842, was directed toward importation,[25] and in 1865 Congress passed a statute prohibiting the sending of obscene materials through the mails.[26]

The apparently growing concern with obscenity notwithstanding, there was little enforcement of state or federal obscenity laws until 1868, when the New York legislature enacted a law prohibiting the dissemination of obscene literature.[27] Shortly after, a grocery store clerk named Anthony Comstock began a one-man crusade to ensure that the law was vigorously enforced; joined by the YMCA, he formed a national organization called the Committee for the Suppression of Vice. In 1873, largely in response to this crusade, Congress broadened the federal mail act[28] and named Comstock a special agent of the Post Office in charge of enforcing it. Many states without obscenity statutes passed them after 1873; by 1900 at least 30 states had some form of general prohibition against the dissemination of obscene materials.

This response to obscenity continued through the first 60 years of this century. Many books, plays, films, and works of art were suppressed as obscene, and countless others had to be obtained, and kept, secretly on the assumption that they would be suppressed if discovered.

Throughout this period the prevailing definition of obscenity was that set forth in the 1868 English case of *Regina v. Hicklin*,[29] in which the court declared that material was obscene if it tended "to deprave and corrupt those whose minds are open to such immoral influences and into whose hands a publication of this sort may fall." This decision meant that for the first time materials could be prohibited solely because of their sexual content, without their attacking the government or religious institutions, and that an entire work could be suppressed as obscene on the basis of a few passages, or if it tended to "deprave and corrupt" only the most immature and susceptible. The *Hicklin* definition prevailed in the United States during the first third of the 20th century.

How have the courts dealt with obscenity in this century?
The first seven decades saw an ever-increasing number of obscenity cases, and confusion about the legal definition of obscenity seemed to increase with every case. More and more courts came to be troubled by shortcomings of the *Hicklin* formulation and the distorted results it gave rise to. In a celebrated case[30] where the federal courts ruled that James Joyce's classic

Ulysses was not obscene and could be admitted into the United States, the word "obscene" was defined as "tending to stir the sex impulses or to lead to sexually impure and lustful thoughts." Also in that case, the court rejected the *Hicklin* definition and ruled that a finding of obscenity had to be based on a reading not of isolated passages but of the whole book, and on the effect of the whole book on a "normal person."

Despite such occasional victories during this period, direct First Amendment challenges to the validity of obscenity laws continued to lose. Other courts were not always as enlightened as the *Ulysses* court in rejecting the restrictive *Hicklin* rules. Books such as *Lady Chatterley's Lover* by D. H. Lawrence,[31] *An American Tragedy* by Theodore Dreiser,[32] and *God's Little Acre* by Erskine Caldwell[33] were found obscene. As late as 1953 the U.S. Court of Appeals in San Francisco upheld obscenity findings against Henry Miller's *Tropic of Cancer* and *Tropic of Capricorn* based on a consideration of isolated passages in those works.[34]

Nonetheless, by the early 1950s some aspects of the *Hicklin* test had been substantially eroded and the basic contours of later constitutionally based standards were taking shape. By 1950 the "whole work," or "dominant theme," standard was accepted by most American courts. Also, the "average person" test was accepted by most courts and the idea that the literary value of a work could be taken into consideration was becoming established. Finally, the doctrine of "community standards" was emerging, generally in a manner that recognized increased sexual tolerance.

What was the *Roth* case?

It was not until 1957—166 years after the First Amendment was adopted—that the Supreme Court directly considered whether various state and federal anti-obscenity laws were constitutional, and if so, what kinds of materials could be suppressed as obscene. Its decision in *Roth v. United States*,[35] however, did not conclusively answer these questions.

Although many argued that all anti-obscenity laws—at least in the absence of proof that obscenity presented a "clear and present danger" of anti-social conduct—were unconstitutional because they violated the First Amendment, a majority of the Supreme Court disagreed. Instead, the Court declared that obscenity was not the kind of material protected by the freedom of speech and press, and therefore a showing of clear and present danger was unnecessary to justify its suppression. As the Court put it, in an opinion by Justice William J. Brennan:

> The protection given speech and press was fashioned to assure unfettered interchange of ideas for the bringing about of political and social changes desired by the people. . . . All ideas having even the slightest redeeming social importance . . . have the full protection of the guaranties, unless they encroach upon the limited area of more important interests. But implicit in the history of the First Amendment is the rejection of obscenity as utterly without social importance.[36]

In defining obscenity, however, the *Roth* majority recognized a number of important principles that had been developing in the lower courts. First, it held that "sex and obscenity are not synonymous," and it seemed strongly to suggest that significant "art, literature and scientific works" must be constitutionally protected. Accordingly, it held that only materials that "appeal to the prurient interest" can be obscene. Second, the Court rejected the *Hicklin* view on isolated passages and adopted the requirement that the obscenity judgment be based on the "dominant theme of the material taken as a whole." Third, the Court held that the obscenity judgment must be based upon the reactions of an average person, not a person peculiarly susceptible to immoral or lustful influences. Finally, the judgment had to be made by "applying contemporary community standards," thus seeming to assure—at least in a permissive era—progress toward fewer restraints upon protected expression.

Justices Douglas and Black dissented, adhering to their nearly "absolutist" view that censorship of any pure expression—"unless so closely brigaded with illegal action as to be an inseparable part of it"—was a violation of the First Amendment.[37] They rejected the effort to define which publications had value and which had not, a role they felt was reserved not to official censors but to the people at large.

In addition, in another case decided that same year, the Court insisted that obscenity statutes be narrowly tailored to the evils they were intended to control. *Butler v. Michigan*[38] concerned a statute that sought to forbid distribution of sexually explicit material to adults because of its potential harm to minors. Though the material in question was explicit, it was not obscene. In an opinion by Justice Frankfurter, the Court stated:

> The State insists that, by thus quarantining the general reading public against books not too rugged for grown men and women in order to shield juvenile innocence, it is exercising its power to promote the general welfare. Surely, this is to burn the house to roast the pig. . . . We have before us legislation not reasonably restricted to the evil with which it is said to deal. The incidence of this enactment is to reduce the adult population of Michigan to reading only what is fit for children.[39]

What happened after *Roth*?

Perhaps inevitably, the Court found itself serving as the "supercensor" of obscenity in the United States. Ironically, in this role, it reversed most of the obscenity convictions that came before it. Moreover, the very basis for excluding obscenity from constitutional protection—its degree of "social importance" —became the means by which constitutional protection was accorded to an ever broader range of sexually explicit materials. The Court was slowly but surely moving toward narrowing permissible obscenity regulation to "hard-core" pornography. In one case the Court established the important rule against "thematic obscenity."[40] In another, the requirement of "patent offensiveness" was articulated.[41] Then, in *Jacobellis v. Ohio*,[42] Justice Brennan first suggested that the concept of "utterly without redeeming social value," which was initially put forward as the reason to deny constitutional protection, should be the benchmark for determining whether material can constitutionally be prosecuted as obscene.

But the "utterly without redeeming social value" test was not accepted by the majority in *Jacobellis* or in the next important case, *Memoirs v. Massachusetts* (the "Fanny Hill" case).[43] In fact, it was never adopted by a majority of the Supreme Court. It nevertheless became the prevailing standard for judging obscenity until *Miller*. As stated by Justice Brennan in *Memoirs*, for a work to be found obscene it had to be proved that

(a) the dominant theme of the material taken as a whole appeals to a prurient interest;
(b) the material is patently offensive because it affronts contemporary community standards relating to the description or representation of sexual matters; and
(c) the material is utterly without redeeming social value.[44]

After *Memoirs*, fewer and fewer obscenity convictions were obtained in lower courts, and when they were obtained they were often reversed on appeal. The Supreme Court continued to be unable to secure a majority for any one legal definition of obscenity, as it candidly acknowledged in 1967 in *Redrup v. New York*.[45] But the Court continued to accept obscenity cases for review, and for the next six years the Justices decided most obscenity cases by reviewing the material in private, applying their divergent standards, and then, when a majority decided that obscenity could not constitutionally be found, issuing orders summarily reversing convictions without writing opinions. These "*Redrup* summary reversals" were issued in 31 cases between 1967 and 1973.[46]

Two developments during this period further encouraged those who believed—and proclaimed—that the "end of obscenity" was at hand.[47] In a major 1969 case, *Stanley v. Georgia*,[48] the Supreme Court struck down a state law that made it a crime to possess obscene materials. "[A] state has no business," declared Justice Marshall, "telling a man, sitting alone in his own house, what books he may read or what films he may watch. Our whole constitutional heritage rebels at the thought of giving government the power to control men's minds."[49] The Court ruled that this privacy right applied even if the obscenity of the material in question was uncontested. *Stanley* seemed to declare the end of legal censorship and, in fact, for a brief period was so interpreted by several lower courts.[50] If a person has the constitutional right to read and view such materials in his own home, they reasoned, there must also be a right to produce and sell the materials. But until the Supreme Court adopted or rejected this interpretation, no one could be sure.

The second development was the report of a special commission created by Congress in 1967 "to investigate the gravity of [the traffic in obscenity and pornography] and to determine whether such materials are harmful to the public." In its report, issued in 1970, the Commission found "no evidence to date that exposure to explicit sexual materials plays a significant role in the causation of delinquent or criminal behavior among youth or adults," and that it "cannot conclude that exposure to erotic materials is a factor in the causation of sex crime or sex delinquency."[51] One of the Commission's principal recommendations was that "federal, state and local legislation should not seek to interfere with the right of adults who wish to do so to read, obtain or view explicit sexual materials" and that "federal, state and local legislation prohibiting the sale, exhibition, or distribution of sexual materials to consenting adults should be repealed."[52]

What happened in 1973?

In 1973 the Supreme Court managed to render its first majority opinion in an obscenity case since *Roth* in 1957. However, primarily because of significant changes on the Court (by reason of death and retirement), there was no final step toward the abolition of obscenity laws. Instead, the new majority, substantially comprised of Nixon appointees, formulated a new—and to a significant extent more regressive—definition of obscenity. The new standards were announced in a series of cases generally referred to by the name of one of them, *Miller v. California.*[53] With only limited elaboration since, the *Miller* formulation has remained the prevailing legal standard of obscenity.

How did the *Miller* majority justify the continued suppression of obscenity?

The *Miller* majority reiterated *Roth*'s conclusion that obscene materials are not protected by the First Amendment. It endorsed the asserted "legitimate interest in prohibiting dissemination or exhibition of obscene material when the mode of dissemination carries with it a significant danger of offending the sensibilities of unwilling [adult] recipients or of exposure to juveniles.''[54] But it refused to limit the reach of obscenity law to unwilling adults and children. Instead, it found that the states have a strong ''interest . . . in the quality of life and the total community environment. . . . [and in] maintain[ing] a decent society.[55] In addition, it rejected the need for ''conclusive proof of a connection between anti-social behavior and obscene material,''[56] and thus rejected (implicitly) the findings by the President's Commission to the contrary. It held that states could simply ''assume'' such a connection.[57]

The *Miller* majority expressed confidence that its new formulation of obscenity would provide ''sufficiently specific guidelines to isolate 'hard core' pornography from expression protected by the First Amendment,''[58] and thus resolve the problems of vagueness, uncertainty, and overbreadth that had plagued the Court—and the law of obscenity—for many years. Finally, the majority found no justification for ''sound[ing] the alarm of repression'' because of continued enforcement of laws against obscenity. ''[P]ublic portrayal of hard-core sexual conduct for its own sake, and for the ensuing commercial gain,'' cannot be equated with ''the free and robust exchange of ideas and political debate'' that is protected by the First Amendment.[59] ''We do not see the harsh hand of censorship of ideas—good or bad, sound or unsound—and 'repression' of political liberty lurking in every state regulation of commercial exploitation of human interest in sex.''[60]

And with these considerations in mind, the majority proceeded to rewrite the law of obscenity.

What was the position of the dissenting Justices in *Miller*?

Four Justices dissented. Perhaps the most significant opinion was that of Justice Brennan, the author of the majority opinion in *Roth* (which first declared that there was such a thing as obscenity that could constitutionally be suppressed). Brennan admitted the errors of his past:

I am convinced that the approach initiated 16 years ago in *Roth* . . . and culminating in the Court's decision today, cannot bring stability to this area of the law without jeopardizing fundamental First Amendment values. . . .[61]

Emphasizing the inherent vagueness and ambiguity of all definitions of obscenity, Brennan declared that the First Amendment "demand[s] that 'sensitive tools' be used to carry out the 'separation of legitimate from illegitimate speech' " and he "reluctantly . . . conclu[ded] that none of the available formulas [of obscenity], including the one announced today, can reduce the vagueness to a tolerable level.[62] So long as such vagueness exists, obscenity laws fail to provide constitutionally required "notice" to persons potentially affected; invite "arbitrary and erratic [law] enforcement"; and "chill" constitutionally protected expression. Accordingly, Justice Brennan urged that the Court reject the total suppression of obscenity, both to protect fundamental First Amendment interests and to prevent the institutional havoc that had been occasioned by 16 years of disagreement on the Court. He concluded:

> I would hold, therefore, that at least in the absence of distribution to juveniles or obtrusive exposure to unconsenting adults, the First and Fourteenth Amendments prohibit the State and Federal Governments from attempting wholly to suppress sexually oriented materials on the basis of their allegedly "obscene" contents. Nothing in this approach precludes those governments from taking action to serve what may be strong and legitimate interests through regulation of the manner of distribution of sexually oriented material.[63]

But the majority had one more vote than the dissenters.[64]

What are the elements of the current legal definition of obscenity?

As defined by the *Miller* majority, expressive matter—including writings, photographs, art, dramatic works, motion pictures, and even live performances—can only be considered legally obscene, and therefore constitutionally subject to legal action, if such matter meets all the following requirements:

1. It must "depict or describe" certain explicit sexual conduct that has been defined as prohibited in applicable state or federal law.

2. The prohibited sexual depictions or descriptions must be "patently offensive" to an "average" person based upon "contemporary community standards."

3. "Taken as a whole," the material must appeal to the "prurient" interest, again when judged against contemporary community standards.

4. Taken as a whole, the material must also lack "serious" literary, artistic, political, or scientific value.[65]

In formulating these elaborate standards, the majority expressly indicated that only "hard core" pornography may constitutionally be proscribed as obscene.

What does it mean to "depict or describe" certain explicit sexual conduct?

In this first *Miller* guideline, it is not clear what "depict or describe" means in all contexts; but most of the time it should be readily apparent to the author or artist.

Evidently, graphic materials such as paintings, photographs, or motion pictures which present or represent sexual activities "depict" those activities. Moreover, under *Miller*, the depictions need not present "actual" sexual activities but may include "simulated" activities as well. "Simulated" presumably means that the depiction has the appearance of presenting sexual activity which may not actually be taking place.

The parallel concept of "description" makes clear that the Court still considers that words alone can be found to be obscene. Indeed, that was the precise holding of another case decided along with *Miller—Kaplan v. California*.[66]

What sexual activities are included in the Supreme Court's definition of obscenity?

The court provided in *Miller* what it called "a few plain examples" of the "hard core" sexual conduct that a state statute could consider obscene. These examples, which the Court indicated were not exclusive, were:

(a) Patently offensive representations or descriptions of ultimate sexual acts, normal or perverted, actual or simulated.
(b) Patently offensive representations or descriptions of masturbation, excretory functions, and lewd exhibition of the genitals.[67]

One year later, in *Jenkins v. Georgia*,[68] the Court held that mere nudity was not enough to render materials legally obscene and overturned a finding of the Georgia courts that the movie *Carnal Knowledge* was obscene. It also ruled that while the examples of sexual conduct provided in *Miller* "did not purport to be an exhaustive catalogue of what juries might find to be patently offensive . . . [they did] fix substantive constitutional limitations" on the "type of material subject to . . . a determination [of patent offensiveness]."[69]

What constitutes "lewd exhibition of the genitals"?

This is not at all clear. Of the examples provided by the Supreme Court of hard-core sexual conduct that can be considered obscene, "lewd exhibition of the genitals" is the most ambiguous.

It is clear from the *Carnal Knowledge* decision that "mere nudity" is not sufficient to constitute "lewd exhibition," but this does little to clarify what lewd exhibition is. In fact, in the *Carnal Knowledge* case the Court observed that the movie contained "no exhibition whatever of the actors' genitals, nude or otherwise."[70] Perhaps all that can confidently be concluded is that lewd exhibition is something more than mere nudity and less than sexual activity.

A leading commentator has provided what may be the best brief explanation of the distinction between mere nudity and lewd exhibition of the genitals, to the extent that any single statement can make sense of inherently subjective and hazy judgments:

"[L]ewd exhibition of the genitals" . . . should be interpreted to include photographs which focus on,

159

exaggerate, or emphasize the genitalia or "erogenous zones." It is this exaggeration or "highlight" on the genitalia which often distinguishes hard-core pornography from mere nudity. Similarly, hard-core pornography often emphasizes suggestive poses or lewdly intertwined bodies, even in the absence of actual sexual activity.[71]

Perhaps because "lewd exhibition of the genitals" is one of the most open-ended *Miller* guidelines, the Court, in its most recent statement on the matter, emphasized the need to limit the definition. In discussing the possible "overbreadth" of a New York child pornography statute which contained a "lewd exhibition" provision, the Court recognized the potential ambiguity and "impermissible application" of the statute, stating:

Nor will we assume that the New York courts will widen the possibly invalid reach of the statute by giving an expansive construction to the proscription on "lewd exhibition[s] of the genitals."[72]

How is "patent offensiveness" defined?

This standard, too, is inherently ambiguous and subjective. According to one observer, it is basically designed to ask the question "Does this material go too far?" Does it go beyond "the current level of society's acceptance of sexual depictions or descriptions"?[73]

The courts offer little guidance; as a result, judging patent offensiveness is often left to the trier of fact—the jury or, where there is no jury, the judge—which must determine, based upon its understanding of the "average" person's views, applying contemporary community standards, whether the material in question is patently offensive. It may, but need not, consider objective evidence on community standards. Its findings are subject to appellate review, but the scope of the review may be limited by the subjectivity of the issue.

Perhaps the best understanding of patent offensiveness is provided by the cases, decided before *Miller*, in which the concept developed. According to Schauer, the Model Penal Code in 1962 introduced the concept of patent offensiveness as a requirement for obscenity.[74] The Code required that in addition to appeal to the prurient interest, the material had also to "go . . . substantially beyond customary limits of candor" in describing or depicting certain sexual activities. The same year, Supreme Court Justice Harlan referred approvingly to this "patent offensiveness" test and indicated that it required "affront" to "current community standards of decency."[75] Still later, a plurality in another Supreme Court case recognized and approved the Model Penal Code language and characterized it as requiring "a deviation from society's standards of decency."[76] Finally (before *Miller*), patent offensiveness was incorporated as the second of three elements of obscenity set forth by the plurality opinion in *Memoirs v. Massachusetts,* requiring proof that "the material is patently offensive because it affronts contemporary community standards relating to the description or representation of sexual matters."[77]

What is the meaning of "prurient interest"?

This requirement did not originate with *Miller*; the Court first used it in *Roth,* where it gave only dictionary definitions to explain what it considered to be prurient.[78] Unfortunately, these definitions include two inconsistent views of prurient appeal. The first requires an appeal to "shameful," "morbid," or "abnormal" interest in sex, while the second merely requires an appeal to sexual response, lust, or desire. According to a leading commentator, it is probably the second definition that the Supreme Court has in mind,[79] although many courts have disagreed on the question.

Who is the "average" person who is to judge patent offensiveness and prurient appeal?

The purpose of this requirement is to assure, as far as possible, that neither deviant nor overly sensitive or insensitive standards are brought to bear in judging obscenity.[80] The average person test is a rejection of earlier legal standards that sought to protect the most sensitive members of the community—children and "weak-willed" adults.[81] These standards have been decisively rejected in American obscenity law, which now requires that the standard be based upon the reactions of an average *adult*.[82] As for materials intended for so-called deviant groups—for example, sado-masochists, flagellists, or fetishists—it has been held that the average person test must be modified to consider whether the materials appeal to the prurient interest of the groups for which they were intended.[83]

How are the contemporary standards of the local community to be defined and applied?

When the concept of contemporary community standards was first recognized by the Supreme Court in 1957,[84] it liberalized obscenity law, in effect, by permitting courts and juries to consider the increasing sexual tolerance in the community at large rather than looking to some fixed (and presumably more regressive) legal concept of obscenity. Application of community standards recognizes the possibility of change and reflects a desire to locate an external standard rather than to rely solely on the personal judgments of the jury or judge. These are admirable ideals, but in practice it has proved difficult to define community standards, either geographically or substantively.

The geographical debate has focused on national versus local standards. In the first important case to consider the issue a national standard was proposed, but only for federal obscenity cases.[85] Then, in 1964, Justice Brennan proposed a national standard for all obscenity cases.[86] To allow a local standard, he argued, would create inconsistent standards that would chill free distribution of material nationwide. "It is, after all a national Constitution we are expounding."[87] The proposed national standard was never adopted by a majority of the Court; nonetheless, national standards were generally applied by the lower courts.[88]

Miller decisively rejected national standards in favor of the standards of the local community:

> It is neither realistic nor constitutionally sound to read the First Amendment as requiring that the people of Maine or Mississippi accept public depiction of conduct found tolerable in Las Vegas, or New York City.[89]

162

The Court also disagreed with the idea that local standards would necessarily be more repressive than national ones. The majority viewed the test as something of a trade-off: some local communities might be more restrictive, but a national standard might prevent those in more liberal communities from receiving materials they would have deemed acceptable.[90]

Most observers agree, however, that the potential dangers of a national community standard are hypothetical, while there is a real possibility that local standards will lead to inconsistent and unpredictable results and a tendency on the part of authors, artists, and their publishers and producers to distribute only what is acceptable to the more repressive communities.

Miller expressly requires that local community standards be applied in deciding the question of appeal to the prurient interest, but the Court did not expressly attach the community standards requirement to the question of patent offensiveness. There seems no reason, however, to conclude that *Miller* intended to preclude such an attachment. Indeed, as one commentator has put it, ''if anything, patent offensiveness is more susceptible to temporal and geographic variations than is prurient interest.''[91] In contrast, local community standards are clearly not to be applied to the question of serious literary value, which has consistently been held a question of law to be considered by the courts.[92]

What is the significance of the "serious value" test?

It remains the most effective protection for the author or artist who deals with sexual subjects. Even if a work is found to arouse prurient interest and to be patently offensive, the author or artist cannot be found guilty of obscenity unless it is also established that the material, taken as a whole, ''lacks serious literary, artistic, political or scientific value.''[93] This standard, unlike the others, is not left to the jury, but is to be decided by courts as a matter of law or ''constitutional fact.''[94]

It is difficult, again, to describe precisely what constitutes serious value, but it is clear that under *Miller* the amount of value must be greater, ''more predominant, more serious, and more pervasive throughout the entire work'' than under the earlier "utterly without" requirement. A more careful examination of the work as a whole will now be required. As has been observed:

> What the addition of the "serious" element does is to allow the jury and the court to look beneath the argued or claimed value of the material to the relationship between the nonpornographic and the pornographic, and to the *intent* upon which the insertion of literary, artistic, political, or scientific material is based. If that intent is to convey a literary, artistic, political, or scientific idea or message, or to impart information, or advocate a position, then the purpose or intent is "serious" as the word appears to be used in *Miller*. If, on the other hand, it appears or is found that the purpose is to "dress up" or try to "redeem" otherwise obscene matter, sold or distributed for its obscenity rather than for its ideas or message, then the value is not "serious."[95]

Has the serious value standard lowered the obscenity threshold to the point where legitimate works by serious authors and artists will be threatened? The answer is probably no. Obscenity prosecutions against even arguably serious works are rare now, although they do occur. The few cases since *Miller* have reached inconsistent results, and do not form a basis for final conclusions. For example, a Louisiana case held that an issue of *Penthouse* did not lack serious value where 67 pages of the magazine contained "articles with serious value" while another 96 pages contained articles lacking serious value.[96] But a federal appellate court found that similar issues of *Penthouse* and *Oui* magazines were obscene: "The issue . . . is close but the numerous pictorials and obscene letters were not saved by articles possessing some literary merit."[97] Two recent cases found that the movie *Caligula*, although explicit and offensive, did not lack serious political or artistic value.[98]

What is the significance of the requirement that to be found obscene, a work must be "taken as a whole"?

The Supreme Court made this requirement explicit in the

Roth case.[99] *Miller* continued the requirement for the "serious value" and "prurient appeal" standards. It is important that an isolated passage, or picture, in an otherwise serious work cannot be taken out of context and viewed separately with the result of finding the work obscene. On the other hand, the courts have developed a rule that prevents a minimal or unrelated addition of material from "redeeming" a work that is otherwise obscene. As the Supreme Court put it in a memorable passage: "A quotation from Voltaire in the flyleaf of a book will not constitutionally redeem an otherwise obscene publication. . . ."[100] The whole-work rule tends to ensure that a careful evaluation of the literary, scientific, political, or artistic purpose and overall theme of a work will be made.

What "criminal state of mind" is required in obscenity cases?

Most criminal laws in this country require proof of some degree of criminal or evil intent (*mens rea* or *scienter*).[101] It is obviously important whether the prosecution in an obscenity case has to prove that the defendant has specific knowledge that the materials complained of are legally obscene. If no such proof is required, the possibility of an obscenity conviction could substantially deter the publication and dissemination of perfectly legal materials. The Supreme Court has held that some degree of criminal knowledge must be proved in order to establish an obscenity offense. In the leading case, *Smith v. California*,[102] the Court found unconstitutional a Los Angeles ordinance that made it a crime for a bookseller to have obscene books in his bookstore. The ordinance had no *scienter* requirement and would have imposed "strict liability" on the bookseller. The Supreme Court held that strict criminal liability is unconstitutional where First Amendment rights are involved. The Court failed in *Smith* to define how much criminal knowledge the Constitution requires. But it has become clear since that some general knowledge of the nature and character of the materials is all that is required and that it need not be proved that the defendant knew or believed the materials were legally obscene.[103] Unlike a bookseller, who may never have read or even glanced at many of the books in his store, the author or artist is obviously fully aware of the content of his or her work. Thus the current *scienter* requirements provide little protection to authors and artists who deal with sexual subjects.

What is "pandering"?

"Pandering" is a legal doctrine created by the Supreme Court. It permits material to be found obscene, although its contents might not otherwise so qualify, because of the manner in which it is sold to the public.[104] Evidence that the advertising or marketing of materials stresses their sexually provocative aspects can be considered in deciding whether the materials are obscene, especially if the issue of obscenity is "close." But materials that are clearly not obscene cannot be transformed into obscene materials, no matter how blatant the pandering.[105]

Authors and artists are usually not in a position to influence advertising and marketing decisions that may ultimately become evidence of pandering; most publishing contracts and customary publishing practice leave these decisions to the publisher. Still, authors and artists of explicit materials that might be considered obscene should at least attempt to obtain some control over advertising or marketing as a protection against potential charges of "pandering."

Are there special rules that apply to the distribution of sexual materials to children?

Yes, many. The definitions of obscenity discussed so far apply to the dissemination of obscene materials to the general (and predominantly adult) public. The author or artist whose materials are intended for or may be distributed to children should be familiar with the special legal standards that apply to the distribution of sexually explicit materials to children.

When the prevailing definition of obscenity looked to the reactions of the "peculiarly susceptible," there was no need for special concern for children. But when the law moved to the "average person" test, children became a matter of considerable legal concern. In *Ginsberg v. New York*[106] the Supreme Court expressly approved the concept of "variable obscenity," upholding New York's "harmful to minors" statute. Materials that would not be obscene for adults—and therefore are constitutionally protected if distributed to them—can be obscene if exposed to children. Since *Miller*, to be obscene for children a work must be patently offensive *for minors*, appeal to the prurient interests *of minors*, and lack serious value *for minors*.[107]

The standard for obscenity is changed, but other procedural protections related to obscenity remain.[108] The Supreme Court has not squarely considered the variable obscenity doctrine since *Miller*, and at least one commentator has expressed doubt that the concept can survive *Miller*'s strict focus on "hard core" materials as the only permissible subject matter for obscenity laws.[109] However, parallel developments since *Miller* strongly suggest that the Supreme Court as now constituted will continue to uphold rules specially devised to protect children, whether or not the rules are logically supportable under *Miller*.[110]

What is "child pornography" and how does it relate to the general rules of obscenity?

The purpose of so called "child pornography" laws is not to limit the dissemination of materials *to* children, which is covered by "harmful to minors" laws, but to prevent the use *of* children in the production of pornographic materials. Thus child pornography is sexually explicit material that displays children engaging in actual (or simulated) sexual activities.[111]

Child pornography laws attempt to proscribe such materials in two ways. First, they impose heavy criminal penalties for the use of children in the creation of sexually explicit (but not necessarily obscene) materials; it has not seriously been argued that such "use" laws violate First Amendment rights. The second way presents far more serious First Amendment concerns by making it a crime simply to publish or sell such materials, even if the publisher or seller had nothing to do with their production and even if the materials are admittedly not obscene.

In 1981 New York's highest court held that a New York statute that made it a crime to sell such non-obscene materials was unconstitutional.[112] But in 1982 the Supreme Court reversed the ruling and held that child pornography materials need not be legally obscene to be constitutionally suppressed.[113] In doing so, the Court expressly created a new exception to First Amendment protection for such non-obscene materials, an exception which does not require the application of the *Miller* standards. It is beyond the scope of this chapter to discuss this at length, but it seems appropriate to note that the Supreme Court has limited the child pornography exception to visual depictions of actual or simulated sexual activity actually being performed by children. Written material, and visual work not based on actual activity by a minor, are not covered by these laws. To the extent that authors and artists do not deal with such matters, they should not be affected by the new exception. However, it is also clear that such laws can affect works of serious value. [114]

What are "minors access" and "minors display" laws?

The desire to protect children is also manifested in laws designed to prevent children from being exposed to or having access to sexual (but not necessarily obscene) materials. Some of these laws make it a crime to sell sexually explicit materials in stores open to children unless the material is in some way bagged, stapled, or otherwise sealed. [115] Other laws require that the materials be kept out of the reach of children. [116] However phrased, they almost inevitably restrict adult access to materials that are seemingly entitled to the full protection of the First Amendment. They also result in a substantial impairment of the First Amendment rights of children.

The constitutionality of these laws has been tested by publishers, booksellers, and distributors. Although the Supreme Court has not yet considered the issue, three "display" or "access" statutes have been struck down as unconstitutional by lower courts. [117] A Georgia display law was invalidated because it prevented the perusal by and limited the sale of constitutionally protected material to adults. [118] Protecting minors was held to be an inadequate justification for such severe interference with adults' First Amendment rights. A Colorado display statute was invalidated because the court concluded that channels for the interchange of literary, political, artistic, and scientific ideas about sex were effectively closed by the statute and that its enforcement would regulate to a commercially unfeasible degree the activities of responsible members of the community. [119] Likewise a California court invalidated a display ordinance which required that commercial establishments seal magazines or books containing sexually explicit but non-obscene pictures, keep them out of the reach of minors, or else bar minors from entering the stores.[120] The ordinance would have affected display in drugstores, grocery stores, and newsstands in addition to "adult" bookstores. The court held that the sealing requirement infringed the freedom of adults to browse and that the entire impact of the statute denied children access to material which they had "an unfettered constitutional right to enjoy."[121] "Whether accompanied by parents or not," stated the court, minors "cannot be denied access to retail establishments which sell a wide variety of literature, or the necessities of life, simply because such establishments also sell some materials sought to be restricted."[122]

How do obscenity laws affect television?

For several reasons, especially industry self-regulation, obscenity laws have rarely if ever had to be applied to traditional radio and television programming.[123] The advent of more explicit programming, to some extent on regular broadcast channels but especially on cable television, has changed this. Because of its unprecedented frankness in dealing with sexual matters, cable TV has emerged as one of the most heated battlegrounds of free expression. The legal issues are complex and volatile, involving not only how cable systems ought to be treated for regulatory purposes but also the proper standards, if any, that should govern the censorship of cable programming. The question of who should define and enforce such regulations is also quite controversial.

Over-the-air broadcasters are subject to licensing and extensive regulation by the Federal Communications Commission; this regulation has been held not to violate the First Amendment rights of broadcasters, although similar government control over other media would be unconstitutional.[124] A dramatic example of the extent of such regulation is the Supreme Court's decision in *FCC v. Pacifica Foundation*.[125] The FCC had imposed sanctions on a radio station that aired a comedic monologue by George Carlin of "words you can't say on the public airwaves." Carlin's routine was clearly not obscene; in fact, it did not describe sexual activities. But even though vulgar language had previously been held not to qualify as obscenity,[126] a divided Supreme Court upheld the FCC's sanctions against such "indecent" language.[127] In so doing, the Court distinguished the standards applicable to broadcasting from those for other media because broadcasting is a "uniquely pervasive" medium that can intrude into the privacy of the home and be readily accessible to children.[128]

It is not yet clear whether extensive regulation of cable television is permissible, as it is of broadcasting. Those who support a maximum of censorship over cable TV say yes. Others argue that cable is distinct technologically and in practice, especially since there is none of the "spectrum scarcity" that has traditionally justified broadcasting regulation. Moreover, cable subscribers must choose to subscribe, and some systems offer devices to prevent access by children without parental supervision. Thus, it is argued, cable is more like a newspaper than over-the-air broadcasting and should be accorded the fullest possible First Amendment protection from governmental supervision and control.[129]

In an important recent commercial pay TV case a court held that cable should receive a higher degree of First Amendment protection then over-the-air broadcasting and declared unconstitutional a Utah statute that made it a crime to transmit "pornographic" or "indecent" material via cable.[130] The court found that the Utah statute failed to meet the *Miller* standards for obscenity and that it could be applied to such serious and non-obscene movies as *The Godfather, Being There, Annie Hall,* and *Coming Home.* It rejected the argument that "indecency" on cable should be treated like "indecency" on television or radio. As the court noted, "[T]here is no law that says you have to subscribe to a cable TV service any more than you have to subscribe to *The Salt Lake Tribune.*"[131] Whether this precedent will be accepted in other pay television cases remains to be seen.

Public access programming on cable presents even more complicated First Amendment issues. Since a Supreme Court ruling that invalidated some federal cable regulations,[132] it is unclear whether and to what extent federal, state, or local agencies have control over cable television. Some states and localities prohibit cable systems from censoring public access programs;[133] but at least some cable companies support legislation that would permit them to censor non-obscene programming on public access channels[134] and many companies have attempted to impose their own systems of censorship, by, for example, inserting restrictive "indecency and obscenity" clauses in contracts with their public access producers.[135]

What is involved in the zoning of sexual materials?

In 1976 a narrowly divided Supreme Court upheld a Detroit zoning scheme that sought to "disperse" bookstores and theaters that specialized in sexually explicit—but not necessarily obscene—materials.[136] The Court's plurality opinion declared:

> Even though the First Amendment protects communication in this area from total suppression, we hold that the State may legitimately use the content of these materials as the basis for placing them in a different classification from other motion pictures.[137]

However, a 1980 decision of the Court casts serious doubt on the future impact of the Detroit decision. In *Schad v. Borough of Mount Ephraim*[138] the Court invalidated a local ordinance that prohibited "live entertainment (including nude dancing) in any establishment." With reference to the zoning issue, the Court flatly declared that

> when a zoning law infringes upon a protected liberty, it must be narrowly drawn and must further a sufficiently substantial government interest.

The Court found that the borough's blanket prohibition of entertainment, by failing this test, violated the First Amendment.

Besides the First Amendment, are there other constitutional limitations on laws addressed to obscenity?

Yes. The fact that speech found to be obscene is not protected by the First Amendment does not mean that it can be regulated or suppressed in disregard of other constitutional protections. Indeed, a legal doctrine sometimes called "First Amendment due process" has been developed to ensure that obscenity cases are handled with special deference to the First Amendment values that are always implicated in them.[139]

Criminal obscenity laws are not the only means government has available to deal with obscenity. Civil proceedings are also available. One such proceeding is a civil action that enables the state to seek a judicial determination that a work is obscene and an order enjoining its distribution and sale, with criminal action possible if it is disseminated in violation of the injunction.[140] The government remains able to censor obscenity, while the individuals who handle such material are not confronted with the potentially drastic consequences of a criminal prosecution. To this extent, "prior civil proceedings" can be seen as being protective of First Amendment rights. Many states have enacted legislation providing for prior civil proceedings, either voluntary or mandatory.[141]

Such civil proceedings are fraught with their own special perils, however. A civil judgment of obscenity can result, as has just been discussed, in subsequent criminal penalties. Moreover, civil actions result in prior restraints against the exercise of free expression. Prior restraints have traditionally been considered the most serious abridgments of First Amendment rights.[142] Civil judgments may also lead to the confiscation and forfeiture of valuable property. Because of these potentially severe penalties, several recent cases make clear the necessity for stringent procedural safeguards.[143]

Prior restraints (injunctions) against publication are very rare. They are permitted in connection with obscenity only because obscene matter is not considered entitled to the protection of the First Amendment. But because non-obscene expression is so protected, careful procedures are constitutionally required before a prior restraint can be issued against obscenity. The leading case is *Freedman v. Maryland*.[144] By the 1960s Maryland was one of the few states to still maintain a motion picture licensing and censorship board. Although the Court in *Freedman* did not rule that such boards were prohibited by the First Amendment, it did declare that "any system of prior restraints of expression comes to this Court bearing a heavy presumption against its constitutional validity."[145] The Supreme Court struck down the Maryland system and listed the minimum procedural safeguards that an obscenity censorship statute must contain in order to comport with the First Amendment:

'Where the transcendent value of speech is involved, due process certainly requires . . . that the State bear the burden of persuasion to show 'that the appellants engaged in criminal speech.' Second, while the State may require advance submission of films, in order to proceed effectively to bar all showings of all unprotected films, the requirement cannot be administered in a manner which would lend an effect of finality to the censor's determination. . . . [B]ecause only a judicial determination in an adversary proceeding ensures the necessary sensitivity to freedom of expression, only a procedure requiring a judicial determination suffices to impose a valid final restraint. To this end, the exhibitor must be assured, by statute or authoritative judicial construction, that the censor will, within a specified brief period, either issue a license or go to court to restrain showing the film. Any restraint imposed in advance of a final judicial determination on the merits must similarly be limited to preservation of the status quo for the shortest fixed period compatible with sound judicial resolution. . . . [T]he procedure must also assure a prompt final judicial decision, to minimize the deterrent effect of an interim and possibly erroneous denial of a license.[146]

The procedural requirements outlined in the *Freedman* case have had far-reaching implications for obscenity law. The absence of such procedures led to the invalidation of a federal postal statute which authorized refusal to deliver mail based on a non-judicial determination of obscenity,[147] as well as state statutes which allowed materials to be seized before judicial proceedings had determined their obscenity.[148] And in 1975 a municipality was held to have unconstitutionally restrained a production of the musical *Hair* because of a procedure that lacked the *Freedman* protections.[149]

In 1976 the Supreme Court considered for the first time the validity of a state's prior civil obscenity proceeding, and it held Alabama's civil action format to be inadequate.[150] An Alabama civil court had determined that a publication was obscene. Thereafter one McKinney—who had no notice of the earlier proceeding—was convicted for selling the publication. When he tried to challenge the determination of obscenity during his criminal trial, the issue was held foreclosed on the basis of the prior civil action. The Supreme Court overturned McKinney's conviction, stating that since he had no notice of the prior proceeding and no opportunity to participate in it or challenge its findings, he should be allowed to have the issue of obscenity fully reconsidered at his trial.[151] In his concurring opinion, Justice Brennan pointed out other difficulties inherent in civil obscenity proceedings, and noted that because of the precious First Amendment values at stake a civil obscenity proceeding should require a stricter standard of proof than the ordinary civil standard of "preponderance of the evidence." "[T]he hazards to First Amendment freedoms inhering in the regulation of obscenity," he stated, require that the state "comply with the more exacting standard of proof beyond a reasonable doubt."[152] Unfortunately, Justice Brennan's position was recently rejected by the Supreme Court, which held that proof beyond a reasonable doubt is not required in a civil obscenity action.[153] The Court did not specifically indicate whether an intermediate standard such as proof by "clear and convincing evidence" would be required, but seemed strongly to suggest that the states were free to chose any burden of proof standard in a civil action, including mere preponderance of the evidence.[154]

What are "nuisance abatement" or "padlock" laws and how do they comport with First Amendment due process requirements?

One of the most recent and most significant developments in civil obscenity law has been the enactment of "nuisance abatement" or "padlock" laws in many cities and states.[15] These statutes invoke a civil court's power to impose unique, far-reaching civil penalties on persons found to be in violation of its injunctions. Relying on traditional civil laws pertaining to "public nuisances," several states have attempted to authorize "abatement" injunctions that operate not only against materials found to be obscene but against the premises where they were made or sold. A civil nuisance action can result, for example, in

174

the suppression of obscene books and the closing of a bookstore that carries them. Although this would seem to violate the First Amendment, the Supreme Court has declined expressly to so hold, choosing to sidestep the broad constitutional issues and to review the statutes in light of the procedural requirements in *Freedman v. Maryland*.

In 1980, in *Vance v. Universal Amusement Co., Inc.*,[156] two Texas nuisance statutes were applied to locations found to have been distributing obscene materials or showing obscene films. One statute authorized the mandatory closing of the premises for one year; the other authorized the granting of injunctions prohibiting the future commercial manufacturing, distribution, or exhibition of obscene material. The Supreme Court held that the injunction statute violated the Consitution but it avoided reviewing the premises-closing statute, since the lower court had held it inapplicable to obscenity cases.[157] The Court was clearly concerned with the issue of procedure. With respect to the injunction statute, the Court recognized

(a) that the regulation of a communicative activity such as the exhibition of motion pictures must adhere to more narrowly drawn procedures than is necessary for the abatement of an ordinary nuisance, and (b) that the burden of supporting an injunction against a future exhibition is even heavier than the burden of justifying the imposition of a criminal sanction for a past communication.[158]

The Court did provide a strong indication that it had significant concerns about the broader First Amendment issues, stating in an important footnote:

Any system of prior restraint . . . "comes to this Court bearing a heavy presumption against its constitutional validity". . . . The presumption against prior restraints is heavier—and the degree of protection broader—than that against limits on expression imposed by criminal penalties. Behind the distinction is a theory deeply etched in our law: a free society prefers to punish the few who abuse rights of speech *after* they break the law than to throttle them and all others beforehand. It is always difficult to know in advance what an individual will say, and the line between legitimate and illegitimate speech is often so finely drawn that the risks of freewheeling censorship are formidable.[159]

As for the procedural improprieties in the Texas statute, the Court noted that it authorized prior restraints of indefinite duration on material that had not been finally found to be obscene. "Presumably," the Court declared, "an exhibitor would be required to obey such an order pending review of its merits and would be subject to contempt proceedings even if the film is ultimately found to be nonobscene. Such prior restraints would be more onerous and more objectionable than the threat of criminal sanctions after a film has been exhibited, since nonobscenity would be a defense to any criminal prosecution."[160]

In 1981 the Supreme Court, in *Brockett v. Spokane Arcades, Inc.*,[161] affirmed a decision by the U.S. Court of Appeals for the Ninth Circuit that invalidated a Washington State nuisance statute similar to the one in the *Vance* case.[162] But the Court acted without an opinion and its decision therefore does not represent a final statement by the Court on the substantive issues.

The nuisance abatement issue was again before the Supreme Court in 1982 in *United States Marketing, Inc. v. Idaho*,[163] but the appeal was withdrawn before the Court had a chance to consider it. The constitutional guidelines remain to be determined.

NOTES

1. Countless books, monographs, treatises, articles, and other writings deal with obscenity, and many of them discuss the impact on obscenity laws upon freedom of expression. Particularly useful and influential are two works by Prof. Thomas Emerson, *The System of Freedom of Expression* 467–515, Vintage, 1970 and "First Amendment Doctrine and the Burger Court," 68 *Calif. L. Rev.* 422 (1980); *see also* L. Tribe, *American Constitutional Law* 656–70, Foundation Press, 1978 (this leading general constitutional treatise is widely cited and provides a useful although brief treatment highly critical of the

Supreme Court's failure to recognize First Amendment rights in the field of obscenity).

2. According to the *Random House College Dictionary* (1972 ed.) the meaning of "obscenity" is: "1—That which is offensive to modesty or decency; lewd. 2—That which causes or intends to cause sexual excitement or lust. 3—That which is abominable or disgusting; repulsive: 'an obscene exhibition of public discourtesy.' " The definition of "pornography" is: "Obscene literature, art or photography, esp. that having little or no artistic merit."

3. The classic statement summarily excluding obscenity—and certain other categories of expression—from First Amendment coverage appears in *Chaplinsky v. New Hampshire*, 315 U.S. 568, 571–72 (1942): "There are certain well-defined and narrowly limited classes of speech, the prevention and punishment of which have never been thought to raise any Constitutional problem. These include the lewd and obscene, the profane, the libelous, and the insulting or 'fighting' words. . . . It has been well observed that such utterances are no essential part of any exposition of ideas, and are of such slight social value as a step to truth that any benefit that may be derived from them is clearly outweighed by the social interest in order and morality." *See also Beauharnais v. Illinois*, 343 U.S. 250 (1952) (libel not covered by First Amendment).

4. *United States v. Reidel*, 402 U.S. 351 (1971); *United States v. Thirty-Seven (37) Photographs*, 402 U.S. 363 (1971).

5. *Stanley v. Georgia*, 394 U.S. 557 (1969); *see* pp. 154-55.

6. *See, e.g., Carey v. Population Services International*, 431 U.S. 678 (1977), which held that a New York statute prohibiting advertising of contraceptives violated the First Amendment. The Supreme Court expressly rejected a contention that the advertisements could be prohibited as being offensive or embarrassing, "at least where obscenity is not involved." The Court appeared to require a consideration of the obscenity of the advertisement and not of the material or transaction being promoted.

7. *See* pp. 166-69.

8. *See* pp. 167-68.

9. Each kind of civil obscenity law is discussed later in the chapter: padlock laws, pp. 174-76; injunctions ("prior restraints"), movie licensing, prior civil proceedings, pp. 172-74; access and display laws, pp. 168-69; zoning, p. 171.

10. Present legal limits on state and local power are reviewed later in the chapter in connection with *Miller v. California*, 413 U.S. 15 (1973), and related Supreme Court decisions.

11. *See* pp. 162-63.

12. State and local laws can vary, sometimes significantly, in their reach and severity and are constantly revised and reinterpreted, although they

must adhere to the constitutional limits defined by the Supreme Court. The Media Coalition, an umbrella group which monitors obscenity law developments, maintains an up-to-date collection of state and local laws. Call Christopher Finan, co-ordinator of the Coalition, at (212) 687-2288 or Michael Bamberger, the Coalition's general counsel. Or write to: Media Coalition, 425 Park Ave., New York, NY 10022.

13. *Joseph Burstyn, Inc., v. Wilson,* 343 U.S. 495 (1952). This was a First Amendment ruling, but the court's rationale focused on the religious freedom clause of the First Amendment: "It is not the business of government in our nation to suppress real or imagined attacks upon a particular religious doctrine whether they appear in publications, speeches, or motion pictures." *Id.* at 505.

14. *Kinglsey International Pictures Corp. v. Regents,* 360 U.S. 684 (1959).

15. *Id.* at 688–89.

16. For a brief review of the historical origins of American obscenity law see generally Schauer, *The Law of Obscenity* 1–29, BNA, 1976 [hereinafter Schauer], and historical materials cited in Schauer at 2 n. 3. This is by far the most useful, authoritative one-volume text on the law of obscenity. The authors gratefully acknowledge their debt to Schauer's fine work, which is cited throughout this chapter. *See also Report of the President's Commission on Obscenity and Pornography,* New York Times ed., 1970 [hereinafter *President's Commission Report*] at 348–54. Although the recommendations of the *President's Commission Report* (which was accompanied by nine volumes of Technical Reports) have been largely ignored if not expressly rejected (*infra* n. 51, 57), it remains a great source of information on obscenity.

17. For example, the first case to reach the law courts (rather than church tribunals) refused to recognize obscenity as a common law rather than religious crime. *Queen v. Read,* 11 Mod. Rep. 142, 88 Eng. Rep. 953 (1708).

18. The Vagrancy Act of 1824.

19. See Schauer at 6–7; *President's Commission Report* at 351.

20. *President's Commission Report* at 352.

21. *Commonwealth v. Holmes;* 17 Mass. 336 (1821) (assumed obscene libel was a common law misdemeanor and upheld a conviction for publishing an edition of *Fanny Hill*).

22. *See* Hentoff, *The First Freedom: The Tumultuous History of Free Speech in America* 55–76, Delacorte, 1980.

23. The First Amendment states as follows: "Congress shall make no law respecting an establishment of religion, or prohibiting the free exercise thereof; or abridging the freedom of speech, or of the press; or the right of the people peacably to assemble, and to petition the government for a redress of grievances."

24. Laws of Vermont, 1824, Chapter XXIII, No. 1, §23.

25. 5 Stat. 566, §28.
26. 13 Stat. 50 (1865).
27. 7 N.Y. Stats. 309 (1868).
28. 17 Stat. 598 (1873) (prohibiting the mailing of obscene publications), currently 18 U.S.C. §1461, still popularly known as the Comstock Act. A later statute extended the scope of federal jurisdiction over obscenity to any matter traveling through or via "interstate commerce." 29 Stat. 512 (1897), currently 18 U.S.C. §1462.
29. [1868] L.R. 3 Q.B. 360.
30. *United States v. One Book Called "Ulysses,"* 5 F.Supp. 182 (S.D. N.Y. 1933).
31. *People v. Dial Press,* 182 Misc. 416 (Magis.Ct. 1944).
32. *Commonwealth v. Friede,* 271 Mass. 318, 171 N.E. 472 (1930).
33. *Attorney General v. Book Named "God's Little Acre,"* 326 Mass. 281, 93 N.E. 2d 819 (1950).
34. *United States v. Two Obscene Books,* 99 F.Supp. 760 (N.D. Cal. 1951), *aff'd sub nom. Besig v. United States,* 208 F.2d 142 (9th Cir. 1953).
35. 354 U.S. 476 (1957).
36. *Id.* at 484.
37. *Id.* at 508–14.
38. 352 U.S. 380 (1957).
39. *Id.* at 383.
40. *Kingsley International Pictures Corp. v. Regents,* 360 U.S. 684 (1959).
41. *Manual Enterprises v. Day,* 370 U.S. 478 (1962).
42. 378 U.S. 184 (1964).
43. 383 U.S. 413 (1966).
44. *Id.* at 418.
45. 386 U.S. 767 (1967).
46. *See Miller v. California,* 413 U.S. 15, 22 n. 3 (1973).
47. *See, e.g.,* Note, "Obscenity from *Stanley* to *Karalexis:* A Back Door Approach to First Amendment Protection," 23 *Vand. L. Rev.* 369 (1970); Katz, "Privacy and Pornography," 1969 *Sup. Ct. Rev.* 203 (1969); Comment, *"Stanley v. Georgia:* New Directions in Obscenity Regulation," 48 *Tex. L. Rev.* 646 (1970); "The Supreme Court, 1968 Term," 83 *Harv. L. Rev.* 7, 147 (1969).
48. 394 U.S. 557 (1969).
49. 394 U.S. at 565. Although there was no dissent in *Stanley,* there was no majority opinion. Justice Marshall's opinion announced the court's judgment and was based upon constitutional protection for "mere private possession of obscene matter," *id.* at 559, with strong First Amendment overtones as well. Justices Stewart, Brennan, and White believed the conviction should be overturned because of an illegal search and seizure and did not join Justice Marshall in deciding the other constitutional issues. Justice Black adhered to his position that all obscenity laws are constitutionally impermissible under the First Amendment.

50. *See, e.g., Karalexis v. Byrne*, 306 F.Supp. 1363 (D. Mass. 1969) (principles of *Stanley* applied to theaters open only to "consenting adults"), *vacated and remanded*, 401 U.S. 216 (1971); *United States v. Thirty-Seven Photographs*, 309 F.Supp. 36 (C.D. Cal. 1970) (principles of *Stanley* applied to importation for personal use), *reversed*, 402 U.S. 363 (1971).

51. *See President's Commission Report* at 32, 59; *see generally* 169–309. These findings have been widely criticized, primarily by those wishing to justify continued enforcement or enactment of obscenity laws. *See, e.g., President's Commission Report* 456–505; 578–623 (dissenting Report of Commissioners Hill, Link, and Keating).

52. *President's Commission Report* at 57.

53. 413 U.S. 15 (1973).

54. *Id.* at 18–19.

55. *Paris Adult Theatre I v. Slaton*, 413 U.S. 49, 58–60 (1973).

56. *Id.* at 60–61.

57. Incredibly, the majority's only citation to the *President's Commission Report* was to the Hill-Link minority report. *Paris Adult Theatre I, supra* at 58 nn. 7–8.

58. *Miller, supra* at 27.

59. *Id.* at 34, 35.

60. *Id.* at 35–36.

61. *Paris Adult Theatre I, supra* at 73.

62. *Id.* at 79, 84.

63. *Id.* at 113.

64. Because the new majority was a narrow one, the game of head-counting became essential in obscenity cases after *Miller*. *Miller* was decided by a 5 to 4 vote, but this one-vote margin has held firm for a decade. Between *Memoirs v. Massachusetts* in 1966 and *Miller v. California* in 1973, five of nine Justices were replaced. Of the six Justices who supported reversal of the obscenity judgment against *Fanny Hill* in *Memoirs* (Black, Warren, Fortas, Brennan, Douglas, and Stewart) only the last three remained. Of the three dissenters in *Memoirs* (Clark, Harlan, and White) only Justice White remained. Four of the five replacement Justices favored continued regulation of obscenity. These four (Chief Justice Burger and Justices Blackmun, Powell, and Rehnquist—all Nixon appointees) joined with Justice White to make up the new majority. Of the new Justices, only Justice Marshall, a Johnson appointee, joined with the carryover Justices who favored limiting obscenity regulation (Brennan and Stewart) or abolishing it altogether (Douglas). In 1976 Justice Douglas retired from the Court and was replaced by Justice Stevens, appointed by President Ford. Justice Stevens promptly joined the four dissenters, at least in opposition to *criminal* obscenity laws affecting adults. *Compare Marks v. United States*, 430 U.S. 188, 198 (1977) (Stevens, J., dissenting) *with Young*

v. American Mini Theatres, 427 U.S. 50 (1976) (Stevens, J.) (favoring civil regulation of obscenity). In 1981 Justice Stewart, another dissenter, retired and was replaced by Justice O'Connor, whose views on criminal obscenity are not yet known. *But see New York v. Ferber,* 102 S.Ct.3348 (1982) (O'Connor, J., concurring) (voting to uphold child pornography law and opposing the views of Justices Stevens, Brennan, and Marshall on the availability of a "serious value" defense for child pornography).

65. *See Miller v. California,* 413 U.S. 15, 24 (1973). Each of these branches of the "*Miller* standard" of obscenity is explored in detail later in the chapter.

66. 413 U.S. 115 (1973). *Kaplan* involved a book that "contains no pictures. It is made up entirely of repetitive [verbal] descriptions of physical, sexual conduct, 'clinically' explicit and offensive. . . ." *Id.* at 116–17.

67. *Miller, supra* n. 65, at 25.

68. 418 U.S. 153 (1974).

69. *Id.* at 160–61. Even depiction or description of sexual intercourse or other similar explicit sexual conduct is not *per se* "hard core" (and therefore obscene). According to Schauer at 112, although normal heterosexual intercourse may be found to be obscene, "most hard-core pornography emphasizes other sexual practices, such as homosexuality, bestiality, flagellation, sado-masochism, fellatio, cunnilingus, and the like."

70. *Jenkins v. Georgia, supra* n. 68, at 161.

71. Schauer at 111–112.

72. *New York v. Ferber, supra* n. 64.

73. Schauer at 104, 103. See also *United States v. Various Articles, Schedule* 2102, 707 F.2d 132 (2d Cir 1983).

74. Schauer at 102, citing A.L.I. Model Penal Code, §251.4 (1962).

75. *Manual Enterprises v. Day,* 370 U.S. 478, 482 (1962).

76. *Jacobellis v. Ohio,* 378 U.S. 184, 191–92 (1964) (Brennan, J.).

77. 383 U.S. 413, 418 (1966).

78. *Roth v. United States, supra* n. 35, at 487 n. 20.

79. Schauer at 98.

80. *See Roth v. United States, supra* n. 35, at 489–90.

81. *Compare* the "particular sensibility" test of *Regina v. Hicklin,* [1868] L.R. 3 Q.B. 360 *with United States v. Levine,* 83 F.2d 156 (2d Cir. 1936) (it was reversible error to instruct a jury that obscenity must be judged in terms of its likely effect on "the young and immature, the ignorant and those who are sensually inclined").

82. The requirement of adult standards was made clear in *Butler v. Michigan,* 352 U.S. 380 (1957), where a statute was invalidated because it would have "reduce[d] the adult population . . . to reading only what is fit for children. *Id.* at 383. *See also Pinkus v. United States,* 436 U.S. 293, 296 (1978) (reversing an obscenity conviction based on an instruction

inviting the jury to consider "young and old . . . men, women and children" in determining the standards to be applied). But *Pinkus* permitted a jury to consider the "sensitive" and the "insensitive" in attempting to determine the standard for a hypothetical average person in the community, apparently on a theory that considering *all* persons in the community will lead to a correct appreciation of the views of an average person.

83. *See Mishkin v. New York,* 383 U.S. 502 (1966); *Hamling v. United States,* 418 U.S. 87, 128–30 (1974); *Pinkus v. United States, supra* n. 82, at 301–03.

84. *Roth v. United States, supra* n. 35, at 489.

85. *Manual Enterprises v. Day,* 370 U.S. 478, 488 (1962) (Harlan, J.).

86. *Jacobellis v. Ohio,* 378 U.S. 184 (1964).

87. *Id.* at 195.

88. Indeed, according to Schauer, every federal court which considered the community standards issue after *Jacobellis* and before *Miller* selected a national standard. *See* Schauer at 119 n. 19 and cases cited therein.

89. 413 U.S. 15, 32 (1973).

90. *Id.* at 32–33 n. 13.

91. Schauer at 123.

92. *See, e.g., Penthouse International, Ltd. v. McAuliffe,* 7 Med. L. Rptr. 1798, 1802 (N.D. Ga. 1981): "It is clear . . . that 'serious value' is not to be judged by the tastes of the 'average person' or measured in terms of 'community standards.' " *Miller v. California,* 413 U.S. at 30; *Smith v. United States,* 431 U.S. at 301.

93. *Miller, supra* n. 65, at 24. The list of "serious" values in *Miller*—literary, artistic, political and scientific—unlike the list of hard-core sexual activities, is said not to be by way of example but to be all-inclusive. Still, the four categories should be viewed expansively; there appear to be other related values that will be expressly or implicitly recognized in appropriate cases. Certainly this would include serious "educational" value, a category which could be subsumed under one or more of the enumerated values. Schauer speculates that the Court may not have included educational value in order to avoid the suggestion that any educational aspect would satisfy the test, since any material however obscene would arguably teach a person something. Schauer at 142. Similarly, the omission of entertainment value should not be read as suggesting that serious works that are also entertaining are not protected. In fact, the Court has on many occasions held that entertainment is protected by the First Amendment, most recently in *Schad v. Borough of Mount Ephraim,* 452 U.S. 61 (1981) (applying First Amendment protection to live entertainment in a zoning case).

94. The community standards test is not applied to the serious value branch of *Miller*. This, combined with the general rule that the question of obscenity is always one of law, or at least of "constitutional fact,"

Obscenity

strongly suggests that the question of serious value should be decided by the court before the jury can decide whether the other elements of the offense are present. Similarly, the factual basis for a judgment of obscenity must be reviewed independently by the appellate courts after trial. Because of the nature of the serious value test, a jury's finding of obscenity would not seem to preclude *de novo* consideration (i.e., a fresh review of all relevant facts) by the appellate court. See Schauer at 147–53.

95. Schauer at 140.

96. *Louisiana v. Walden Book Company*, 6 Med. L. Rptr. 1696 (La. 1980).

97. *Penthouse Int'l, Ltd. v. McAuliffe*, 610 F.2d 1353, 1372 (5th Cir. 1980). Serious value is particularly difficult to assess for magazines or other collections of generally unrelated poetry, short stories, or articles. It is not easy to judge such works as a whole and courts are put to the task of weighing the relative merits of more and less valuable matter.

98. *Mitchell v. Delaware*, 6 Med. L. Rptr. 1988 (Del. Super. 1980) (serious political value in movie *Caligula*, although it lacks serious literary, artistic, or scientific value); *Penthouse International, Ltd. v. McAuliffe*, 7 Med. L. Rptr. 1798 (N.D. Ga. 1981) (serious political and artistic, but not literary and scientific, value in *Caligula*). This decision was reversed in part on appeal, 9 Med. L. Rptr. 1502 (11th Cir. 1983) but the entire appeals court then agreed to reconsider the appeal. See 9 Med. L. Rptr. No. 27, News Notes, Aug. 2, 1983.

99. *Roth v. United States, supra* n. 35 at 489.

100. *Kois v. Wisconsin*, 408 U.S. 229, 231 (1972).

101. *See Lambert v. California*, 355 U.S. 225 (1957).

102. 361 U.S. 147 (1959). The requirement of *scienter* relates primarily to criminal laws; in general, it has limited relevance to civil obscenity regulations.

103. *Hamling v. United States*, 418 U.S. 87 (1974), citing *Rosen v. United States*, 161 U.S. 29 (1896), with approval. *See also, Young v. Abrams*, 698 F. 2d. 131 (2d Cir. 1983).

104. The pandering doctrine was first fully developed in *Ginzburg v. United States*, 383 U.S. 463 (1966), and has been expressly upheld by the Supreme Court in two cases since: *Hamling v. United States*, 418 U.S. 87 (1974), and *Splawn v. California*, 431 U.S. 595 (1977).

105. *See Papish v. Board of Curators of University of Missouri*, 410 U.S. 667 (1973), where the lower court found pandering but the Supreme Court reversed on the ground that the subject materials were clearly protected by the First Amendment. Pandering is not a separate criminal offense, but merely "evidence" of obscenity. *See* Schauer at 80–87.

106. 390 U.S. 629 (1968).

107. *See* Schauer at 89.

108. This would include the requirement of specificity in statutory offenses defining matter harmful to minors; due process safeguards; protections for ideas, vulgar language, or mere nudity; and limitation to sexually explicit matter rather than violence or other "thematic" obscenity. *See* Schauer at 89–91.

109. Schauer at 94–95.

110. *See, e.g., FCC v. Pacifica Foundation*, 438 U.S. 726 (1978); *New York v. Ferber*, 102 S.Ct. 3348, 50 U.S.L.W. 5077 (1982).

111. *See, e.g.*, N.Y. Penal Law §263.00 *et seq.*

112. *People v. Ferber*, 52 N.Y. 2d 674 (1981).

113. *New York v. Ferber*, 102 S.Ct. 3348, 50 U.S.L.W. 5077 (1982).

114. *See, e.g., St. Martin's Press v. Carey*, 605 F. 2d 41 (2d Cir. 1979), which involved an unsuccessful attempt by the publisher of the sex-education book *Show Me!* to enjoin enforcement of the New York statute against that book. After the Supreme Court upheld the statute, the publisher withdrew the book from circulation.

115. *See, e.g.*, City of Paramount, Calif. Ord. No. 478, Paramount Mun. Code, Chapter 11A, *discussed in American Booksellers Association v. Superior Court*, 8 Med. L. Rptr. 2014 (Cal. Ct.App. 1982).

116. *Id..*

117. *American Booksellers Association v. McAuliffe*, 7 Med. L. Rptr. 2288 (N.D. Ga. 1981); *American Booksellers v. Superior Court, supra* n. 114; *Tattered Cover, Inc. v. Tooley*, Case No. 81 CV 9693 (Dist. Ct. Denver Co.) (unreported decision of Jan. 7, 1982).

118. *American Booksellers Association v. McAuliffe, supra*. n. 116.

119. *Tattered Cover, Inc. v. Tooley, supra* n. 116.

120. *American Booksellers Association v. Superior Court, supra* n. 114.

121. 8 Med. L. Rptr. at 2017–18.

122. *Id.* at 2017.

123. *But see* a small number of Federal Communications Commission proceedings cited in *FCC v. Pacifica Foundation*, 438 U.S. 726, 741 n. 16 (1978).

124. *Compare Red Lion Broadcasting Co. v. FCC*, 395 U.S. 367 (1969) (upholding FCC broadcast regulations on "fairness," personal attack, and political editorializing against a First Amendment challenge) *with Miami Herald Publishing Co. v. Tornillo*, 418 U.S. 241 (1974) (overturning a state statute requiring a kind of public access to newspapers to reply to certain publications, on First Amendment grounds).

125. 438 U.S. 726 (1978).

126. *See, e.g., Cohen v. California*, 403 U.S. 15 (1971).

127. Justices Brennan, White, Marshall, and Stewart dissented, making this another of the Supreme Court's narrow 5 to 4 decisions. The opinion was even more divided in that two of the majority (Justices Powell and Blackmun) disassociated themselves from a key portion of the majority opinion that would have adopted a hierarchy of levels of protection

depending upon a judicial analysis of the "value" of the expression. *Compare* Part IV(B) of Justice Stevens's majority opinion with Part II of Justice Powell's concurring opinion.

128. 438 U.S. at 748.

129. This position was recently advocated in a major paper by the National Cable Television Association.

130. *Home Box Office, Inc. v. Wilkinson*, 8 Med. L. Rptr. 1108 (D. Utah 1982). *See also Community Television of Utah, Inc. v. Roy City*, No. NC 82-0122J and NC 82-0171J (D. Utah 1982); 9 Med. L. Rptr. No. 24, News Notes, July 12, 1983.

131. 8 Med. L. Rptr. at 1117–18.

132. *FCC v. Midwest Video Corporation*, 440 U.S. 689 (1979). Because it invalidated the FCC regulations on other grounds, the Supreme Court did not reach the question of how cable systems ought to be treated for First Amendment purposes.

133. E.g., N.Y. Exec. L. §829.

134. See Tell, "Cable TV's Sex Problem," *Nat'l L. Journal*, Feb. 15, 1982, p. 1.

135. *Ibid.*; see also, Gunther, "The Debate Over Sex on TV," *TV Guide* Mar. 28–Ap. 3, 1981, p.5.

136. *Young v. American Mini Theatres*, 427 U.S. 50 (1976).

137. *Id.* at 70–71.

138. 452 U.S. 61, 68 (1981). *See also Basiardanes v. City of Galveston*, 682 F. 2d 1203 (5th Cir. 1982); *Alexander v. City of Minneapolis*, 798 F. 2d 936 (8th Cir. 1983); *CLR Corp. v. Henline*, 702 F. 2d 637 (6th Cir. 1983).

139. *See* Monaghan, "First Amendment 'Due Process'," 83 *Harv. L. Rev.* 518 (1970).

140. Chief Justice Burger, in *Paris Adult Theatre I v. Slaton*, 413 U.S. 49, 55 (1973), approved a prior civil injunction proceeding instituted by the state of Georgia, stating that "such a procedure provides an exhibitor or purveyor of materials the best possible notice, prior to any criminal indictments, as to whether the materials are unprotected by the First Amendment and subject to state regulation." Justice Douglas, dissenting in *Miller*, also placed his imprimatur on such civil proceedings: "[U]ntil a civil proceeding has placed a tract beyond the pale, no criminal prosecution should be sustained." 413 U.S. at 41.

141. An example of a "mandatory" civil proceeding, requiring a civil determination of obscenity before any criminal action can be commenced, is MASS. ANN. LAWS, Chapter 272, §28c. An example of a non-mandatory proceeding is ALA. CODE TIT. 14, §374.

142. *See, e.g., New York Times Co. v. United States*, 403 U.S. 713 (1971) (the "Pentagon Papers" case).

143. *See, e.g., Blount v. Rizzi*, 400 U.S. 410 (1971); *Roaden v. Kentucky*, 413 U.S. 497 (1973); *Lee Art Theatre v. Virginia*, 392 U.S. 636 (1968) (*per curiam*).

144. 380 U.S. 51 (1965).

145. *Id.* at 57.

146. *Id.* at 58–59 (citations omitted).

147. *See, e.g., Blount v. Rizzi,* 400 U.S. 410 (1971).

148. *See, e.g., Roaden v. Kentucky,* 413 U.S. 497 (1973); *Lee Art Theatre v. Virginia,* 392 U.S. 636 (1968) *(per curiam).*

149. *Southeastern Promotions Ltd. v. Conrad,* 420 U.S. 546 (1975).

150. *McKinney v. Alabama,* 424 U.S. 669 (1976).

151. *Id.* at 676–77.

152. *Id.* at 683–84.

153. *Cooper v. Mitchell Brothers,* 454 U.S. 90 (1981) *(per curiam)* (nuisance abatement). As might be expected, Justice Brennan dissented, along with Justices Marshall and Stevens, although Justice Stevens did not express his views on the First Amendment issue.

154. *Id.* The Court sent the case back to the California state courts, which then adopted the "clear and convincing evidence" test as required by both state and federal constitutional law. 128 Cal. App. 3d 937, 180 Cal. Rptr. 728 (Ct. App.) *cert. denied,* 103 S. Ct. 259 (1982).

155. *See, e.g.,* Articles 4666 and 4667, Texas Revised Civil Statutes, discussed in *Vance v. Universal Amusement Co., Inc.,* infra n. 156.

156. 445 U.S. 308 (1980).

157. *Id.* at 314 n. 8.

158. *Id.* at 315–16.

159. *Id.* at 316 n. 13 (citations omitted).

160. *Id.* at 316.

161. 454 U.S. 1140 (1982) (noting probable jurisdiction).

162. 631 F.2d 135 (9th Cir. 1980).

163. The opinion of the Idaho Supreme Court appears at 631 P.2d 622 (Idaho 1981).

VI

Business and Tax Matters Affecting Authors and Artists

Authors and artists who sell their work or otherwise derive a financial benefit from it are "in business," and must make decisions on the way they conduct their businesses. They are also taxpayers—federal, state, perhaps local—and should be aware of how tax laws affect them and what steps they can take to minimize their taxes.

A full discussion of these issues is beyond the scope of this chapter. Instead, we will discuss some of the most common business and tax questions that affect authors and artists.[1]

What are the available ways of doing business?

One author or artist can conduct business as a sole proprietorship or as a corporation. If the author or artist joins forces with one or more colleagues, a third method—a partnership—becomes available.

What is a sole proprietorship?

This way of doing business—the one used by most authors and artists—means that the author or artist is in business for him- or herself, period. There are no other business entities (except, perhaps, agents or galleries) that stand between such authors and artists and everyone they deal with, including the purchasers of their work.

This is the simplest form of doing business, but it may not

be the wisest or the most economical. A sole proprietor is personally responsible for everything he or she does, including purchasing supplies, renting a studio, hiring secretaries or other staff, and countless other everyday activities. If debts cannot be paid, or if there is an accident in the studio and someone is hurt, or if a secretary defrauds a publisher or a gallery, the sole proprietor may be held personally liable, with creditors or victims collecting what is due from the proprietor's personal income and assets. This unlimited personal liability is a principal reason why many people prefer to do business as a corporation, where the individual's liability is more limited. If, however, the risks of unlimited liability are not significant or can be insured, incorporation is less attractive.

Corporations are separate entities for tax purposes, and authors and artists who incorporate must prepare separate returns—and pay separate taxes—for the corporation and for themselves as individuals. However, because of the difference in tax rates between corporations and individuals, and because of other differences in tax law, an author/artist who incorporates may pay less total tax than would have been paid as a sole proprietorship. (Tax laws affecting authors and artists are discussed later in this chapter.)

Incorporation entails expense that a sole proprietorship does not, it is a more cumbersome way of doing business, and many authors and artists do not get significant tax or other benefits from it. Those who are in doubt about whether to incorporate should consult an accountant or lawyer familiar with such matters.

What does incorporation entail?

A corporation is in a sense a legal fiction—an entity, created by the law, that exists only in the eyes of the law. It cannot be seen or touched or talked to. It can conduct business, and hire and fire employees, but only if and when the people who own it tell it to.

Although it is more complicated than a sole proprietorship, a corporation is relatively easy to create. Forming one does not even require the services of a lawyer. Essentially, one need only pick a corporate name, make sure the name is available by checking with the appropriate state agency (usually the Secretary of State), and prepare appropriate documents—the forms for which can usually be obtained from the agency—and deliver them, with the necessary fees, to the agency.

In most states, it is legal, and common, for a corporation to have only one shareholder, who is also its board of directors and staff. The individual author/artist, having formed a corporation, need not involve anyone else in the conduct of its business. To the outside world, he or she would look no different from the sole proprietorship through which that business was conducted the day before. But to the law, and to those with whom the corporation does business, the differences are real and important.

Individual shareholders, directors and employees of corporations are not generally personally liable for the debts or obligations of the corporation. Creditors or accident victims or the like can only look to the corporation for satisfaction, and the assets a small corporation has available to provide that satisfaction are usually far more limited than those owned by the individual. In effect, those individuals are insulated from per sonal liability in many—but not necessarily all—of those situations in which the sole proprietor would be fully liable. There would be no such insulation for accidents actually caused by the individual, or where the individual personally guaranteed payment of the corporation's obligations, which frequently is required with respect to small corporations.

The corporate structure works like this: Mary Artist has just formed Mary Artist, Inc. She becomes its only shareholder. As such, she elects the Board of Directors, which consists solely of herself. As the Board of Directors, she designates herself as president and secretary (indeed, the entire staff) and as the authorized check signer on the corporate bank account. She opens that account in the name of the corporation with a deposit of, say, $250 of her own money, which is treated as payment for the shares of stock issued to her, which is how she became the sole shareholder. A work schedule and salary are agreed upon, with perhaps even a written employment contract, and Mary gets to work. Legally, she now works for the corporation, and not herself. The paintings she creates belong to the corporation, which can decide when and for how much to sell them. Proceeds from sales belong to the corporation and are used to pay Mary's salary, the rent, and other bills for her studio and supplies. If any profits remain, they can be applied in a number of ways.

The corporation and Mary must each file an income tax return. Mary only has to report the salary she received from the corporation, and the corporation can deduct that salary from its reported income. It can also deduct many other uses of its income: for example, providing fringe benefits such as health and life insurance for Mary, placing part of the gross income in profit-sharing or pension plans for Mary's benefit, or mounting an exhibition of Mary's work. In this way, Mary can control her personal reportable income and at the same time enjoy fringe benefits that the corporation can deduct from its taxes, benefits which would not be deductible by Mary if she acquired them as a sole proprietor.

Incorporation can provide meaningful tax benefits in some cases. But such benefits are much less significant, and even non-existent, for the individual who must use a limited income just to make ends meet.

What about partnerships?

Partnerships are essentially sole proprietorships consisting of more than one proprietor. They do not provide the limited liability protection of corporations; indeed, each partner can be held liable for obligations incurred by the others in the course of the partnership business. And they do not provide some of the tax advantages available from corporations. But they do enable several persons to pool their resources for their mutual benefit and to share profits and losses in accordance with any formula they choose.

What is the impact of tax laws on authors and artists?

It has been graphically described as follows, in a statement which refers to artists but is just as applicable to authors:

> The federal tax laws appear to have a singularly devastating effect on artists, in large part due to the unique nature of their profession. Artists create products which result in ordinary income (not capital gain) upon sale. Unlike most taxpayers, they usually do not have a

steady stream of income from year to year. Their often wildly fluctuating income makes tax planning a necessity; yet in many cases they do not have access to the shelters afforded by the tax laws to other persons.

For subjective reasons, too, the tax laws are frequently viewed as inequitable by artists. Artists are often aware of their contribution to society and what they have "suffered" to produce these contributions. Some may feel that they have given enough already and should not be called upon to contribute again in the form of taxes. Fuel is added to the fire when an artist witnesses the "damage" that the tax structure can render to an artist's estate, the representation of an entire lifetime of creative efforts.[2]

The most important aspect of this "devastating" impact is probably the refusal of the tax laws to classify the creations of authors and artists as capital assets. Profits derived from the sale of a capital asset—shares of stock, real estate, an invention, even works of art created by others—are treated as capital gains and generally taxed at lower rates than ordinary income. In the view of many, the creations of authors and artists, particularly where they have required much time and effort to produce and where their value may appreciate substantially after they are created but before they are sold, should be treated as capital assets. But our tax laws have long provided that "a copyright, a literary, musical, or artistic composition, a letter or memorandum, or similar property held by . . . a taxpayer whose personal efforts created such property" is ineligible for capital gains treatment.[3]

As a result, all gains are treated as ordinary income, in the year in which the gain is realized. This is true whether the creator is a sole proprietor or a corporation, although if it is a corporation there is some flexibility to soften heavy tax burdens.

What expenses are deductible?

Like all taxpayers, authors and artists—as individuals or corporations—may deduct their "ordinary and necessary expenses incurred during the taxable year in carrying out any trade or business. . . ."[4] The Internal Revenue Code provides three examples of such expenses:

> (1) a reasonable allowance for salaries or other compensation for personal services actually rendered;
> (2) traveling expenses (including amounts expended for meals and lodging other than amounts which are lavish or extravagant under the circumstances) while away from home in the pursuit of a trade or business; and
> (3) rentals or other payments required to be made as a condition to the continued use or possession, for purposes of the trade or business, of property to which the taxpayer has not taken or is not taking title or in which he has no equity.[5]

An author or artist who wishes to make such deductions must be engaged in the business of creating; those who create as a hobby cannot deduct expenses. It is not always easy to know whether an author or artist will be treated as a business or as a hobbyist, but the Code contains a presumption that if gross income exceeded expenses in two of the previous five years the taxpayer is in business and can deduct expenses.[6]

To be deductible, expenses must be "ordinary and necessary." This requirement has been described as follows:

> That is, in general, they must be normal, usual, and customary in the business in which the individual is involved, whether one is an author or in any other business. *Ordinary* might be defined as an expense that arises with some degree of consistency in the business of the individual involved, and *necessary* means that it is appropriate or helpful to the development or conduct of the trade or business. I think there is one other criterion that the expense would probably have to satisfy—it must be reasonable. Assuming that all of these three criteria were established, the expense would be deductible against the current income of the individual involved.[7]

Many of an author or artist's expenses are clearly deductible. But others are more questionable, including especially those for travel, research, entertainment, and a home office. For out-of-pocket expenses, it is usually necessary that the taxpayer have detailed receipts and records confirming the amount and business purpose of the expense. For claimed home-office expenses, the Code requires (1) that the space be used exclusively for business; (2) that it be used for business purposes on a regular basis; (3) it must be the principal place of the taxpayer's business; and (4) the taxpayer cannot deduct expenses that exceed the gross income from the business use, so that if there is no income there can be no such deductions.

What can authors and artists do to minimize tax burdens?

First, they should keep detailed records of their deductible expenses. If they don't and if there is an audit, the claimed deductions may well be disallowed.

Second, they can take advantage of tax-saving programs that are available to all. For example, moneys placed in Keogh or IRA plans are deductible from current income and are not taxable until the individual takes them out, usually at retirement when income (and tax rates) are presumably lower. The appreciation of and income earned on the funds is also not taxable until the money is taken out.

Third, they may be eligible for "income averaging," which enables a taxpayer to soften the tax burdens of a particularly good year by averaging it with the four previous years. In particular, "[I]ncome averaging can benefit an author or artist whose income increases sharply after a period of three or four lean years."[8] Furthermore, [D]epending upon the actual income fluctuations, the benefit may continue after the first year for two or three years, or even indefinitely, if the author's or artist's income continues to accelerate sharply."[9]

Fourth, they can take steps to control the amount of money they receive in a given year. An author can arrange with a publisher, or an artist with a gallery, not to be paid more than a fixed amount in a given year. If tax is paid on the basis of income received (which is what most taxpayers do), there will be no tax (yet) on income held by the publisher or gallery. Such arrangements may minimize tax exposure, but they have drawbacks: It is unlikely that the publisher or gallery will agree to pay interest, or enough interest, on moneys held, and the author or artist will lose money because of this; also, the publisher or gallery may go out of business or otherwise become insolvent and be unable to pay.

Finally, authors and artists may be able to shift the income to be derived from created works to members of their families who are in lower tax brackets. One way to do this is to give a work, or perhaps one or more of the exclusive rights that comprise the copyright in that work, to a member of the family. The family member, as the owner of the work and/or rights, can arrange for its dissemination and receive (and be responsible for the taxes on) the income derived. It should be emphasized, however, that the Internal Revenue Service will scrutinize such transfers carefully to determine whether they are bona fide gifts or merely devices to shift tax burdens. For this kind of transfer to be effective, it is necessary that the gift be made before the work is sold, or, in most cases, the publishing agreement is signed, or any income accrues.

A variation is for the author or artist to create a trust for the benefit of, say, a member of the family and assign the work or exclusive rights in the work to the trust. If the trust passes muster with the IRS—which is not always easy—the income derived by the trust is attributable to its beneficiaries and not to the author or artist. It may be possible, too, to create a short-term trust—which must be of at least ten years' duration—whose assets are returned to the creator at the end of that term.

The tax laws impose stringent guidelines for such plans, which the author or artist must comply with. Almost certainly the assistance of an accountant or lawyer will be necessary.

What can a corporation do to minimize taxes?

Corporations, at least those with limited income, pay significantly lower tax rates than individuals do. Moreover, corporations only pay taxes on profits, i.e., the amount, if any, that remains after salaries, expenses and retirement investments, etc., are made. With proper planning, it is entirely possible that the corporation will pay little or no tax and the author or artist will pay significantly less tax than he or she would have paid as a sole proprietor. However, as the taxable income of the corporation increases, which means that the applicable tax rate also increases, the amount of total tax savings will decrease and the tax benefits of incorporation become less significant.[10]

The corporation can control the amount it pays the individual each year, thus giving better foreknowledge and control of the individual's taxable income. By choosing a different "tax year" from that of the individual, the corporation can in effect defer to a later time moneys paid to the individual.

There are also tax benefits on fringe benefits, as discussed earlier in the chapter.

Finally, corporations can create pension and profit-sharing plans to defer and minimize taxes. Like individual Keogh and IRA plans (discussed above), these plans segregate and invest moneys on which the employee does not have to pay taxes until later. As a result of the Tax Equity and Fiscal Responsibility Act of 1982 (TEFRA), the amount of money that may be placed in tax-deferred pension plans is the same for individuals and corporations.

These proposals are fraught with technical requirements that must be complied with. The services of an accountant or lawyer will probably be necessary. If done properly, they can bring significant savings to the author or artist.

What about an author's or artist's estate?

Estate problems, particularly those of an artist, are significant. As one commentator has noted:

The accumulated life's work of the working artist is [most] troubling. Most working artists do not focus on the problems that will be presented to their estate in disposing of their work in an effective way. If the artist has achieved limited public acceptance prior to death, the issue is not a major one. The Internal Revenue Service may ignore concern as to the value of the work for estate tax purposes and may permit a modest estate the value claimed without any dispute. If, however, the artist had publicly reported sales in any significant numbers, the problem can be acute and if the family of the artist has any concern in perpetuating the name of the artist—and generating any significant proceeds by the sale of his work—the problem can be severe and the methods of solving the problem can have substantial disparate results.[11]

The problem is that for federal estate tax purposes the assets of the decedent must be valued as of the date of death or six months thereafter. If an artist leaves a significant number of valuable works, the resulting high estate tax will create severe burdens and pressures on the estate, which may be forced to sell works immediately to pay the tax. Naturally, a forced sale does not maximize the income of the estate, nor does it otherwise well serve the reputation and future value of the work. The Internal Revenue Code has provisions that would enable an estate to defer the payment of estate taxes under certain circumstances, particularly if specified percentages of the estate are attributable to a "closely held business."[12]

Recent changes in federal tax law have reduced estate tax burdens for many. The amount of an estate that will be exempted from federal estate tax was increased to $225,000 in 1982 and will ultimately be $600,000 in 1987. Similarly, the marital exemption—i.e., the inheritance of a surviving spouse that will be exempted from estate tax—has been revised so that the entire inheritance is now exempt. This means that the surviving spouse will pay no estate tax on his or her inheritance, but the estate will be taxed on the survivor's death.

All authors and artists, but especially those who may leave sizable estates on their death, should plan now for the handling of their work and the payment of estate taxes when they die. They should certainly have wills that dispose of their estates in an orderly way consistent with their desires, and they should also consider transfers or gifts during their lifetimes that may serve the best interests of their families and their work. In their wills, they may name special executors or curators to handle the disposition of their work, if they can be trusted.[13]

NOTES

1. For a more comprehensive discussion of these matters see Duffy, *Art Law: Representing Artists, Dealers, and Collectors,* Practicing Law Institute, New York, 1977 [hereinafter Duffy]; Davidson and Blue, *Making It Legal: A Law Primer for the Craftmaker, Visual Artist, and Writer,* McGraw-Hill, 1979; Horwitz, ed., *Law and the Arts,* Lawyers for the Creative Arts, Chicago, 1979; and Crawford, *The Writer's Legal Guide,* Hawthorn Books, 1977.
2. Duffy at 171. Interestingly, no taxes are payable in the Republic of Ireland on income derived from literary or artistic creations.
3. Internal Revenue Code, §1221(3).
4. Internal Revenue Code, §162.
5. *Id.*
6. *Id.* at 183(d).
7. Remarks of Francis Neuwirth at "Symposium on Taxation" sponsored by the Authors Guild on December 8, 1981, copies of which are available from the Guild.
8. Duffy at 187.
9. *Id.*
10. See Duffy at 204.
11. Feldman, "Marketing Fine Art: Selling the Right Thing the Wrong Way," *Communications and the Law,* Vol. 1, No. 1, at 71.
12. Internal Revenue Code, §§6166, 6166A.
13. See, e.g., *Matter of Rothko,* 43 N.Y.2d 305 (1977). The Authors League *Symposium on Author's Wills and Estates,* which is published in the Author's Guild's Spring 1983 *Bulletin,* contains an extensive discussion of issues raised in connection with authors' and artists' wills and estates.

Appendix A—

THE ARTISTS' AUTHORSHIP RIGHTS ACT
OF THE STATE OF NEW YORK

Section 1. Legislative findings and declaration of purpose. The legislature finds that New York state is the home of many artists of international repute and that the physical state of a work of fine art is of enduring and crucial importance to the artist and the artist's reputation.

The legislature further finds that there have been cases where works of art have been altered, defaced, mutilated or modified thereby destroying the integrity of the artwork and sustaining a loss to the artist and the artist's reputation.

The legislature therefore finds that there are circumstances when an artist has the legal right to object to the alteration, defacement, mutilation or other modification of his or her work which may be prejudicial to his or her career and reputation and that further the artist has the legal right to claim or disclaim authorship for a work of art.

§ 2. Short title. This act shall be known and may be cited as the "artists' authorship rights act."

§ 3. The general business law is amended by adding a new article twelve-J to read as follows:

ARTICLE 12-J
ARTISTS' AUTHORSHIP RIGHTS
Section 228-m. Definitions.
228-n. Public display, publication and reproduction of works of fine art.

§ 228-m. Definitions. *Whenever used in this article, except where the context clearly requires otherwise, the terms listed below shall have the following meanings:*

1. "Artist" means the creator of a work of fine art;

2. "Conservation" means acts taken to correct deterioration and alteration and acts taken to prevent, stop or retard deterioration;

3. "Person" means an individual, partnership, corporation, association or other group, however organized;

4. "Reproduction" means a copy, in any medium, of a work of fine art, that is displayed or published under circumstances that, reasonably construed, evinces an intent that it be taken as a representation of a work of fine art as created by the artist;

5. "Work of fine art" means any original work of visual or graphic art of any medium which includes, but is not limited to, the following: painting; drawing; print; photographic print or sculpture of a limited edition of no more than three hundred copies; provided however, that "work of fine art" shall not include sequential imagery such as that in motion pictures.

§ 228-n. Public display, publication and reproduction of works of fine art. *Except as limited by section two hundred twenty-eight-p of this article, no person other than the artist or a person acting with the artist's consent shall knowingly publicly display or publish a work of fine art of that artist or a reproduction thereof in an altered, defaced, mutilated or modified form if the work is displayed, published or reproduced as being the work of the artist, or under circumstances under which it would reasonably be regarded as being the work of the artist, and damage to the artist's reputation could result therefrom.*

§ 228-o. Artists'. authorship rights. *1. Except as limited by section two hundred twenty-eight-p of this article, the artist shall retain at all times the right to claim authorship, or, for just and valid reason, to disclaim authorship of his or her work of fine art. The right to claim authorship shall include the right of the artist to have his or her name appear on or in connection*

200

with the work of fine art as the artist. The right to disclaim authorship shall include the right of the artist to prevent his or her name from appearing on or in connection with the work of fine art as the artist. Just and valid reason for disclaiming authorship shall include that the work of fine art has been altered, defaced, mutilated or modified other than by the artist, without the artist's consent, and damage to the artist's reputation could result or has resulted therefrom.

2. The rights created by this section shall exist in addition to any other rights and duties which may now or in the future be applicable.

§ 228-p. Limitations of applicability. 1. Alteration, defacement, mutilation or modification of a work of fine art resulting from the passage of time or the inherent nature of the materials will not by itself create a violation of section two hundred twenty-eight-n of this article or a right to disclaim authorship under subdivision one of section two hundred twenty-eight-o; provided such alteration, defacement, mutilation or modification was not the result of gross negligence in maintaining or protecting the work of fine art.

2. In the case of a reproduction, a change that is an ordinary result of the medium of reproduction does not by itself create a violation of section two hundred twenty-eight-n of this article or a right to disclaim authorship under subdivision one of section two hundred twenty-eight-o of this article.

3. Conservation shall not constitute an alteration, defacement, mutilation or modification within the meaning of this article, unless the conservation work can be shown to be negligent.

4. In the case of work prepared under contract for advertising or trade use, the rights granted by this article may be waived contractually or otherwise at any time.

5. The provisions of this article shall apply only to works of fine art knowingly publicly displayed, published or reproduced in this state.

§ 228-q. Relief. 1. An artist aggrieved under section two hundred twenty-eight-n or section two hundred twenty-eight-o of this article shall have a cause of action for damages, exemplary damages where appropriate, equitable relief and reasonable attorney's and expert witness's fees; provided, the court may, in

its discretion, award attorney's and expert witness's fees to the defendant upon dismissal of any action on the grounds such action was frivolous and malicious.

2. No action may be maintained to enforce any liability under this article unless brought within three years of the act complained of or one year after the constructive discovery of such act, whichever is longer.

§ 4. This act shall take effect on the first day of January next succeeding the date on which it shall have become a law and shall apply to claims based on proscribed acts occurring on or after that date to works of fine art whenever created.

Appendix B—Libel—

"RED FLAG" WORDS*

The following selected "red flag" words and expressions are typical of the numerous words and expressions which may lead to a libel lawsuit if not carefully handled in news stories.

A
adulteration of products
adultery
altered records
ambulance chaser
atheist
attempted suicide

B
bad moral character
bankrupt
bigamist
blackguard
blacklisted
blackmail

blockhead
booze-hound
bribery
brothel
buys votes

C
cheats
collusion
communist (or red)
confidence man
co-respondent
corruption
coward
crook

*Excerpted from *Synopsis of the Law of Libel and the Right of Privacy* by Bruce W. Sanford (Rev. ed. 1981). Copyright 1977, 1981 by Baker & Hostetler, Washington, D.C. Reprinted by permission. The Sanford *Synopsis* is the leading brief and inexpensive guide to libel and privacy problems. It is widely used by journalists and news professionals nationwide. Copies can be purchased from World Almanac Publications, 200 Park Avenue, New York, New York 10166, Jane D. Flatt, Publisher.

D
deadbeat
deadhead
defaulter
disorderly house
divorced
double-crosser
drug addict
drunkard

E
ex-convict

F
false weights used
fascist
fawning sycophant
fool
fraud

G
gambling house
gangster
gay (in context of
    "homosexual")
gouged money
grafter
groveling office seeker

H
humbug
hypocrite

I
illegitimate

illicit relations
incompetent
infidelity
informer
intemperate
intimate
intolerance

J
Jekyll-Hyde personality

K
Kept woman
Ku Klux Klan

L
liar

M
mental disease
moral delinquency

N
Nazi

P
paramour
peeping Tom
perjurer
plagiarist
price cutter
profiteering
pockets public funds

Appendix B

R
rascal
rogue

S
scam
scandalmonger
scoundrel
seducer
sharp dealing
short in accounts
shyster
skunk
slacker
smooth and tricky
sneak
sold his influence
sold out to a rival

spy
stool pigeon
stuffed the ballot box
suicide
swindle

U
unethical
unmarried mother
unprofessional
unsound mind
unworthy of credit

V
vice den
villain

Any words or expressions imputing:
a loathsome disease;
a crime, or words falsely charging arrest, or indictment for or confession or conviction of a crime;
anti-Semitism or other imputation of religious, racial or ethnic intolerance;
connivance or association with criminals;
financial embarrassment (or any implication of insolvency or want of credit);
lying;
involvement in a racket or complicity in a swindle;
membership in an organization which may be in ill-repute at a given period of time;
poverty or squalor;
unwillingness or refusal to pay or evading payment of a debt.

Appendix C—Libel—

STATE STANDARDS OF FAULT IN "PRIVATE FIGURE" CASES*

Alabama	unclear
Alaska	actual malice
Arizona	negligence
Arkansas	negligence
California	unclear
Colorado	actual malice
Connecticut	unclear
Delaware	no case law
Florida	divided authority leaning toward negligence
Georgia	unclear
Hawaii	negligence
Idaho	no case law
Illinois	negligence
Indiana	actual malice
Iowa	unclear
Kansas	negligence
Kentucky	negligence
Louisiana	negligence
Maine	no case law

*Compiled from LDRC 50-State Survey 1982: Current Developments in Media Libel and Invasion of Privacy Law (Libel Defense Resource Center, 1982). Covers developments approximately through September 1982. Note that these characterizations are not always the complete story. In many instances, the LDRC Survey or local law should be consulted for more detail.

Maryland	negligence
Massachusetts	negligence
Michigan	actual malice
Minnesota	no case law
Mississippi	no case law
Missouri	no case law
Montana	unclear but leaning toward negligence
Nebraska	no case law
Nevada	no case law
New Hampshire	negligence
New Jersey	unclear
New Mexico	negligence
New York	gross irresponsibility
North Carolina	unclear
North Dakota	no case law
Ohio	negligence
Oklahoma	negligence
Oregon	no case law
Pennsylvania	unclear
Rhode Island	no case law
South Carolina	unclear
South Dakota	no case law
Tennessee	negligence
Texas	negligence
Utah	negligence
Vermont	no case law
Virginia	unclear
Washington	negligence
West Virginia	negligence
Wisconsin	negligence
Wyoming	no case law
District of Columbia	negligence
Guam	negligence
Virgin Islands	negligence

ADDITIONAL TITLES IN ACLU HANDBOOK SERIES

The books are all available from the ACLU, 132 W. 43 St., New York, N.Y. 10036

AMERICAN CIVIL LIBERTIES UNION HANDBOOKS